TRAVANCORE INSCRIPTIONS

TRAVANCORE INSCRIPTIONS

A TOPOGRAPHICAL LIST

R. VASUDEVA PODUVAL

GYAN

Published by

GYAN

Gyan Publishing House
5, Ansari Road
Daryaganj, New Delhi-110002
Phone: 011-47034999, 9811692060
E-mail: books@gyanbooks.com

Distribution Network
gyanbooks.com
India, USA, Canada, UK, Australia, France

ISBN : 978-81-212-4139-7 (PB)
First Published, 1941

2nd Impression 2020

Printed at: Gyan Press, Delhi.

Travancore Inscriptions
Author: R. Vasudeva Poduval

TOPOGRAPHICAL LIST OF TRAVANCORE INSCRIPTIONS.

LIST OF INSCRIPTIONS IN TRAVANCORE.

Aḍūr.. (*Kunnattūr*)

No.	Place of inscription.	Dynasty.	King.	Date.	Language and Alphabet.	Remarks.
1	On a stone built into the floor just near the north gateway of the Kaṅkālanāthasvāmin temple at Paḷḷikkal near Aḍūr. (107/1092)	...	...	...	Tamil.	Refers to the construction of the steps. (T. A. S. Vol. VII. p. 109)
2	On two sides of a pillar in the eastern *Vaḷiyambalam* of the same. (108/1092)	...	...	...	Malayalam Vaṭṭeḻuttu.	Mentions a certain Kurupu who constructed some stone work. (T. A. S. Vol. VI. p. 109)
3	On the east base of the central shrine of the same. (109/1092)	...	...	...	Malayalam. Vaṭṭeḻuttu.	Contains the name "*Iravi Mangalattanar*. (T. A. S. Vol. VII. p. 109)
4	On the outer pillar of the eastern corner of the Viṣṇu temple in Koṭu-maṇ near Aḍūr. (6/1104)	...	...	...	Tamil.	Damaged — nothing could be traced.

Agastīśvaram.

1	On the west and south base of the central shrine of the Agastya-liṅgasvāmin temple at Agastīśvaram. (44/1086)	Pāṇḍya.	Tribhuva Srīvallabh dēva.	2nd.	Tamil.	Introduction begins with திருமகள் etc. When the king was in the palace at Tiruppuvanam, near the Rājasiṅgakkulam, seated upon the cot called Aḻakiya-pāṇḍya ……… Mentions a number of officers of the king.
2	On the west and south base of the central shrine of the same. (45/1086)	...	Do.	4th.	Do.	The king was residing in the same place as in the above inscription. Incomplete.
3	On the south base of the central shrine of the same. (46/1086)	...	Jaṭāvarman Srīvallabha-dēva.	2 plus 1st.	Do.	Grant of a village.
4	On the north wall of the same. (47/1086)	...	...	...	Do.	Mentions one சிவிக்கிரமாதி who seems to have made a gift of paddy for the celebration of the ஆடித்திருவோணம் festival.
5	On a rock lying in a field south of the Agastīśvaram temple, Agastīśvaram (6/1103)	...	...	Kollam 614 Makaram 4.	Do.	Few lines are underground. Records the first colonisation in the village of Agastisvaram by the command of the king and mentions the land set apart for men of different castes and occupations.

Agastīśvaram (*contd.*)

No	Place of inscription.	Dynasty.	King.	Date.	Language and Alphabet.	Remarks.
6	On the same rock. (7/1103)	Pāṇḍya.	Jaṭāvarman Śrīvallabha-dēva.	Kollam 613 Makaram 4.	Tamil.	A portion of the epigraph is underneath the ground. Registers the gift of land to *Caturvēdibhaṭṭakaḷ* etc., of Agastīśvaram, settled there by the Royal Command.
7	On a rock lying south of Agastīśvaram temple, Agastīśvaram. (1/1106)	Travan-core.	....	...	Do.	This record is a continuation of 6 of 1103.
8	On the same rock. (2/1106)	...	...	...	Do.	Is a continuation of 7 of 1103.
9	On the west base of the central shrine of Agastyaliṅga shrine, Agastīśvaram. (1/1112)	Pāṇḍya.	Śrīvallabha.	2nd year.	Do.	Begins with திருமடந்தையும் ஜயமடந்தையும் and refers to Munnūṟṟuvamaṅgalam.

10	Do. (2/1112)	Pāṇḍya.	Srīvallabha	4th year.	Tamil.	States that while the king was seated in Aḻakiya-pāṇḍiyarājan Paḷḷikkaṭṭil in Tiruppūvanam, provision was made for feeding of 50 persons returning after bath in Kanyātīrtha.
11	On the north base of the central shrine of the same. (3/1112)	...	...	...	Do.	Fragmentary. Mentions Śivindiravādi a person who contributed something to the temple on the day of *Tiruvōṇam* in the month of *Āṭi*.
12	On the south base of the central shrine. (4 1112)	...	...	2 plus 1.	Do.	Damaged! Refers to the grant of a village.

Aḻakiyapāṇḍyapuram. (*Tōvāḷa*)

1	On the west base of the central shrine of the Venkatācalapati temple at Aḻakiyapāṇḍya-puram. (14/1087)	Pāṇḍya.	Srīvallabha.	Jupiter in Mithunam, Kollam 299.	Tamil.	Gift of land to Kōnkēralan as an *aṭṭippēru*. Mentions Atiyaman and Aḻakiya-pāṇḍyapuram in Nānjināṭu. (T.A.S. Vol. III. p. 58)

Aḻakiyapāṇḍyapuram. (contd.)

No.	Place of inscription.	Dynasty.	King.	Date.	Language and Alphabet.	Remarks.
2	On the west and south bases of the central shrine of the Veṅkaṭācalapati temple at Aḻakiyapāṇḍyapuram. (15/1087)	**Pāṇḍya.**	Srīvallabha.	Jupiter in Mithunam, Kollam 299.	Tamil.	End built in. Gift of money for lamps to the temple at Aḻakiyapāṇḍyapuram. (T. A. S. Vol. VII. p. 107)
3	On the south of the central shrine of the same. (16/1087)	...	...	...	Do.	End built in. Provides rice for daily requirements of the same temple. Mentions Sērakōnār. (T. A. S. Vol. VII. p. 107)
4	On the north base of the central shrine of the same. (17/1087)	...	...	Kollam 252	Do.	Kaṇṇan Dēvan *alias* Uttamapāṇḍya Sīlaiśeṭṭi provided for offerings to the temple of Pavitramāṇikka Viṇṇakar Āḻvar. (T. A. S. Vol. III. p. 57)

5	Do. Do. (18/1087)	...	...	...	Tamil.	Fragment. Relates to certain grants made for offerings. (T. A. S. Vol. VII. p. 107)
6	On the north and west of the central shrine of the same. (19/1087)	...	....	...	...	Records grants of lands made for lamps to the same temple by the *Nagarattār* of the place. (T. A. S. Vol. VII. p. 106)
7	On a rock lying in Nanjakuravan vila at Kurattiyara, near Aḻakiyapāṇḍyapuram. (7/1105)	...	...	...	Tamil. Vaṭṭeḻuttu.	Damaged. இ்பயாண்டு நா ஞ்சிகாட் traceable. (T. A. S. Vol. VIII. p. 26)
8	On a stone set up in the Pillaiyarkoil at Kurattiyara, near Aḻakiyapāṇḍyapuram. (8/1105)	...	....	...	Tamil.	Damaged. Refers to gift of land to Kannivināyakar Pillaiyār, Ambalattāṭuvār etc. (T.A.S. Vol. VIII. p. 25)
			Ālaṅkoṭu (*Kalkuḷam*)			
1	On a stone beam in a wayside *ambalam* at Ālaṅkōṭu. (64/1098)	...	...	Kollam 871 Mithunam 11 Monday, Hastam.	Tamil.	Damaged. Registers gift of lands by Uṭaiyan Uṭaiyan of Neyyūr in Paṭaippānāṭu for the maintenance of a *paṇḍāram* for the wayside choultry.

Āḷūr. (*Kalkuḷam.*)

No.	Place of inscription.	Dynasty.	King.	Date.	Language and Alphabet.	Remarks.
1	On the south base of the Central shrine of the Cēra-Pāṇḍya Mahādēva temple, Āḷūr, Kalkuḷam Taluk. (5/1112.)	...	...	Ko. 435 A. D. 1260.	Tamil.	Gift of money for a perpetual lamp by a person named Nakarattu Peṟṟān Mālan.
2	On a stone built into the floor of the Maṇimaṇḍapa of the same temple. (6/1112.)	...	...	Ko. 1062. A. D. 1887.	Do.	Records the Aṣṭabandhanam of Mahādēvar and the Prāṇapratiṣṭha of Sabhāpati, Sivakāmi Amman and Karaikkal Ammai by the trustee Nakaram Tāṇumālayapperumāl.
3	On the four sides of a pillar set-up in front of the Aliśaṭi Vināyakar Temple belonging to Īḻava Community at Sekkaravilai, Āḷūr, Kalkuḷam taluk. (.0/1112)	...	...	Ko. 990 A. D. 1815.	Do.	Gift of land for *Uccapūja* and offerings by Īccaran Piccan and Aṇainci Māya Laccimi.

	Ancal. (Pattanāpuram.)					
1	On a pillar in the maṇḍapa in front of the central shrine of the Sāstā temple at Panavañjeri near Ancal. (1/1094)	...	...	...	Tamil.	Contains the name Malaikumaran. (T. A. S. Vol. VII. p. 66)
2	Do. Do. (2/1094)	...	...	...	Do.	This is the gift of Mariyaperumal Seṭṭi *alias* Aṇṇiñca Perumāl. (T. A. S. Vol. VII. p. 66)
	Aṅkamāli. (Kunnattunāṭu.)					
1	On a slab of stone built into the south wall near the holy of holies of the Jacobite Syrian church in Aṅkamāli. (79/1086)	...	...	...	Syriac.	States that when the church was rebuilt in the year the bones of Givargis Archdeacon who died in A. D. 1640 were re-interred in the Church. Same as 103 of 1100 (T. A. S. Vol. VII. p. 153)
2	On a stone built into the floor in front of an Altar on the south side of the front hall of the Jocobite Syrian church at Aṅkamāli. (80/1086)	...	...	...	Malayalam Vaṭṭeḻuttu.	

Aṅkamāli. (contd.)

No.	Place of inscription.	Dynasty.	King.	Date.	Language and Alphabet.	Remarks.
3	On a stone built into the flight of steps leading into the eastern Romo Syrian church at Aṅkamāli. (81/1086)	...	...	...	Malayalam Vaṭṭeḻuthu	Mutilated. Fragment
4	On a stone used at present as the stepping stone in front gate of the Jacobite Syrian church at Aṅkamāli. (82/1086.)	...	...	...	Do.	Fragmentary.
5	On a stone used as stepping stone in the northern gate of the eastern Romo Syrian church at Aṅkamāli. (83/1086.)	...	...	...	Do.	Do.

6	On a cadjan in the possession of the trustees of the Jacobite Syrian church at Akapparambu near Aṅkamāli. (104/1086.)	Cochin.	Do.	Ko. 926.	Do.	The Raja ordered the *Puttankūṟṟukārs* to divide the property belonging to their church equally with the *Paḻaiyakūṟṟukārs* to avoid any further disturbance of peace which was often taking place. (T. A. S. Vol. VII. p. 154.)
7	On another. (105/1086.)	Do.	Do.	Do.	Do.	The division is effected in the presence of the officer deputed by the Raja. (T. A. S. Vol. p. 155.)
8	On a tombstone in the R. C. church at Aṅkamāli. (102/1100)	...	Do.	Ko. 835 A. D. 1662 Mithunam 14.	Malayalam. Vaṭṭeluttu.	Refers to the death of Māṇi-Pauloda of Velapparambil. (T. A. S. Vol. VII. p. 153.)
9	On another tombstone in the same church. (103/1100.)	...	Do.	A. D. 1667 Kollam 84 (2) Makaram 28	Do.	Refers to the demise of Avaran Anna of Velapparambil. (T. A. S. Vol. VII. p. 153.)

Aṅkamāli. (contd.)

No.	Place of inscription.	Dynasty.	King.	Date.	Language and Alphabet.	Remarks.
10	On the right side doorway in the same church. (104/1100.)	...	...	...	Malayalam. Vaṭṭeḻuttu.	Built in at one end and fragmentary. Mentions Avuran, Pauloda, Kattanar and a few others. (T. A. S. Vol. VII. p. 153)
11	On a slab in the altar of the Jacobite church at Aṅkamāli. (105/1100)	...	...	...	Syriac.	Is said to record that when the church was rebuilt in (1900 ?) the bones of Givargis who died in A. D. 1640 were re-interred there. (T. A. S. Vol. VII. p. 153.) same as 79 of 1086.
12	On a slab set up in the left altar. (106/1100)	...	...	Kollam 776 Makaram 29	Malayalam. Vaṭṭeḻuttu.	Records the death of Itti Cheriyada. (Vol. VII. p. 156.)

Ānkōṭu. ***(Kalkuḷam.)***

1	On the south wall of the central shrine in the Siva temple at **Aṅkōṭu.** (104/1096.)	...	...	Kollam 7 (22).	Malayalam. Vaṭṭeḻuttu.	Damaged. Seems to record the construction of the temple and of covering it with copper sheets. (T. A. S. Vol. VII. p. 115.)
2	On the yāḻi panel of the steps in front of the same shrine. (105/1096.)	...	...	...	Malayalam.	Kaṇḍan Gōvindan of Vilaiyannūr caused the steps to be made. (T. A. S. Vol. VII. p. 115.)
3	On the rock in the south-west corner of that same temple. (106/1096.)	...	...	...	Tamil.	Contains the statement "This is the Muḻam (cubit) of Tiruvattaru." Nearby is a mark engraved on stone. (T. A. S. Vol. VII. p. 115.)
4	On the same rock. (107/1096.)	...	...	...	Tamil. Vaṭṭeḻuttu.	Do. Do. Do.
5	On the same rock. (108/1096.)	...	...	...	Tamil.	Mentions the exact half of Muḻam. Do.

Arippāṭu. (Karttik op pally).

No.	Place of inscription.	Dynasty.	King.	Date.	Language and Alphabet.	Remarks.
1	On the east base south of the entrance into the first prākāra of the Subrahmaṇya temple at Arippāṭu. (8/1088.)	.....	...	.....	Malayalam. Vaṭṭeḻuttu.	States that a certain Matisūtan Kaṇḍan of Akaḻakam gave away to the temple of Arippāṭu all his rights in Koṟṟanāṭṭukari for having wronged (?) the god. (T. A. S. Vol. VI. p. 40.)
2	On the same base. (9/1088.)	.....	.....	Jupiter in Karkaṭaka Tulāṃ.	Do.	Unfinished. Seems to record gift of land made by Nārāyaṇan Śrīkumāran of Seṅgaḻunīrpalli to the same temple. (T. A. S. Vol. VI. p. 40.)
3	On the same base. (10/1088.)	...	.....	...	Do.	Records that Maṇivaṇṇan Nāśerman of Taḻaiyūr gave, as fine, 10 parai of land to the temple for the fault of having misappropriated some of the temple lands. (T. A. S. Vol. VI. P. 40)

4	Do. Do. (11/1088.)	..	..	...	Do.	Records that Maṇivaṇṇan Pāvanan of Taḷaiyūr sold away to the temple all his lands for not having paid the share due to the temple on the temple lands held by him. (T. A. S. Vol. VI. p. 41.)
5	Do. (12/1088.)	..	..	..	Do.	Records sale of land to the temple by Subrahmaṇyan Nāgasaruman of Kalpakanallūr. (T. A. S. Vol. VI. p. 41.)
6	Do. (13/1088.)	..	..	--	Do.	Records that Kaṇḍan Nāgasaruman of Taḷaiyūr and his eldest son gave their *kārāṇmai* right on Pulimpaḷañni to the God at Arippaṭu. (T. A. S. Vol. VI. p. 42.)
7	(14/1088.)	..	..	...	Do.	Records a similar sale by Maṇiya Nārāyaṇan of Kalppaḷḷi. (T. A. S. Vol. VI. p. 42.)

Arippāṭu. (contḍ.)

No.	Place of inscription.	Dynasty.	King.	Date.	Language and Alphabet.	Remarks.
8	On the east base north of the entrance into the first prākāra of the Subrahmaṇya temple at the same place. (15/1088.)	Ōṭanāṭu chief.	Raman-Ādiccan.	Jupiter in Simha, Tulām.	Tamil.	Refers to a gift made during the time of two other Ōṭanāṭu chiefs named Ravi Ādiccan and Ravi Kēraḷan to the temple of Ārippāṭṭudēva. (T. A. S. Vol. VI. p. 39.)
9	On the east and north bases of the Kūttambalam in the same temple. (16/1088.)	...	...	Kollam 944 Mīnam 8, Friday Punarvasu, Su 10.	Tamil.	Records that a number of persons including Kumāran Tampi constructed the Kūttambalam as a Vaḻipāṭu to the temple of Arippāṭu (Peruntirukkōil). (T. A. S. Vol. VI. p. 42.)

			Aruvāmoḻi. ***(Tōvāḷa).***			
1	On the face of a rock of the hill at Āruvāmoḻi. (86/1099)	Travancore.	Bālamārtāṇḍa Varman *alias* Ciraivāy-Muttavar.	Kolam 923 Arpaśi 30.	Tamil.	Incomplete. States that according to royal order, Agastīśvaram temple and Kumārakōvil from Kollam 921 Kārttikai 2 (T. A. S. Vol. VI. p. 100.)
2	On a slab sent up at Aralikkutti in the same village. (87/1099.)	...	...	Saka. 1618 Kollam 871 Tai-17, Su 2 Varīyan Yōgam Pulikkaraṇam Aviṭṭam.	Do.	Records certain gifts of land made by Nallakutti Aṇḍār of Āraivāymoḻi in Nāñjināṭu for conducting worship to the image of Nallavināyaka Pillaiyār set up in the stone maṭham built by his father-in-law Udaiyavanadi Jñāniyār on the bund of the Akalikaiyūṟṟu. (T. A. S. Vol. VI. p. 97.)
			Aruvikkarai ***(Neṭumaṅgāṭu).***			
1	On the Malaiketti stone in the Bhagavati temple. (38/1095.)	...	...	...	Malayalam Vaṭṭeḻuttu.	Damaged. (T. A. S. Vol VII. p. 99.)
2	On the pillars of the same. (39/1095.)	...	...	...	Malayalam.	Mentions some private individuals who, probably must have contributed something to the temple. (T. A. S. Vol. VII. p. 99.)

Aruvikkarai. (Kalkulam)

No.	Place of inscription.	Dynasty.	King.	Date.	Language and Alphabet.	Remarks.
1	On the north wall of the central shrine in the Kṛṣṇa temple at Aruvikkarai. (48/1096)	...	...	Kollam 413 Karkaṭakam	Malayalam Vaṭṭeluttu.	Registers a gift of land by a certain Araiyan-Serikkaṇḍan Jātavēda Bhaṭṭan for offerings and garlands to the temple of Puruṣottamattudēva at Aruvikkarai. (T. A. S. Vol. VII. p. 114)
2	On the north, west and south walls of the same shrine. (49/1096)	...	...	Kollam 416 Mīnam	Do.	Registers a gift of land to the same temple, by certain residents of Karpakamaṅgalam. (T.A.S. Vol. VII. p. 114)
3	On the west and south walls of the same shrine. (50/1096)	...	...	Kollam 411 Mithunam	Do.	Gift of land to the same temple by certain residents of Pālakkōtu in Tiruviṭāṅkōṭu. (T. A. S Vol. VII. p. 113)

4	On a pillar in the south Cuṟṟambalam in the same temple. (51/1096)	...	...	Kollam 830 Āni 30	Tamil.	Records that Jātavēdan Sāvitri Palakkottu Ammai built one of the rows of the ceiling. (T. A. S. Vol. VII. p. 113)

Aruvittura. (Minaccil)

1	On a tombstone in the church at Aruvittura (67/1099)	...	...	Kollam 766 Mithunam 11	Malayalam Vaṭṭeḷuttu	Records the death of Itticheriyadu Mappilla of Oraṟrukūru. (T.A.S. Vol. VI. p. 91)
2	On another tombstone of the same. (68/1099)	...	...	Kollam 708 Mithunam 25	Do.	Do. of Olisemma of Oraṟṟukūru. (T.A. S. Vol. VI. p.91)
3	On a third tombstone, in the same. (69/1099)	...	...	Kollam 853 Makaram 26	Do.	Do. of Kuññacci. (T. A. S. Vol. VI p. 91)
4	On a fourth tombstone in the same. (70/1099)	...	...	Kollam 889 Vṛscikam 30	Do.	Do. of Sākaṇatti. (T. A. S. Vol. VI p. 91)

Atiramviḷa. (Minaccil)

No.	Place of inscription.	Dynasty.	King.	Date.	Language and Alphabet.	Remarks.
1	On a tombstone at Atiramviḷa. (8/1099)	...	...	Kollam 804 Karkaṭakam 30	Malayalam Vaṭṭeḻuttu.	Records the death of Kocca Mariyam. (T. A. S. Vol. VI. p. 92)
2	On a tombstone in the church at Atiramviḷa. (71/1099)	...	...	Kollam 775 Mīnam 9	Do.	Records the death of Māṇi Ayippa Mappilla. (T. A. S. Vol. VI. p. 92)
3	On another tombstone. (72/1099)	...	...	Kollam 798 22	Do.	Records the death of Cheriyan Varkki. (T. A. S. Vol. VI. p. 82)
4	On a third tombstone. (73/1099)	...	...	Kollam 781 Dhanu 22	Do.	Records the death of Ayippa Māṇi. (T. A. S. Vol. VI. p. 92)

Āṟṟiṅgal. (Cirayinkīḻ).

1	On the margin of the parapet round the well in the Kṛṣṇasvāmin temple at Āṟṟiṅgal. (1/1085)	...	...	Ko. 628	Malayalam Vaṭṭeḻuttu.	Records that one Viṣṇu Viṣṇu of Nilaveli constructed the stone-work of the well. (T. A. S. Vol. VI. p. 80)
2	On the south base of the central shrine of the Siva temple at Āvaṇī-svaram in Āṟṟiṅgal. (2/1085)	...	...	Ko. 752	Malayalam or Grantha.	Records that the queen of the Kūpaka country constructed the temple and set up the image. (T. A. S. Vol. VI. p. 82)
3	On the balikkal in front of the Siva temple at Vīraḷam in Āṟṟiṅgal. (3/1085)	...	...	...	Tamil Vaṭṭeḻuttu.	Records that Dēvadharan Vīra Kēraḷa Varma set up the *balikkal*. (T. A. S. Vol. VI. p. 81)
4	On the front base of the central shrine proper left of the entrance of the same. (4/1085)	...	...	Ko. 388 Jupiter in Kanni, Iṭavam 2.	Do.	Mentions the *Kīiappērūr Illam*. (T. A. S. Vol. VI. p. 81)
5	On the east base of the cuṟṟumaṇḍapa in the Subrahmaṇyasvāmin temple at Maṇambūr near Āṟṟiṅgal. (5/1085)	...	...	Ko. 800	Malayalam. Kōleḻuttu.	Records that the temple works were begun in the year 800 and finished in 811 Kollam. (T. A. S. Vol. VI. p. 82)

Arumanallūr. (Tōvāḷa.)

No.	Place of inscription	Dynasty.	King.	Date.	Language and Alphabet.	Remarks.
1	On a stone set up in front of the Ammankoil Vīravanallūr near Arumanallūr. (51/1086)	...	...	...	Tamil.	Damaged.
2	On a slab of stone fixed in the wall proper right of entrance into the inner prākāra, of the Siva temple at the same place. (52/1086)	...	...	...	Do.	Grant of land for the *pūja*, offerings etc. to the gods, Karpakavināyakar, Piḷḷaiyār, Tirunellaināthar and the goddess Aḻakiyanācciyar of the temple at Vīrakēraḷanallūr, the eastern suburb of Anumaketananallūr.

3	On a slab fixed into the front wall of *maṇḍapa*, built some distance from the Siva temple on the roadside at the same place. (53/1086)		...	S. 1605. Ko. 859	Do.	Grant of land for the same. Mentions Parākrama Pāṇḍipperumāḷ *alias* Dikkellāmpukaḷumperumāl.
	On a second slab in the same. (54/1086)	...	...	Illegible.	Do.	Grant of land to the Maṭha built by Pāṇḍyanāyanār, the daughter ... Nayanar ; mentions Siva Pāṇḍiyāṇḍār and Parakrama Pāṇḍipperumāl *alias* Dikkellāmpukaḷumperumāl.
5	On a third slab in the same. (55/1086)		...	S. 1600 Ko. 854.	Do.	Grant of land to the same Maṭha.
6	On a stone lying in a *maṇḍapa* on the northside of the second *prākāra* of the Siva temple at the same. (56/1086)	...	...	Ko. (829)	Do.	Damaged. Mentions Tirunelvēlipperumāl *alias* Venbamalaipperumal, appears to record grants made for the celebration of 3 festivals on pradōṣam, Amāvāsya and other days.

Āṟṟūr. (Kalkulam.)

No.	Place of inscription.	Dynasty.	King.	Date.	Language and Alphabet.	Remarks.
1	On the south wall of the Siva temple at Āṟṟūr. (42/1096)	...	...	Ko. 571 Mēṣa 27.	Tamil.	Records that Maṇiya Nārāyaṇan and Rāman Śūlan executed some works in the temple. (T. A. S. Vol. VII, p.112)
2	On the slab in a field near Āṟṟūr. (43/1096)	...	...	...	Do.	Much damaged. Seems to relate to the construction of an ambalam by one Tankammai and to provide for keeping the premises clean. (T. A. S. Vol. VII. p. 112)

Āykuṭi. (Cenkōṭṭa)

No.	Place of inscription.	Dynasty.	King.	Date.	Language and Alphabet.	Remarks.
1	On a stone built into the well in the Śiva temple at Āykuṭi. (58/1087)	...	...	Ko. 88.	Tamil.	Fragment; modern characters. Contains only a few syllables.

2	On a stone set up in a paddy field known as the *Vibhūti-Kaṭṭaḷa,* east of the Village of Āykuṭi. (59/1087)	...	...	..	Do.	Fragment. Top lost. Seems to register a gift of land to the shrine of Subrahmaṇya.
3	On two sides of a stone set up in the garden known as the *Karaiyāḷantōppu* east of the village of Āykuṭi. (60/1087)	...	...	Ko. 932 Cittirai Friday.	Do.	Records gift of land made in favour of the temple of Subrahmaṇya by a certain Śaṅgu Pillai, son of Pinamalai Karaiyāḷan. Mentions Āykuṭi in Kallakanāṭu. (T. A. S. Vol. VII. p. 110)
			Bharaṇaṅgānam. (*Mīnaccil*)			
1	On a tombstone in the Roman Catholic Church at Bharaṇaṅgānam. (80/1100)	Travancore.	...	Kollam 790 Karkaṭakam (2) Sunday.	Malayalam Vaṭṭeḻuttu.	States that Ayippa Māttu died. (T. A. S. Vol. VII. p. 62.)
2	On another tombstone in the same church. (81/1100)	...	...	Kollam 812 Iṭavam 29	Do.	Records the death of Okkan Kuriyan of Mārāmaṟṟam. (T. A. S. Vol. VII. p 63.)

Bharaṇaṅgānam. (contd.)

No.	Place of inscription.	Dynasty.	King.	Date.	Language and Alphabet.	Remarks
3	Do. Do. (82/1100)	...	...	...	Do.	This slab contains three damaged epitaphs. The Middle one is completely effaced. Another mentions Ittu...kken Mappilla's death in Kollam 7[illegible] while the third refers to the death of Mātten in Kollam 8*8. (T. A. S. Vol. VII. p. 63.)
4	On the base of the maṇḍapa in front of the Siva temple at Bharaṇaṅgānam. (83/1100)	...	...	Kollam 704	Do.	A few letters are damaged at the end. Refers probably to the erection of the maṇḍapa by Tiṭala Iśakki. (T. A. S. Vol. VII. p. 92.)

5	On the base of the *dvajastambha* in the same temple. (84/1100)	...	...	Kollam 1040 Makaram 23	Do.	States that Krishṇa Pillai of Iṭamaṟṟam contributed the stone work of the basement and that the Kalaśa ceremony was performed at the expense of the Devasvam.

Bharaṇikkāvu. (Māvēlikkara.)

1	On the lintel of the north gateway of the Bhagavati temple at Bharaṇikkāvu. (101/1092)	...	...	...	Malayalam.	Mentions Namban Aṇanjaperumāl paṇḍāram one of the Jōgīccurar. (T. A. S. Vol. VII. p. 108.)
	On the lintel of the north gateway of the Bhagavati temple at Bharaṇikkāvu. (102/1092)	...	..	...	Tamil.	Do. but in Tamil. (T. A. S VII. p. 108)
2	On the lintel of the north gate-way of the central shrine of the Bhagavati temple at Bharaṇikkāvu. (103/1092)	...	...	...	Tamil Vaṭṭeḻuttu.	Contains the Syllables. "இட்டிக்குமொர வைச்சனர் கட்டன"

Bharaṇikkāvu. (contd.)

No.	Place of inscription.	Dynasty.	King.	Date.	Language and Alphabet.	Remarks.
3	On the lintel of the eastern gate of the same. (104/1092).	...	...	...	Tamil Vaṭṭeḻuttu.	Contains the syllables இப்படிக்கு மொசவைச சறு...ள (T. A. S. Vol. VII. p. 108.)
4	On the north base proper right of the entrance of the central shrine of the same. (105/1092)	...	...	Kollam 818	Do.	Contains only the year. (T. A. S. Vol. VII. p. 109.)

Bhūtappāṇḍi. (Tōvāḷa.)

No.	Place of inscription.	Dynasty.	King.	Date.	Language and Alphabet.	Remarks.
1	On two sides of a stone set up in front of the central shrine of the Bhūtaliṅgasvāmin temple at Bhūtappāṇḍi. (55/1085)	Trāvancore.	Iravivarman Ciravāy Mūtta Tampirāṉ.	Kollam 834	Tamil.	Records that certain tenants of the temple lands were released on their tenancy at their own request. (T. A. S. Vol. VII. p. 91.)

2	On the south wall of the Amman shrine of the same. (56/1085)		...	Kollam 794 Āvaṇi 7	Tamil.	Records that a private person made permanent arrangements for the celebration of a festival on Cittirai Pūrani. Mentions the large street named after *Ravivarma Kulasekharapperumāl* of Tiruvitāmkōṭu in the Malai maṇḍalam. (T. A. S. Vol. VII. p. 89.)
3	On the south wall of the Amman shrine of the same. (57/1085)	...	...	Kollam 783 Mārkaḷi 4 Tueśday Uttiraṭṭāti	Tamil.	Gift of money by a private person for Tiruppaḷḷi eḻucci and for offerings etc. (T. A. S. Vol. VII. p. 85.)
4	Do. Do. (58/1085)	...	...	Kollam 790 Cittirai 13	Do.	Arrangements made by a private person for the celebration of a festival during new-moon days. (T. A. S. Vol. VII. p. 88.)
5	On the north wall of the same. (59/1085)	...	...	Kollam 759 Cittirai 8 Saturday	Do.	Gift of money for the performance of *pūja* for Dakṣiṇāmūrti by a private person. (T. A. S. Vol. VII. p. 83.)
6	On the east wall of the same. (60/1085)	...	...	Kollam 757 Āṭi 2 Sunday	Do.	Gift of money by a private person for the celebration of the ***Aṣṭami** Pūja*. (T. A. S. Vol. VII. p. 82.)

Bhūtappāṇḍi. (contd.)

No.	Place of inscription.	Dynasty.	King.	Date.	Language and Alphabet.	Remarks.
7	On the east wall of the same. (61/1085)	...	...	Kollam 754 Paṅkūni 2	Do.	Gift of money for lamps. (T. A. S. Vol VII. p. 81)
8	Do. Do. (62/1085)	...	...	Kollam 757 Kārttikai 21	Do.	Gift of land for the festival of Cittrai vasantan. (T. A. S. Vol. VII. p. 86.)
9	On a stone set up in a corner where two lanes meet in Bhūtappāṇḍi. (63/1085)	...	...	Kollam 867 Tai 19	Do.	An order of the king permitting the Sāliyars to live in the northern portion of the town. (T. A. S. Vol. VII. p. 93.)
10	On the stone set up in a corner where two lanes meet in Bhūtappāṇḍi. (64/1085)	...	...	Kollam 692	Do.	The street is called Udaiyamārttāṇḍan street alias Bhūtalarāman street. (T. A. S. Vol. VII. p. 81)
11	On the south wall of the Amman shrine at Bhūtappāṇḍi. (83/1099)	...	...	Kollam 794 Āvaṇi 7 ba 12 Friday, Punarpūsam	Do.	Same as 56/1085. (T. A. S. Vol. VII. p. 89.)

			Caṭayamaṅgalam. (Koṭṭārakkara.)			
1	On the base of the south western *Viḷakku-māṭattara* of Māhādēva temple at Pōrēṭam near Caṭayamaṅgalam. (5/1104)	...	...	Kollam 634 Expressed by the chronogram ചെങ്കൊ	Sanskrit in Malayalam.	States that Kaṇḍan Cēnnan of Maṇalettu constructed the *Viḷakkumāṭattara*. (T. A. S. Vol. VIII. p. 11.)
			Caṅganāśśri.			
1	On a tombstone on the altar of the church Caṅganāśśeri. (26/1098).	...	...	A. D. 1823 December 22.	English.	States that Rev. Mar Paulos Archbishop of Cranganore died at Quilon on 20-12-1823 and was buried at Caṅganāśśeri on the 22nd of the same month. (T. A. S. Vol. VII. p. 60.)
2	On the same slab. (27/1098).	...	...	Kollam 968 Dhanu 16.	Malayalam.	Contains the same particulars as above. (T. A. S. Vol. VII. p. 60.)
3	On the base of the flag-staff in front of the same church. (28/1098).	...	...	Kollam 1074.	Do.	States that the flag-staff was set up in commemoration of the Jubilee of the Pope by the Roman Catholic Syrian Christians of Caṅganāśśeri. (T. A. S. Vol. VII p. 60.)

Canganāśēri. (contd.)

No.	Place of inscription.	Dynasty.	King.	Date.	Language and Alphabet.	Remarks.
4	On the yāḻi panel of the Sāsta temple at Sât-takōṭṭam, Caṅganāśēri. (46/1099).	...	...	Jupiter in Kanni, Mithu-nam.	Tamil in Vaṭṭeḻuttu.	Incomplete. Records that Suvākaran Kumārasvāmi of Maṅgalacēri made some donation of land for the provision of daily offering to the God of Śāttakōttam. (T. A. S. Vol. VII. p. 135.)
5	On the other panel of the temple. (47/1099).	...	...	...	Do.	Damaged. Seems to refer to some rights of cultivation of temple lands. (T. A. S. Vol. VII. p. 135.)

Cāttannūr. (Quilon.)

No.	Place of inscription.	Dynasty.	King.	Date.	Language and Alphabet.	Remarks.
1	On the base of the Sāsta temple at Cāttan-nūr near Quilon. (3/1099 S. A. 17/1107)	...	...	Kollam 446 Jupiter in Vṛścikam, Mēṭam.	Tamil Vaṭṭeḻuttu.	States that the work on the temple was begun in the month of Mēṭam in Kollam 446 and was finished in Mēṭam in Kollam 448. Dēvan Rudran a vāriyan of Cāttan-nūr and Śaṅkaran Sāttan are mentioned.

Ceṅgamanāṭu—(Parur.)

1	At the left of entrance into the Śiva temple at Ceṅgamanāṭu. (132/1096).	...	...	...	Malayalam Vaṭṭeḻuttu.	Records that a certain son of Viman contributed towards paving. (T. A. S. Vol. VII. p. 101.)
2	On a slab built into the well in the same temple. (133/1096).	...	...	Kollam 1049 Iṭavam 4.	Malayalam.	Mentions Raman Namburi of Taḷiyil. (T. A. S. Vol. VII. p. 101.)
3	On the base of the dvajastambha in the same temple. (134/1096).	...	...	Kollam 1086 Kumbha 23.	Do.	Mentions Puttanvīṭṭil Raman Pillai. (T. A. S. Vol. VII. p. 101.)

Ceṅgannūr.

1	On the left side of the passage into the Kunnumēl Śiva temple at Ceṅgannūr. (37/1090 Same as 1/1097 and 1/1100.)	...	...	Jupiter in Kanni, Saturn in Katakam	Tamil Vaṭṭeḻuttu.	Registers a gift 100 accu by Ravi of Vañjippuḷai for the requirements of worship on the *Śivarātri* day in the temple of Kunṟattudēvar at Vālakaccēri.
2	Do. (38/1090 Same as 2/1097 and 2/1100.)	...	...	Kollam 643.	Do.	Registers some agreement relating to the tenancy rights of some temple lands.

Ceṅgannūr—(contd.)

No.	Place of inscription.	Dynasty.	King.	Date.	Language and Alphabet.	Remarks.
3 to 6	On the right and left side of the passage into the Cāttankuḷaṅṅara at Ceṅgannūr. (39, 40, 41 and 42/1090).	...	...	Jupiter in Karkatakam Mēṭam.	Do.	Dēvan Śaṅkaran of Melkkāṭu repaired the temple at Cāttankulaṅṅara and provided for the feeding to be conducted in it on all *Dvādaśi* days with funds assigned by several people. (T. A. S. Vol. IV. p. 162.)
7	On the floor of the eastern entrance of the Siva temple at Ceṅgannūr. (7/1104).	...	...	...	Malayalam.	Mentions Kēraḷan Kumāran who is represented very near by a stone figure. (T. A. S. Vol. VIII. p. 22.)
8	On the left side of the passage into the shrine of the Siva temple at Ceṅgannūr. (8/1104).	...	...	...	Tamil.	Runs as சங்கு சூழா சேனை. (T. A. S. Vol. VIII. p. 12.)

9	On the right *kaivari* stone at the entrance to the central shrine of Kṛṣṇasvāmi temple of Adimiṟṟattu maṭham, Budhanūr near Ceṅgannūr. (9/1104).	...	...	...	Tamil Vaṭṭeḻuttu.	Mentions Adimiṟṟattu Kaṇḍa Nārāyaṇan.
10	On the left *kaivari* stone of the same. (13/1104).	...	...	...	Do.	Do.
			Ceṅkōṭṭa.			
1	On the south base of the Central shrine of the Viṣṇu temple at Ceṅkōṭṭa. (1/1086)	Pāṇḍya.	Mar. Tribh. Srīvallabhadēva.	14th.	Tamil.	Records the grant of land for the Niccitta Kaṇḍa Viṇṇakar Emperumān by Ponnan Śīrālan *alias* Sundara Pāṇḍya- Kalandaikkōn, the builder of the temple. The temple is said to be situated in Nallūr *alias* Mahīpālakulakālapuram. (T. A. S. Vol. VII. p. 54.)

Ceṅkōṭṭa—(contd.)

No.	Place of inscription.	Dynasty.	King.	Date.	Language and Alphabet.	Remarks.
2	On the north base of the same. (2/1086).	Do.	Do.	11th.	Do.	The king, while he was seated on the cot called the *Munaiyadaraiyan*, in his palace at Kaḷakkuṭi, Jatavēda Bhaṭṭa of Māṛābharapaccaturvēdimaṅgalam and Ponnau Baga.....Śrivallabhakkanattu Vēlān requested the king to the grant tax on oil mills for lamps to be burnt in the Niccittakaṇḍa Viṇṇakar Emperuman temple. (T. A. S. Vol. VII. p. 54.)
3	On the west base of the same. (3/1086).	Do.	Jatil. Tribh. Aḷakanperumāḷ Srīvalabhadēva.	2 + 1*	Do.	One Taṅgacci-Venrumālaiyiṭṭa-perumāḷ, which might also be the Biruda of the king repaired completely one temple of Viṇṇakar-emperumān of Ceṅkōṭṭai belonging to Nallūrpaṟṟu. Records a grant of some villages to the temple by the king. (T. A. S. Vol. VII. p.55.)

4	On the north wall of the maṇḍapa in front of central shrine of the same. (4/1086).	Pāṇḍya.	Kulaśēkharadēva *alias* Parākrama Pāṇḍya, son of Abhirāma-Parākrama Pāṇḍya.	S. 1467 * 3rd Viśvāvasu.	Tamil.	Grant of land to the God of the temple of Kulaśēkhara Viṇṇakar in .... Nayakac-caturvēdimaṅgalam. (T.A.S. Vol. I. p. 266.)
5	On the door-post at the front entrance into the same temple. (5/1086).	...	...	Ko. 1064.	Do.	Records that the front *maṇḍapa* was built by the villagers by raising public subscription. (T. A. S. Vol. VII. p. 57.)
6	On the south wall of the central shrine of the Kulaśēkharamuṭaiyār temple, Ceṅkōṭṭa. (6/1086)	Do.	Do.	S. 1467 3rd Visvāvasu, Arpaśi 30, su. 11, Friday, Uttiram.	Do.	Records the grant of land to the temple of Kulaśēkharam-uṭaiyar of Ceṅkōṭṭai. (T. A. S. Vol. I. p. 103.)
7	On the south wall of the *Kalyāṇamaṇḍapa* of the same. (7/1086)	Do.	...	S. 1754, Ko. 1004, Kīlaka.	Tamil.	Records that by the order of Dēvan Venkaṭarāyar, Tahsildar Sokkappa Mudaliyar and Supparamaṇiya Pillai of Tekkumedu in Puḷiyarai and Maniyara (Rāma) Samiyappillai constructed the *Kalyāṇamaṇḍapa* and performed Kumbhābhiṣēka. (T. A. S. Vol. VII. p. 57.)

Citarāl—(Vilavankōṭu.)

No.	Place of inscription.	Dynasty.	King.	Date.	Language and Alphabet.	Remarks.
1	On a stone built into the flight of steps leading to the tank in front of the Bhagavatī temple of the Tiruccaṇāttumalai near Citarāl. (62/1087) and-(31/10:6).	...	...	...	Sanskrit Grantha.	Records that Vijayabhadravipascit set up the stone entrance. (T. A. S. Vol. IV. p. 148.)
2	On four faces of a pillar built into the steps leading to the kitchen of the same. (63/1087)	...	...	Kollam 54 (8) Mēṭam	Tamil Vaṭṭeḻuttu.	Records certain arrangements were made for performing temple services. (T. A. S. Vol. I. p. 297.)
3	On a rock to the south west of the Bhagavati temple on the same. (64/1087).	Āy.	Vikramāditya Varaguṇa.	28th year.	Do. Vatteḻuttu.	States that Guṇantāṅgikurattikal the disciple of Arattanēmi-bhaṭāra of Pērayakkuṭi gave some golden ornaments to the Bhaṭāriyār of the Tiruccaraṇattumalai. (T. A. S. Vol. I. p. 194. and T. A. S. Vol. II. p. 125)

4	On the same. (65/1087 and 30/1096)	Ay	Vikramāditya Varaguṇa.	Year 17 + 4.	Do. Vaṭṭeḻuttu	Gift of gold for a lamp to the Jaina shrine at Tiruccaraṇam. (T. A. S. Vol. IV. p. 147.)
5	On the boulder to the south west of the Bhagavatī temple on the same. (66/1087)	...	...	Kollam 425 Māsa and also Kollam 440.	Tamil.	Provides for the requirements of the temple of Bhagavati at the Tiruccaranāttu malai by a certain Tamiḻappallavaraiyan.
6	Below an image cut on the boulder to the north of the Bhagavati temple on the same. (67/1087)	...	...	...	Tamil Vaṭṭeḻuttu.	States that the image got sculptured by Varaguṇan. (T. A. S. Vol. II. p. 126.)
7	Do. Do. (68/1087).	...	...	...	Do.	Damaged. The following is only traceable. ஸ்ரீம . . . னக்க . . . . க்கு செய்ப்பித்த திருமேனி
8 to 10	Do (69, 70, & 70a/1087).	...	...	...	Do.	Damaged.

Citarāl—(contd.)

No.	Place of inscription		Dynasty.	King.	Date.	Language and Alphabet.	Remarks.
11	Do.	Do. (72/1087).	...	...	...	Tamil Vaṭṭeḻuttu.	Records at the image has sculptured by Uttaṇandi. (T. A. S. Vol. II. p. 126.)
12	Do.	Do. (73/1087).	...	...	...	Do.	States that the image got sculptured by Accaṇandi. (T. A. S. Vol. II. p. 126.)
13	Do.	Do. (74/1087).	...	...	...	Do.	States that the images got sculptured by Vīraṇandi. (T. A. S. Vol. II. p. 126.)
14	Do.	Do. (75/1087).	...	...	...	Do.	Damaged. Only a few syllables are preserved.

Cōḷapuram. (Agastīsvaram.)

1	On the south base of the maṇḍapa in front of the central shrine of the Coḷēśvara temple at Cōḷapuram. (74/1084)	...	...	Kollam 396 Mithunam.	Tamil.	Records that the mother of Mālan Paradan set up the image of Kunṛamenṛinda Pillaiyār (Subrahmaṇya) and that he gave some gold pieces for offerings for the same. (T. A. S. Vol. VI. p. 22 and Indian Ant. 1897. p. 115).
2	Do. (75/1084)	...	...	Kollam 428 Mīnam 8 Sunday.	Do.	A dancing girl belonging to the same temple set up the image of the goddess, the wife of Kunṛamarinda Pillaiyār and gave money for offerings for the same. (T. A. S. Vol. VI. p 24.)
3	Do. (76/1084)	...	...	Kollam 392 Ka. 4317 Vṛścikam.	Do.	Gift of money by a private individual for perpetual lamp. (T. A. S. Vol. VI. p. 21 and Indian Ant. Vol. XXVI. p. 144).
4	On the east wall, proper right of the entrance of the Cōḷēśvara temple at Cōḷapuram. (77/1084)	Pāṇḍya.	Jaṭāvarman Tribhuvana Cakravarti Parākrama Pāṇḍyadēva	5th—10th year. S. 1293 Makaram Su 3 Friday Catayam.	Tamil.	Records that the king repaired the temple of Rajēndracōḷēśvaram Uṭaiya Nayanār. (T. A. S. Vol. VI. p. 28).

Cōḻapuram. *(contd.)*

No.	Place of inscription.	Dynasty.	King.	Date.	Language and Alphabet.	Remarks.
5	On the north, west and south bases of the central shrine of the Cōḻēśvara temple, Cōḻapuram. (11/1086)	Cōḻa.	Rājakēsarivarman Tribh. Kulōttuṅga Cōḻadēva I.	(2) 9th year 180th day and 30th year.	Tamil.	While the king was seated in the western (or upper) maṇḍapa called Rajēndracōḻa near the theatre in the palace at Kāncīpuram gift of a village was made to the God Rajēndra Cōḻēśvara set up in the temple built at Kōṭṭāru alias Mummuṭiccōḻanallūr by Araiyan Madurāntakan Alias Kulōttuṅga Cōḻa Keraḷarajan of Pālaiyūr in Maṇṇināṭu, a sub-division of the Cōḻa manḍalam. (T. A.S. Vol. I. p. 245 and Vol. VI. p. 14)
6	On the south base of the cen ral shrine of the same. (12/1086)	...	...	Kollam 428 Mīnam 17 Tuesday.	Do.	Gift of land by the Kulavan Vaṭukan alias Rajēndracōḻavaiśravaṇṇan. (T. A. S. Vol. VI. p. 25)

7	On the south base of the central shrine of the same. (13/1086)	Do.	Rājakēsari varman u-lōttuṅgacōḷadēva I.	39th year.	Tamil.	Gift of sheep for a lamp by Araiyan Gaṅgaikoṇḍān alias Cōḻa Viccadara Pallavaraiyan of Iraiyur. Mentions Kōṭṭāṟṟu Nilaippadai. (T. A. S. Vol. I. p. 246)
8	On the south base of the maṇḍapa in front of the central shrine of the same. (14/1086)	...	...	Kollam 440 Karkaṭakam 23.	Do.	Gift of money for a lamp. (T. A. S. Vol. VI. p. 26)
9	On the south base of the central shrine of the same. (15/1086)	...	...	Kollam 592 Mithunam.	Do.	Fragmentary. (T. A. S. Vol. VI. p. 29)
10	On the west base of the same. (16/1086)	Travancore.	Vīra-Kēraḷa Varma, ruling Vēṇāṭu.	Kollam 301 —1 year.	Do.	Grant of taxes etc., for offerings and lamp. Mentions the following officers of the king, Danañjayan Kaṇḍan of Varukkaippalli, Cakrayudan alias Sri Tongapallavaraiyan of Mannūr, Sivalaviman, Kannan Govindan and Kunrinmel Vikraman. Kunran alias Kēraḷaśiṅgappallavaraiyan. (T. A. S. Vol. IV. p. 17. Indian Ant. XXIV. 253)

Cōḷapuram. (*contd.*)

No.	Place of inscription.	Dynasty.	King.	Date.	Language and Alphabet.	Remarks.
11	On a stone (facing west) at the north base of the maṇḍapa in front of the same. (17/1086 and 99/1099)	Cōḷa Pāṇḍya.	Jaṭāvarman Sundaracōḷa Pāṇḍya.	19th	Tamil.	Registers gift of 12½ cows by a female ascetic named Nārpatteṇṇāyira Maralidēvi of Tirukkōṭṭāru for burning half a lamp in the same temple. The names of the two persons who received the cows were Suryan-Rajasimhan and Suryan-Rajamallan. (T. A. S. Vol VI. p. 13)
12	On the east and north bases of the maṇḍapa in front of the same. (18/1086)	Do.	Jaṭāvarman Sundaracōḷa Pāṇḍyadēva.	(2)	Do.	Gift of land.
13	On the south prākāra wall of the same. (44/1090)	...	...	3rd and 7th year.	Do.	Beginning lost. Registers gift of land made at the instance of the king's Officer Malavarayan. (T. A. S. Vol. VI. p. 6)

14	On the south wall of the same. (93/1099)	...	...	Kollam 419 Mēṭam	Tamil.	Records gift of land by Āṭuvān alias Alālasundarapperuman of Merppāṭi living in Gaṅgaimaṅgalam alias Madurōdaiyapperunteruvu in Kuṭanāṭu. (T. A. S. Vol. VI. p. 22)
5	On the west wall of the central shrine of the same. (94/1099)	...	...	...	Do.	Contains the name of Madhurāntakan who was probably the builder of the temple. (T. A. S. Vol. VI. p. 5)
16	On the north wall of the same shrine. (95/1099)	...	...	...	Do.	Contains the name "Gaṅgaikoṇṭacōḻa Tamiḻappallavaraiyan" who was probably the builder of the temple. (T. A. S. Vol. VI. p. 5)
17	On the south base of the mahāmaṇḍapa of the same temple. (96/1099)	Cōḻa Pāṇḍya	Jaṭāvarman alias Sundara Cōḻa Pāṇḍyadēva	11th year	Do.	Records gift of 50 sheep by Dēvan Viccādiran alias Cōḻamārāyan one of the nobles (Perundanam) of Uṭaiyar (probably the Cōḻa-Pāṇḍya Viceroy) for burning a perpetual lamp in the temple of God Rājēndracōḻēsvaram Uṭaiyār of Tirukkōṭṭāru alias Mummuṭicōḻanallūr in Nāñjināṭu a district of Uttamacōḻavaḷanāṭu. (T. A. S. Vol. VI. p. 9)

Cōḷapuram. (*contd.*)

No.	Place of inscription.	Dynasty.	King.	Date.	Language and Alphabet.	Remarks.
18	On the same base. (97/1099)	Cōḷa Pāṇḍya.	Jaṭāvarman alias Sundara Pāṇḍya dēva.	11th year	Tamil.	Records gift of 50 sheep by Ādittan Iraṇasiṅgan of Koṭuṅkuḷam in Rājarāja tennāṭu for a perpetual lamp to the same temple. (T. A. S. Vol. VI. p. 10)
19	On the base of the same. (98/1099)	Do.	Do.	Do.	Do.	Registers gift of 25 cows by Sarvalōkāsraya Viṣṇuvardhana Mahārāja alias Caḷukki Vijayādittan Vikkiyaṇṇan for a perpetual lamp to the same God. It is noteworthy that the district in which the temple was situated is called Nāñjilnāṭu, the land of ploughshares. (T. A. S. Vol. VI. p. 8)

20	On the same base. (100/1099)	Do.	Do.	Do.	Do.	Records gift of 50 sheep by Candraśēkhara Bhaṭṭan of Damattūr (a suburb of) Koccaṭaiya Srivalanāṭu alias Āṭavalasundara Caturvēdimaṅgalam, a Brahmadēya of Kil-Sembiya valanāṭu, for a perpetual lamp to the same temple. (T. A. S. Vol. VI. p. 11).
21	On the east base of the same maṇḍapa. (101/1099).	Cōḷa Pāṇḍya.	Jaṭāvarman *alias* Sundara Cōḷa Pāṇḍya dēva.	...	Tamil.	Built in at the end by a porch. Seems to refer to a sale of land in Terkurumbaluvu *alias* Aḻakiyacōḷanallūr in Nāñjināṭu. (T. A. S. Vol. VI. p. 13).
22	On the north base of the same maṇḍapa. (102/1099).	Do.	Do.	1_th year.	Do.	Registers sale of land by the assembly of Srivallabhamaṅgalam *alias* Kēraḷakulāsani-Caturvēdimaṅgalam to the temple, officials of Rājēndracōlîsvaram Uṭaiyār, and mentions certain arrangements made regarding the payment of taxes, etc. (T. A. S. Vol. VI. p. 11).

Cōḷapuram. (*contd.*)

No.	Place of [illegible]ription.	Dynasty.	King.	Date.	Language and Alphabet.	Remarks.
23	On the capital of a pillar in the maṇḍapa in front of the same shrine. (103/1099)	...	...	...	Tamil.	States that the pillar and bracket were contributed by Periyan Kuḍitāngi *alias* Sundara Pāṇḍya Nanjinad-alvar. (T. A. S Vol. VI. 27).
24	On a door-jamb of the ruined entrance of the temple at Cōḷapuram. (52/1100)	Cola Pāndya.	Jātavarman *alias* Sundara Cola Pāṇdya deva.	...	Do.	The door-jamb which was recently removed from a ruined mandapa is broken. The available record seems to refer to some gift of land. (T. A. S. Vol. VI. Appendix A.)
	Culḷiyūr. (Neyyāṟṟinkara)					
	On a stone set up near a paddy field in the village of Culḷiyūr, Neyyāṟṟinkara. (19/1084)	...	...	...	Malayalam.	Damaged. Seems to record that a private individual made a gift of land for a way-side Charitable Institution. Mentions Caṭācci Mārttāṇḍan.

Darsanankoppu (Tovala).

1	On the south base of the central Shrine of the Rāghavēsvara temple at Darśanankōppu. (50/1085)	Cōḷa.	Rājakēsari varman (Rājarāja deva).	(8)	Tamil Vaṭṭeḻuttu.	Records an arrangement made by the assembly of Karaṇattārs of the temple of Tiruvarankōlppu. Mentions Periya tali (T. A. S. Vol. I. I. p. 238).
2	Do. (51/1085)	Do.	Do.	10	Do.	Gift by the *sabha* of a lamp on behalf of Pulla Narayanan. (T. A. S. Vol. I. p. 239.)
3	On the south base of the central shrine in the same. (52/1085 and 84/1099).	Travancore.	Ādiccavarmar Ciraivāymūttatu	Kollam 734	Do.	Grant of land for Uccasandhi and Srīveli.
4	On the east wall proper right of the entrance of the Amman shrine in the same. (53/1085)	Do.	Udayamārttāṇḍavanmar Tiruppāppūr Mūttavar	Kollam 744	Tamil.	Grant of land for celebrating monthly the dhārai ceremony and for offerings.

Darśanankōppu. *(contd.)*

No.	Place of Inscription.	Dynasty.	King	Date.	Language and Alphabet.	Remarks.
5	On the east wall proper left of the entrance of the same. (54/1085)	...	...	S (mistake for Kali) 4545	Do.	Gift of money for offerings by a person named Nenmēni Kaliyuga Rāman perumāl.
	Ericcakuḷam. (Tōvāḷa).					
1	On the east wall of Siva temple at Ericcakuḷam. (54/1102)	Travancore.	Mūtta Tambirān of Jayatuṅganāṭu.	Kollam 804 Āni 17	Tamil.	Registers a gift of land by Kēraḷan-Eṭuttāyitamuṭaiyan of Ter *alias* Aḷakiyacōḷanallūr in Nañjināṭu for providing garlands daily to god Udaiyamārttāṇḍēśvaram Uṭaiyār at Ericcakuḷam. The king, on personal representation, was pleased to grant some tax exemptions. (T. A. S. Vol. VII. p. 95).

Erumānūr. (Koṭṭayam).

1	On three sides of the base of the *dvajastambha* in the Siva temple of Errumānūr. (1/1090)	van-core.	H. H. Sri Mula Rama Varma Maharajah.	1063 M. E.	Malayalam.	Records that the *dvajastambha* was set up on this day when Dewan T. Rama Rao and Dewan Peishkar T. Rajarama Rao, Deputy Peishkar V. Madhavan Pillai, Tahsildar Ramasvamy Aiyar and Committee Superintendent Subba Rao were the officers of the king.
2	On the west base of the central shrine (south of the steps) of the Śiva temple. (3 & 4/1090 and 39/1099)	...	...	...	Do.	Records that the repairs of the temple were begun in Kollam 717 and that the consecration ceremony was performed in Kollam 720. Mentions Punnekal Turutti-kkāṭu. (T. A. S. Vol. VII, p. 139)
3	On a stone built into the paved walk round the 2nd prākāra near the *dvajastambha* in the Śiva temple at Errumanūr. (5/1090 and 41/1099)	...	...	Ko. 945 Kumbha 6	Do.	States that a portion of the flooring was paved by Muttu-kumarasvami on behalf of Hariharaputra. (T. A. S. Vol. VII, p. 140)

Ēṟṟumānūr. (*contd.*)

No.	Place of inscription.	Dynasty.	King.	Date.	Language and Alphabet.	Remarks.
4	On the hill called Vēdagiri near Ēṟṟumānūr. (38/1099)	...	...	...	Modern Tamil.	Contains some syllables. (வெதகிரிபுண்ணியஸ்தலம்) (T. A. S. Vol. VII. p. 139.)
5	On a pillar in the Śiva temple at Ēṟṟumānūr. (40/1099)	...	...	...	Malayalam.	States that as a woman who was guilty of adultery and the woman who had administered medicine to her had died, some *prāyaścittam* was performed in the Ēṟṟumānūr. temple on behalf of the deceased. (T. A. S. Vol. IV. p. 140)
6	On the copper bull in the *Namaskāramaṇḍapa* of the same temple. (42/1099)	...	...	Kollam 876 Tulām 20	Do.	Records that the bull was the gift of Dēvanārāyaṇan. (T. A. S. Vol. VII. p. 140)

			Iḷamba. (Cirayinkīḻ)			
1	On the west base of the maṇḍapa in front of the Śiva temple at Iḷamba. (123/1096)	Travancore.	Sri Vīra-mārttāṇḍa Ravivarman	Kollam 781 Ṛṣabha.	Malayalam.	Records that the officers of the king paved the floor and constructed the walls and *maṇḍapa* of the temple at Iḷamba. (T. A. S. Vol. V. p. 167)
2	On the pillar in the *nālambalam* in the same temple. (124/1096)	...	...	...	Do.	Registers that a certain Ramappilla presented the pillar. (T. A. S. Vol. V. p. 167)
3	On another pillar in the same place. (125/1096)	...	...	...	Do.	Registers that Srīkumāran Kēśavan presented the pillar. (T. A. S. Vol. V. p. 168)
4	On a third pillar in the same place. (126/1096	...	...	...	Do.	Registers that Nāni Celvarayappillai presented the pillar. (T. A. S. Vol. V. p. 167.)
5	On a fourth pillar in the same place. (127/1096)	...	...	...	Tamil.	Mentions one Nallaperumāl (T. A. S. Vol. V. p. 168)
			Ilantūr. (Pattanamtiṭṭa)			
1	On the east base of the *maṇḍapa* in front of the central shrine of the Peruvan-devasvam temple at Ilantūr. (106/1092)	...	...	...	Malayalam Vaṭṭeḻuttu.	Mentions one Paṅṅināyar. (T. A. S. Vol. VII. p. 109)

Ilattūr. (Cenkōṭṭa).

No.	Place of inscription.	Dynasty.	King.	Date.	Language and Alphabet.	Remarks.
1	On the south wall of the central shrine of the Tēnīśvara temple at Ilattūr. (37/1087)	Pāṇḍya.	Kulaśēkharadēva.	17th year.	Tamil.	Fragment. Mentions Ilattūr *alias* Aḻakiyapāṇḍiyanallūr.
2	Do. (38/1087)	Do.	Māravarman	...	Do.	Built in. Registers a sale of land.
3	Do. (39/1087)	Do.	Do.	...	Do.	Do.
4	A fragment on the south base of the same. (40/1087)	...	...	...	Do.	Mentions Irunjerai *alias* Indrasamānanallur. Note :—Cf with No. 39.
5	On the west base of the central shrine of the Tēnīśvara-temple at Ilattūr (41/1087)	Pāṇḍya.	Jaṭāvarman *alias* Tribhu. Sri Vīra-Pāṇḍyadēva	4th year Puraṭṭāti.	Do.	Records gift of land, by purchase, by the natives of the village of Ilattūr *alias* Aḻakiyapāṇḍiyanallūr. Mentions Vīran Ponnan Śīvalavanman.

6	On the south base of the central shrine of the Kāṭṭuperumālkōyil at Ilattūr. (42/1087)	Pāṇḍya.	Aḻakan Perumāḷ Ativīra-Pāṇḍya Kulaśēkha-ran.	...	Tamil	Damaged
7	In front of the *maṇḍapa* of the Kṛṣṇasvāmin temple at Ilattūr. (43/1087)	...	...	Kollam 962 Avaṇi 27	Do.	Mentions Kiṭṭiṇankōyil
			Iraṇiel. (Kalkuḷam).			
1	On four sides of a stone set up in the yard of the Viṣṇu temple at Āḻvārkōyil near Iraṇiel. (43/1093)	Travan-core.	Sri-Vira-kēraḷa Mārttāṇḍa-varma-Tiruvaṭi of Kīḷappērur.	Saka 1325 Sakraloka Kollam 578 Mēṭam 26 Saturday Amāvāsya Bharaṇi.	Tamil.	Records gift of land for the performance of the *uṣappūja* offerings and flower garlands to the temple Sivagiri Mahādēva at Iraṇasing-anallūr. (T. A. S. Vol. VI. p. 30 and Indian Antiquary Vol. XXV. p. 107.)
2	On a stone set up in the yard of the same. (44/1093)	...	...	...	Tamil. Vaṭṭeḻuttu.	Mutilated and damaged. Seems to register a gift of land for offerings and lamps to the temple.

Iraṇiel. (*contd.*)

No.	Place of inscription.	Dynasty.	King.	Date.	Language and Alphabet.	Remarks.
3	On the east and south bases of the Curru-maṇḍapa of the Śivagiri Śiva temple at Āḻvār-kōyil. (45/1093 and 52/1095)	...	...	Jupiter in Kanni Mēṭam	Tamil.	Provides for feeding *agni-hotrins* living between Nel-vēli and Sucīndram. (T. A. S. Vol. III. p. 217.)
4	On a pillar in the newly constructed shed in front of the Śivagiri Siva temple at Āḻvār-kōyil. (46/1093)	...	...	Kollam 1081 Māsi 10	Tamil.	Records that the shed in front of the temple Sivagiri mahadeva was constructed by Muttayya Pillai Aruṇācalam Pillai and others.
5	On another pillar. (47/1093)	...	...	...	Sanskrit Grantha.	Contains the syllables ஸ்ரீ[illegible] ||

6	On the west wall of the Central shrine of the Rāmasvāmin temple at Kaippiṭi near Iraniel. (66/1093)	...	...	Kollam 728 Mārkaḷi 20 sudi. 3, Sunday Tiruvōṇam.	Tamil.	Records provisions made for conducting worship and feeding Brahmans in the temple of Tirumallisvaramuṭaiya mangalam in Kaṭikaipaṭṭinam a village in Kurunāṭu which was a sub-Division of Raja Raja-Tennāṭu (T. A. S. Vol. VII. p. 32)
7	On a pillar set up in the bazaar street at Irañiel (50/1095).	Travancore.	...	857 Mārkaḷi 21	Do.	Records that the incomes derived from the stalls built at Cenpakarāman Putukkaṭai in Iraṇasinganallūr shall be divided between the *maṭhas* in the eastern and western streets. (T. A. S. Vol. III. p. 219.)
8	On a slab set up near the Piḷḷaiyār shrine in the same village. (51/1095)	...	...	Saka 1675 Jupiter in Karkatakam Kollam 929 Tai 1 Thursday, Pūya (pushya) Ba 3 19th year	Do.	Registers a gift made by a certain Kattumari-āṭum-Perumal Piccai Piḷḷai, of lands for offering, worship, lamps and feeding, to the temple of Mahādēva and Piḷḷaiyār and for maintaining a flower-garden. (T. A. S. Vol. III. p. 223.)

Kaṭamaṟṟam—(**Mūvāṟṟupuḻa.**)

No.	Place of inscription.	Dynasty.	King.	Date.	Language and Alphabet.	Remarks.
1	On a tablet cross set up in the altar of the Jacobite church at Kaṭamaṟṟam. (37/1099).	...	...	...	Pahlavi.	This has been deciphered by Dr. J. J. Modi B. A. C. I. E. of Bombay as containing the words *Le sicah vai min Ninav val denman. Napist Mar Shapu. Lernum ahrob Mashiab Avakshahi az khar bokht.* (T. A. S. Vol. VI. p. 72).

Kaṭatturutti—(Vaikam) TC

No.	Place of inscription.	Dynasty.	King.	Date.	Language and Alphabet.	Remarks.
1	On a slab found in the Ceriya paḷḷi church at Kaṭatturutti. (20/1097).	...	...	Kollam 768 Mīnam 8	Malayalam Vaṭṭeḻuttu.	Records that Kaṭavil Maṇi Māttu Kattanār died on this day. (T. A. S. Vol. VII. p. 152).
	On another slab in the same church. (21/1097).	...	...	Kollam 753 Mēṭam 24	Do.	Registers the death of a certain Mattuvan. (Do.)

3	On a slab in the Valiyapaḷḷi church in the same place. (22/1097)	...	...	Kollam 836 Vṛścikam 30	Do.	Do. of Vilakeyil Iṭṭiyera. (T. A. S. Vol. VII p. 149).
4	Do. (23/1097)	...	...	Kollam 827 Mīnam 24	Do.	Do. of Vaṭakkeṭattu Māttu. (Do.)
5	Do. (24/1097)	...	...	Kollam 793 Tulām 23	Do.	Do. of Kuriyol. (Do.)
6	Do. (25/1097)	...	...	Kollam 836 Mithunam 21	Do.	Do. of Accāmāp-piḷa. (Do.)
7	Do. (26/1097)	...	...	Kollam 796 Iṭavam 16	Do.	Do. of Thomman Pōtten. (Do.)
8	Do. (27/1097)	...	...	Kollam 770 Karkaṭakam 3	Do.	Do. of Annamma. (Do.)
9	Do. (28/1097)	...	...	Kollam 782 Kumbham 7	Do.	Do. of Kuññaśeri Kuññanmāppiḷa. (Do.)
10	Do. (29/1097)	...	...	Kollam 823 Ciṅgam 7	Do.	Do. of Alungal Tommā ccen. (T. A. S. Vol. VII. p. 150.)

Kaṭatturutti—(contd.)

No.	Place of inscription.	Dynasty.	King.	Date.	Language and Alphabet.	Remarks.
11	On a slab in the Valiyapaḷḷi church in the same place. (30/1097).	...	...	Kol'am 765 1590 after the birth of Messiah Kumbham 23 Sunday	Do.	Mar Aburametrān and 4 kattans had the Church enlarged, put up the chapel after demolishing the old one. (T. A. S. Vol. VII. p. 151.)
12	Do. (31/1097).	...	...	Kollam 732 Ciṅgam 20	Do.	Records the death of Madacci Koera. (T. A. S. Vol. VII. p. 150.)
13	Do. (32/1097).	...	...	Kollam 792 Tulām 30	Do.	Do. of Madattil Mātten. (Do)

Kaṭukkarai—(Tōvāḷa.)

No.	Place of inscription.	Dynasty.	King.	Date.	Language and Alphabet.	Remarks.
1	On a stone lying near the Aramboli wall on the bank of the river Allatturai near Kaṭukkarai. (73/1084).	...	...	Kollam 9 (49)	Tamil.	Gives the measurements of stone works. (T. A. S. Vol. VII p. 112.)

2	On a rock lying in the Tiruveṅkaṭapperumāḷ temple at Kaṭukkarai. (1/1107.)	...	...	Śa, 1628 Kollam 882 Tai 16 Bahula Pañcami Thursday	Tamil.	Kegisters a Visva jayina praınana executed by Saravaṇaperumāl *alias*-Veṟṟivēlum Tampirānkutti Tāṇuvan in favour of God Tiruvēnkaṭapperumāḷ of Pañcagiri Pārvataccal at Kaṭukkarai in Aḷakiyapāṇḍiyapuram and states that some lands were set apart for pūjas, feeding, lighting etc. (T. A. S. Vol. VIII. p. 29.)
3	On another rock in the same. (2/1107).	...	....	Sa. 1628 Kollam 882 Tai 16 Sunday	Do.	Refers to a gift of land by *Kaṇakku* Āṇḍār Māṟayakutti Ullittar to Nainar Kāśīviśvanātha Nainar, Sivakami Amman and Tiruvēnkatapperumal for conducting *pūjas* and for offering *Tiru amutu* garlands, lights etc.
4	On a stone pillar standing north east of Panantāraviḷākam village near Kaṭukkarai. (3/1107).	...	...	Sa. 1633 Kollam 887 Tai 14	Do.	Refers to the gift of land conducting the *pujas* of Vīrakēraḷa Piḷḷayār of Panantaraviḷākam by Kāri Cattankutti and Aṇañcaperumāḷ Mārtāṇḍan Kuṭṭi Ullittar, and states that the villagers, Darmakartta and Paṇḍāram will be the Trustees for the proper maintenance of the charity. (T. A. S. Vol. VIII. p. 30.)

Kaḻakkūṭṭam—(Trivandrum)

No.	Place of inscription.	Dynasty.	King.	Date.	Language and Alphabet.	Remarks.
1	On the south base of the Siva temple at Kaḻakkūṭṭam. (33/1035)	...	...	Kollam 645 Makaram 25	Tamil Vaṭṭeḻuttu.	Records that Dāmodiran-Kaṇḍan of Mudaiyamanba gam in Aṟṟinkil, Śaṅkara-Devan of Cirrūr and Nārāyaṇan Devan of Mambaḷḷi built of stone the *tiruccuṟṟu-maṇḍapa*, covered certain parts with copper and performed the consecration ceremony of the god in Kollam 546, Makara 8. (T. A. S. Vol. VI. p. 34)

Kalāngāṭu—(Ceṅkōṭṭa)

No.	Place of inscription.	Dynasty.	King.	Date.	Language and Alphabet.	Remarks.
1	On the south base of the central shrine of the Venkāṭacalapati temple at Kalāngāṭu. (44/1087)	Pāṇḍya.	Kōnēriṉmai Koṇḍān.	Śaka 1647	Tamil.	Damaged. Contains the introduction commencing with the words *Bhuvanaika-vīra, Candrakulapradīpa* and the portion secured runs up to the name of the king.

2	On the south base of the central shrine of the Venkaṭācalapati temple at Kalāngāṭu. (45/1087)	...	...	...	Do.	Fragmentary. Pieces built upside down.
3	On the north base of the same. (46/1087)	Pāṇḍya.	Kōnērinmai Koṇḍān.	8th year Prajōlpatti	Tamil.	Registers the gift of land. (T. A. S. Vol. I. p. 278)
4	Do. (47/1087)	Do.	Do.	9th year	Do.	Do. Do.
5	Do. (47a/1087)	..	...	Prajōlpatti Yuva Āni 25	Do.	Records that the *Villagers Karaiyāḷar* and *Bhaṭṭas* of Kalāngāṭu ordered the income from the sale of fishing rights in the Periyakuḷam tank should be utilised in deepening it. (T. A. S. Vol. VII. p. 50)
6	On the south wall of the Mahāmaṇḍapa of the Jamadagniśvara temple at Kalāngāṭu. (48/1087)	Pāṇḍya.	Tribhu. Kulaśēkhara dēva.	Saka 1416 15th year Mīnam 10	Do.	Records a gift of land. (T. A. S. Vol. I. p.265)

Kalāṅgāṭu—(*contd*)

No.	Place of inscription.	Dynasty.	King.	Date.	Language and Alphabet.	Remarks.
7	On the south wall of the *Mahāmaṇḍapa* of the same. (49/1087).	Pāṇḍya.	Māravarman *alias* Tribhu. Sundara Pāṇḍyadēva who having taken the Cōḷa country was pleased to perform the anointment of victors at Muṭikoṇḍacōḷapuram.	20th opposite Kārttikai, Thursday	Tamil.	Registers gift of land in Kelaiponnarai for two lamps to the temple of Tiruvekkīśvara-nāṭu. Mentions Veliyāmūr. (T. A.S. Vol. VII. p.48)
8	Do. (50/1087)	Do.	Do.	Do.	Do.	Mentions the temple noticed in No. 49 and is left unfinished. (T.A. S. Vol. VII. p. 48)

9	On the north wall of the *Mahāmaṇḍapa* of the Jamadagnīśvara temple at Kalāngāṭu. (51/1087)	Do.	Parākrama pāṇḍya dēva.	Śaka 1470	Do.	Registers a gift of land for a festival. (T. A. S. Vol. I. p. 267)
10	Do. (52/1087)	Do.	Do.	Śaka 1472	Do.	Refers to the appointment of the herēditory accountant of the temple. (T. A. S. Vol. I. p. 270)
11	On the east wall of the *Mahamaṇḍapa* (proper right of the entrance) of the same. (53/1087)	Do.	Ḻakanperumāḷ alias Ativīrarāma.	Śaka 1480 5th year	Do.	Records that one Sri Kailāyamutaiyān was appointed as the accountant. (T. A. S. Vol. I. p. 275).
12	On a stone set up in front of the Jamadagnīśvara temple at Kalāngāṭu. (54/1087)	...	...	Śaka 1665 Kollam 919 Tai 21	Tamil.	Records gift of land for morning service and festivals in the temple of Jamadagnīśvara. (T. A. S. Vol. VII. p. 51)
13	On a stone set up in front of the same temple. (55/1087)	...	...	Kollam 961 Arpaśi 11 Monday Punarvasu	Do.	Records a provision of lands made for midday-service in the same temple. Mentions Periya Mutaliyār. Incomplete. (T. A. S. Vol. VII. p. 52).

Kalāṅgāṭu. (*contd.*)

No.	Place of inscription.	Dynasty.	King.	Date.	Language and Alphabet.	Remarks.
14	On a stone set up in the garden north of the river near Kalāṅgāṭu. (56/1087)	...	...	...	Do.	Mentions Parākrama Pāṇḍiyanallūr. (T. A. S. Vol. VII. p. 51)
15	On a stone set up underneath a Banyan tree to the east of the village Kalāṅgāṭu. (57/1087)	Pāṇḍya.	Aḻakanperumāḷ alias Ativīrarāma.	Saka 1522 38th year	Do.	States that the king colonised the village of Kalāṅgāṭu by remitting taxes on the house site for six months. (T. A. S. Vol. I. p. 280)

Kaḷḷiyankāṭu. (Kalkulam)

No.	Place of inscription.	Dynasty.	King.	Date.	Language and Alphabet.	Remarks.
1	On the sides of a pillar set up in the Bhagavati temple at Kaḷḷiyankāṭu. (14/1084)	Travancore.	...	Ko. 864	Tamil.	Gift of land for the pūja and offerings by a native of Kaḷḷiyankāṭu near Vīranārāyaṇasseri in the Kurunāṭu—a sub division of Tennāṭu. (T. A. S. Vol. V. p. 153.)

Kalluṣēri. (Tiruvalla)

1	On a slab in the court yard of the Kalluṣēri Church, Kalluṣēri. (11/1097)	...	...	Ko. 873 Makaram 26 Saturday	Tamil in Vaṭṭeḻuttu	Kuññacci died on the evening of this day. (T. A. S. Vol. VII. p. 144).
2	Do. (12/1097)	...	...	Ko. 869 Vṛścikam 20	Do.	Ippanmannathil-Cakkanatti died on this day.

Kaṇḍānāṭu. (Vaikam)

1	On a tomb stone kept in the Jacobite Church at Kaṇḍanaṭu. (18/1099)	...	...	Ko. 807 Makaram 3	Tamil in Vaṭṭeḻuttu.	Records the death of Vittavatta Kuriyakkos. (T. A. S. Vol. VI. p. 72).
2	On a second tomb stone. (19/1099)	...	...	A. D. 1656 Ko. 831 Cingam 28	Do.	Damaged at the end.
3	On a third tomb stone. (20/1099)	...	...	Ko. 807 Mithunam 3	Do.	Records the death of Mattuvan Kuriyan. (T. A. S. Vol. VI. p. 72).

Kaṇḍanāṭu. (*contd.*)

No.	Place of inscription.	Dynasty.	King.	Date.	Language and Alphabet.	Remarks.
4	On a fourth tomb stone. (21/1099)	...	...	A. D. 1665, Ko. 839 Cingam 2	Tamil in Vaṭṭeḻuttu.	Do. of Koccokken Chakko Kuriyada. (T. A. S. Vol. VI. p. 73).
5	On a fifth tomb stone. (22/1099)	...	....	A. D. 155* Ko. 83* Kumbham 2	Do.	Do. of Tommen Okkanda. (T. A. Ś. Vol. VI. p. 72).
6	On the sixth tomb stone. (23/1099)	...	...	Ko. 803 Mēṭam 24	Do.	Do of Okanda Tomman. (T. A. S. Vol. VI. p. 71).
7	On a seventh tomb stone. (24 1099)	...	...	Ko. 831 Cingam 18	Do.	Do. of Chommar Velan nane. (T. A. S. Vol. VI. p. 72.)
8	On an eighth tomb stone. (25/1099)	...	...	Ko. 825 Mīnam 7	Do.	Do. of Muttuvan-Accar (T. A. S. Vol. VI. p. 73.)

9	On a ninth tomb stone. (26/1099)	...	...	Ko. 834 Karkaṭakam 7	Tamil in Vaṭṭeḻuttu.	Records the death of Chandi Kuriyan. (T. A. S. Vol. VI. p. 73)
10	On a tenth tomb stone. (27/1099)	...	...	Ko. 815 Mithunam 25	Do.	Do. of Annama. (T. A. S. Vol. VI. p. 72).
11	On an eleventh tomb stone. (28/1099)	...	...	Ko. 897 Mīnam 28	Do.	Do. of Mariyam. (T. A.S. Vol. VI. p. 74).
12	On the twelfth tomb stone. (29/1099)	...	...	A. D. 1656 Ko. 831 Cingam 22	Do.	Damaged at the end. Mentions Ettuppa (T. A S. Vol. VI. p. 73.)
13	On the baptismal font in the same Church. (30/1099)	...	...	A. D. 1682	Do.	States that the baptismal font was presented by Koccokkan and others. (T. A. S. Vol. VI. p. 74.)
			Kaṇṭiyūr. (Māvēlikkara)			
1	On the east base (proper left (of the entrance of the *mahāmaṇḍapa* of the Śiva temple at Kaṇṭiyūr. (4/1087)	...	...	...	Do.	Much damaged. There are only a few pieces.
2	On the same. (5/1087)	Ōṭanāṭu. and Vēṇāṭu	Raman Gōdavarman.	Ko. 392	Do.	States that Raman-Godavarman rebuilt the temple. (T. A. S. Vol. I. P. 290.)

Kaṇṭiyūr. (*contd.*)

No.	Place of inscription.	Dynasty.	King.	Date.	Language and Alphabet.	Remarks.
3	On the east base of the *maṇḍapa* in front of the central shrine of the same. (6/1087)	Ōṭanāṭu	Vīra Kēraḷa Varman.	...	Do.	The maṇḍapa was constructed in this king's reign.
4	On a pillar in the platform at right of the entrance into the first *prākāra* of the same temple. (7/1087)	...	...	...	Do.	Contains the words :— (1) தெபரப். (2) பாக்கத்த. (3) சவெறென்.
5	On a stone lying in front of the same temple. (8/1087)	...	...	123rd year of the god	Do.	Records the gift of land to the temple. (T. A. S. Vol. I. p. 293.)
6	On the base of the balikkal in the same. (9/1087)	...	...	...	Do.	Order of pieces not marked.

Kānjirappaḷḷi. (Canganāsēri)

1	On the pedestal of the open-air cross at Kānjirappaḷḷi. (43/1099)	...	...	Ko. 816 Minam 1	Tamil in Vaṭṭeḻuttu.	Records that open-air cross was set up during the time of Vicar of Kulalkkāttu Tekkemuri-Kattanar. (T.A. S. Vol. VII. p. 148.)
2	On a slab set up in front of the Mīnākṣi-amman temple in the same village. (44/1099)	...	...	...	Do.	A chief called Māvali Vāṇādarāyar, who is introduced with the epithets '*Samara-kolahalan*' and *Madiyada-manna-manavalan*' stipulated that not more than 1/16 (visam) shall be levied on each bull.
3	On three stones in the maṇḍapa near the same temple. (45/1099)	...	...	...	Do.	Mentions the names Kuppa-ceṭṭiyār, Marudacceṭṭiyār and Guru Namaśivāya Mūrti.

Kāñjūr. (Vaikam).

1	On a slab embedded in the wall of the church at Kāñjūr. (74/1099)	...	...	Ko. 796 Mīnam 24.	Tamil Vaṭṭeḻuttu.	Records the death of Kappiyār Chacko. (T. A. S. Vol. VI. p. 92)

Kāñjūr. (*contd.*)

No.	Place of inscription.	Dynasty.	King.	Date.	Language and Alphabet.	Remarks.
2	On another slab embedded in the wall of the church at Kāñjūr. (75/1099)	....	...	Ko. 864, Kanni 3, Monday	Tamil Vaṭṭeḻuttu.	Records the death of Kaittottungal Accunniyamma. (T. A. S. Vol. VI. p. 92)
3	On a third slab. (76/1099)	...	...	Ko. 889, Mithunam 20 Saturday.	Do.	Do. of Kaittottungal Varikit yapalo(t). (T. A. S. Vol. VI. p. 92)
4	On a fourth slab. (77/1099)	...	...	Ko. 884, Karkaṭakam 20.	Do.	Do. of Varikit olacci. (T. A. S. Vol. VI. p. 92)
5	On a fifth slab. (78/1099)	...	...	Ko. 750, Dhanu 24	Do.	Do. of Kurisakko Cummar-taragan. (T. A. S. Vol. VI. p. 92-)
6	On a sixth slab. (79/1099)	....	...	Ko. 872, Mithunam 7, Monday.	Do.	Do. of Aburan Varkida. (T. A. S. Vol. VI. p. 93)

Kanyākumāri (Agastīśvaram.)

1	On the south wall, (inside) of the second *prākāra* of the Kanyābhagavati temple at Kanyākumāri. (111/1084)	Pāṇḍya.	Jaṭāvarman Pārāntaka Pāṇḍya.	9th	Tamil.	Grant of the village of Kallur to Kanyābhaghavati for offerings. (T. A. S. Vol. I. p. 23.)
2	On the north base of the *arddhamaṇḍapa* of the Guhānāthāsvāmin temple at Kanyākumāri. (10/1085)	Cōḷa.	Parakēsari varman Rājēndra Cōḷadēva.	31st year	Do.	Gift of 50 sheep for a perpetual lamp by one Manarkadan *alias*, Naṭuvunilai Danmaccetti of Manalur on the bank of the Vaigai (Beginning built in). (T. A. S. Vol. I. p. 241.)
3	On the same. (12/1085)	Do.	Rājakēsari varman Rajādhirājadēva.	Lost	Do.	Beginning built in ; incomplete. Mentions *Rājarājaśālai* and its śālābhōgam, the village of Manarkuṭi and the *Nārpatteṇṇāyirapanmaheśvaras*. (T. A. S. Vol. I. p. 242.)

Kanyākumāri. (*contd.*)

No.	Place of inscription.	Dynasty.	King.	Date.	Language and Alphabet.	Remarks.
4	On the north base of the *arddhamaṇḍapa* of the Guhānāthasvāmin temple at Kanyākumāri. (12/1085)	Cōḷa.	Rājakēsari varman Rajādhirāja dēva who took the head of Vīra Pāṇḍya and śālai of Cēra.	30th	Tamil.	Records the revival of the old arrangement for the supply of salt required for the Śrīvallabhapperuncālai, *alias*, Rājarājapperuñcālai, from the salt pans of Maṉarkuṭi at the request of Tittai Arikulakēsari Pavittira Māṇikkatongapperaraiyan, *alias* Tiruppaḷḷittongal Uṭaiyan. (T. A. S. Vol. I. p. 163.)
5	On the south base of the *arddhamaṇḍapa* of the Guhānāthasvāmin temple, Kanyākumāri. (13/1085)	Do.	Parakēsari–varman Rājēndra cōḷadēva.	24th	Do.	Gift of a perpetual lamp by the queen who cooked for the king; her name is said to be Tittai Cōḷakulavalli. (T. A. S. Vol. I. p. 161.)
6	On the south base of the *arddhamaṇḍapa* of the same. (14/1085)	Do.	Māravarman Vikkirama Cōḷa Pāṇḍya Dēva.	29th	Do.	Records a resolution of the *sabha* of the temple of Rājarājēśvaram. End built in. (T. A. S. Vol. I. p. 249.)

7	On the south and west bases of the central shrine of the same. (15/1085)	Cōḷa.	Parakēsarivarman, Rājēndra-Cōḷadēva.	29th	Tamil.	Gift of 25 sheep for a perpetual lamp. (T. A. S. Vol. I. p. 240.)
8	On the west base of the same. (16/1085)	Do.	Rājādhirājadēva.	Lost.	Do.	Introduction beginning with திங்களேரார் etc. End lost. Mentions the King of Kūpaka. (T. A. S.Vol. I. p. 242.)
9	Do. (17/1085)	Do.	Parakēsarivarman Rājēndra Cōḷadēva.	28th	Do.	Gift of sheep for lamp by a female servant of the temple. (T. A. S. Vol. I. p. 240.)
10	Do. (18/1085)	..	...	...	Do. Verse.	One Ayyan Maṅgalakkalman made arrangements for the supply of paddy for the upkeep of a water shed. (T. A. S. Vol. I. p. 170.)
11	Do. (19/1085)	...	...	...	Tamil Verse.	Records that Ayyanambi, *alias*, Mangalakkalman, the minister of the Cōḷa king established a water shed. (T. A. S. Vol. I. p. 169.)

Kanyākumāri. (*contd.*)

No.	Place of inscription.	Dynasty.	King.	Date.	Language and Alphabet.	Remarks.
12	On the west base of the central shrine of the *arddhamaṇḍapa* of the Guhānāthasvāmin temple Kanyākumāri. (20/1085)	Cōḷa.	Rājakēsari-varman Rājādhirāja-dēva (?)	31st.	Tamil.	Records the sale of land for establishing on it a water shed named after Jayankoṇḍa Cōḷadēva. Mentions Cakratīrtham . Uttamacōlappērēri, and the temple of Ayyappan Vēdiya Sāsta. (T. A. S. Vol. I. p. 118.)
3	On the west base of the central shrine of the same. (21/1085)	...	...	...	Do.	Fragmentary. (T. A. S. Vol. VI. p. 141.)
14	On the south base of the central shrine of the same. (22/1085)	Cōḷa.	Parakēsarivarman Rājēndradeva.	5th.	Do.	Gift of sheep for one perpetūal lamp. Mentions *Pavittiramāṇikkam* as the name of the standard measure used in the temple of Rājarājēśvaram. (T. A. S. Vol. I. p. 248.)

15	Do. (23/1085.	Cōḷa.	Parakēsarivarman Rājēndra Cōḷadēva.	28th	Tamil.	Gift of sheep for a perpetual lamp. (T. A. S. Vol. I. p. 239.)
16	Do. (24/1085)	Do.	Do.	(30th)	o.	Do. (T. A. S. Vol. I. p. 241.)
17	On a stone once used as a parapet for a flight of steps. (25/1085)	...	Lost.	31st	Do.	Beginning lost. Mentions the śaṭṭaperumakkaḷ of Rājarājēśvaram. (T. A. S. Vol. I. p. 150.)
18	On a stone built into the floor of the narrow prākāra round the central shrine of the same. (26/1085)	Cōḷa.	Ko-p Para Kēsarivanmar.	31st	Tamil Vaṭṭeḻuttu.	End built in. (T. A. S. (Vol. I. p. 237.)
19	On a small stone built into the wall adjacent to the door post of the outer-most gateway in the same. (27/1085)	Do.	Rājarāja kēsari.	13th	Do.	Fragmentary. (T. A. S. Vol. VI. p. 142.)

Kanyākumāri. (*contd.*)

No.	Place of inscription.	Dynasty.	King.	Date.	Language and Alphabet.	Remarks.
20	On the east wall (inside) of the first prākāra of the Kanyābhagavati temple at Kanyākumāri. (28/1085)	Pāṇḍya.	Parāntaka Pāṇḍyadēva.	9th	Tamil Vaṭṭeḻuttu.	Records the gift of villages for celebration of a festival and for offerings. (T. A. S. Vol. I. p. 23.)
21	On the north wall of the same. (29/1085)	Do.	Ko-c Caṭaiya-Māran.	2 + 14th	Do.	Gift of a lamp by a private individual. (T. A. S. Vol. VI. p. 141.)
22	Do. (30/1085)	...	...	...	Tamil.	Fragment. (T. A. S. Vol. VI. p. 141.)
23	Do. (31/1085)	Cōḷa.	Rājakēsari Rājarāja I.	(2) 7th	Do.	Damaged very badly.
24	Do. (32/1085)	Pāṇḍya.	Māraṉcaṭaiyan.	2 plus 8th.	Tamil in Vaṭṭeḻuttu.	Records certain gift made to the temple by a private individual. (T. A. S. Vol. VI. p. 141.)

25	On the west and north walls of the same. (33/1085)	Cōḷa.	Kōnēr-in-mai koṇḍān Parakēsari Rājēndra-dēva.	4th	Tamil.	When the king was seated in his palace at Gaṅgaikoṇḍa-cōḻapuram he ordered that certain taxes be made over for (1) a festival to be celebrated on the *Hasta* nakṣatra, the nakṣatra of birth of his Queen Kilānaṭi, (2) the services of the temple of Rājarājēśvara and (3) the *Rājarājan Sālai.* (T. A. S. Vol. I. p. 164.)
26	On the west wall of the same. (34/1085)	...	...	...	Tamil in Vaṭṭeḻuttu.	Fragmentary. (T. A. S. Vol. 142.)
27	Do. (35/1085)	...	...	...	Tamil.	Do. (T. A. S. Vol. VI. p. 141.)
28	Do. (36/1085)	...	...	...	Do.	Do. (T. A. S. Vol. VI. p. 142.)
29	On the south wall of the same. (37/1085)	...	...	...	Tamil in Vaṭṭeḻuttu.	Gift for the celebration of the *Mahānavamī* festival.
30	Do. (38/1085)	...	Rājarāja I.	(12)	Do.	Fragmentary. (T. A. S. Vol. VI. p. 142.)

Kanyākumāri.. *(contd.)*

No.	Place of inscription.	Dynasty.	King.	Date.	Language and Alphabet.	Remarks.
31	On the south wall (inside) of the first prākāra of the Kanyābhagavathi temple at Kanyākumāri. (39/1085)		Rājarāja I.	Illegible.	Tamil in Vaṭṭeḻuttu.	Gift of paddy. Very much damaged.
32	On the four faces of a pillar at the *Bhairav-anaṭai* of the same. (40 1085)	Travancore.	Vīra Udaya Mārtāṇḍuvarman, *alias* Tiruppāppūr Mūttavar of Jayatuṅganāṭu.	Kollam 708.	Tamil.	Gift of the village of Putukkulam in the Tāḻaikuṭipparru of Nāñjināṭu for the performance of the *Uṣappūja* daily under the name of *Vira Mārtāṇḍas Sandhi* (T. A. S. Vol. VI. p. 126.)
33	Do. (41/1085)	...	—	S. 1529* Kollam 782.	Do.	Gift of a village called Kakkaraikkulam in the Pullalankurucci for the *Kala Sandhi* set up in the name of Tirunelvēlipperumal by a private person (?) by the order of Visvanātha Nāyakarayyan. (T. A. S. Vol V. p. 195.)

34	On the central pillar (Northern side) of Maṇi maṇḍapam in the same. (42/1085)	Cōḷa.	Vīrarājēndra.	...	Grantha in Sanskrit.	Records the conquests of the king. (T. A. S. Vol. III. p. 87)
35	On the western pillar (Northern side) of the same. (43/1085)	Do.	Do.	...		Do. Do.
36	On the eastern pillar (Northern side) of the same. (44 1085)	Do.	Do.	...	Do.	Do. Do.
37	On the eastern most pillar (North side) of the same. (45/1085)	Do.	Do.	...	Do.	Do. Do.
38	On the central pillar of the same. (6/1085)	Do.	Do.	...	Do.	Do. Do.

Kanyākumāri. (*contd.*)

No.	Place of inscription.	Dynasty.	King.	Date.	Language and Alphabet.	Remarks.
39	On the western pillar (southern side) of the same. (47/1085)	Coḷa.	Vīrarājēndra	...	Grantha in Sanskrit	Records the conquests of th King (T. A.S. Vol. III. p. 87)
40	On the stone set up near the Parava quarters in Kumarimuṭṭam near Kanyākumāri. (48/1085 & 50/1099)	...	...	Kollam 669	Tamil.	See page 92.
41	Do. (49/1085 & 51/1099)	Travancore.	Cīravāy Mūtta tampiranar.	Kollam 701	Do.	Do.
42	On three sides of a stone set up in a *maṇḍapa* near Cakra Tīrtham at Kanyākumari. (50/1086)	Nayaka.	Cokkanātha Nāyakkaraiyan.	Sa. 1589 Krōdhin	Do.	Grant of land to Tirujnānasambandha Paṇḍāram of the maṭha near the Cakra-tīrtham by Tirumalai Kolundu Pillai for the merit of Cokkanātha Nāyakkarayyan and Vadamalai Pillai. (T. A S. Vol. V. p. 199)

43	On the east wall of the second Prākāra(Proper right of the entrance) of the Kanyābhagavati temple at Kanyākumāri. (20/1087)		...	Kollam 376, Māṭam 21 Saturday	Tamil.	Records gift of money by Maṇiyan Gōvindan a merchant of Kurakkāni Kollam for a lamp to the temple of Kanyābhagavati at Kumari in Tenvaranavasi- nannāṭu, which was a district of Pāṇḍināṭu. (*T. A.S. Vol. IV. p.65*).
44	On the east wall of the second *prākāra* (proper right of the entrance) of the Kanyābhagavati temple at Kanyākumāri. (21/1087)	...	...	...	Sanskrit in Grantha.	Fragment. Records a gift of lamp to the same temple.
45	On the east wall of the second *prākāra* of the same. (22/1087)	...	...	Kollam 376 Māṭam	Tamil.	Provides for a lamp to the same temple by a merchant of Kurakkāṇikkollam.
46	On the east wall of the second *prākāra* (proper left of the entrance) of the same. (23/1087)		...	...	Telugu.	Fragmentary

Kanyākumāri. (*contd.*)

No.	Place of inscription.	Dynasty.	King.	Date.	Language & Alphabet.	Remarks.
47	Do. (24/1087)	Cōḷa.	Rājēndra Cōḷa.	5th	Tamil.	Fragmentary. gift of land. (T. A. S. Vol. VI p. 147. FN
48	Do. (25/1087)	...	...	...	Do.	Fragment. Mentions Singan Dēvan and records gift of sheep for lamps. (T. A. S. Vol. p. 152 F. N.)
49	On the east wall of the second prākāra (proper left of the entrance) of the same., (26/1087)	Cōḷa Pāṇḍya.	Jāṭavarman Sundara Pāṇḍya.	8th year	Do.	Much damaged and mutilated. Mentions Kumari in Purattāyanāṭu. (T. A. S. Vol. p. 152 FN)
	Do. (27/1087)	...	...	...	Sanskrit in Grantha.	Fragment. Registers gift of a lamp.
51	Do. (28/1087 and 9/1095)	Cōḷa.	Parakēsari-varman Rājēndra Cōḷa 1.	5th year	Tamil.	Registers gift of a lamp to the temple of Kanniyābhagavatiyār at Kumari in Purattāyanāṭu, a sub-division of Rājarāja Maṇḍalam. (T A. S. Vol. p. 147.)

52	On the four sides of the base of the *dvajas-tambha* of the same. (29/1087 & 14/1107)	...	...	..	Sanskrit in Grantha.	Furnishes the genealogy of the second dynasty from Isvaranayaka. Relates to the setting up of the Dvajas-tambha.
53 to 55	On a stone which forms the door post of the gate leading down to Pāpanāśam tank at Kanyākumāri. (30 to 32/1087)	...	...	...	...	Mere scratches. Nothing could be made out.
56	On a slab of stone lying in the yard of the church newly built in the fishermen's quarters at Kanyākumāri. (33/1087 and 53/1093)	...	...	A. D. 1763 March 13.	Dutch.	See page 93.
57	On the lintel of the entrance into the Kāśi-Viśvanātha temple Kanyākumāri. (34/1090)	...	...	...	Tamil.	Containing the syllables ; [illegible]. (T. A. S. Vol. V p. 201)

Kanyākumāri. (*contd.*)

No.	Place of inscription.	Dynasty.	King.	Date	Language and Alphabet	Remar
58	Above the figure of a male devotee in the *maṇḍapa* in front of the Kāśi Viśvanātha temple at Kanyākumāri. (15/1090)	...	...	...	Tamil	Contains the name of a certain person. . Vol. V. p. 201)
59	Above the figure of another male devotee in the same. (16/1090)	...	...	...	Do.	Figures which make 15 on all sides. 4 | 9 | 2 3 | 5 | 7 8 | 1 | 6 Another piece contains the name of the person that presented the pillar. (T. A. S. Vol. V. 201)
60	Above the figure of another male devotee in the same. (17/1090)	...	...	...	Tamil.	Contains some names. (T. A. S. Vol. V. p. 201)
	Do. (18/1090)	...	...	...	Tamil in Vaṭṭeḻuttu.	Fragment.

62	Near the drawing of prostrating figure engraved on the floor of the Mahāmaṇḍapa of the same. (19/1090)	...	...	...	Tamil (Modern)	Mentions the name of a private person. (T. A.S. Vol. V. p. 201)
63	On another pillar of the same temple. (20/1090)	...	...	...	Tamil.	See 16/1090.
64	On the six pillars in front of the temple of Kanyā Bhagavati at Kanyākumāri (1 to 48/1092; 42 to 47/1085; and 12/1095)	Cōḷa.	Vīrarājēndra Cōḷa.	7th	Sanskrit in Grantha and Tamil.	Contains the genealogy the Cōḷa and registers gift land to the temple at Kanyākumāri. (T.A. S. Vol. III. 87)
65	On the boundary stone at Muṭṭam near Kanyākumāri. (49/1092)	...	...	Kollam 706 Pankuni 20	Tamil.	Damaged.
66	On the boundary stone near the Teppakulam at Kanyākumāri (50/1092)	...	...	...	Do.	Contains the words:—பண்டசாலைக்கு அஞ்சினான் புகலிடமாக காலெல்லைக்குள் பட்டதங்கேதம் and some symbols such as Chatra Cāmara, Ankuśa, Sankha and a staff.

Kanyākumāri. (*contd.*)

No.	Place of inscription.	Dynasty.	King.	Date.	Language and Alphabet.	Remarks.
67	On the wall of Pāpanāśam tank at Kanyākumāri. (51/1092)	...	...	Ko. 627 Āvaṇi	Tamil	Seems to register a gift of two lamps. (T. A. S. Vol. VII. p. 65)
68	On the north wall of the second *prākāra* of the Kanyābhagavati temple at Kanyākumāri. (1/1095)	Cōḷa Pāṇḍya.	Māravarman alias Uṭaiyār Sri Vikrama Cōḷa Pāṇḍya Dēva.	20th year	Do	Mentions Kōṭṭāru *alias* Mummuṭiccōḷanallūr in Nānjināṭu and the temple of Kanyāpaṭāriyār at Kumari in Purattāyanāṭu; incomplete. (T. A. S. Vol. VI. p. 152)
69	On the same wall (2 1095)	Do.	Do.	27th year	Do.	Damaged and incomplete. Registers a gift made by Nārāyaṇa Tiruccirrambalamuṭaiyan, a native of Pērayarkuṭi in Mulaikkattunāṭu a sub division of Arumoḷidēvavalaāāṭu which was a district of Cōḷamaṇḍalam, to the temple mentioned in No. 1 above. (T. A. S. Vol. VI. p. 152)

70	Do. (3/1095)	Do.	Jaṭāvarman *alias* Sri Sundara Cōla Pāṇḍya Dēva.	13th year	Tamil.	Damaged. Registers gift of sheep for a lamp to the same temple by a private individual. Mentions Karuṅkuḷanāṭu. (T. A. S. Vol. VI. p. 141)
71	Do. (4/1095)	Cōḷa.	Rājarāja varman Rājarāja Dēva.	6th year	Do.	Incomplete. Registers gift of money for a lamp. Contains the introduction திருமக ள்போல and mentions the conquests of Vēṅgaināṭu Gangapāṭi, Nulambapaṭi, Taṭiyapāṭi, Kuṭamalaināṭu, Kollam, Kalingam and Iḷamaṇḍalam. (T. A. S. Vol. p. 142)
72	On the west wall of the same *prākāra*. (5/1095)	Do.	Rājarāja I.	...	Tamil in Vaṭṭeḻuttu.	Fragmentary. Mentions Kumarimangalam in Purattāyanāṭu, a sub division of Rājarāja Vaḷānaṭu. Seems to provide for a lamp. (T. A. S. Vol. VI. p 145/F N)

Kanyākumāri. *(contd.)*

No.	Place of inscription.	Dynasty.	King.	Date.	Language and Alphabet.	Remarks.
73	On the same wall. (6/1095)	Cōḷa Pāṇḍya.	Jaṭāvarman *alias* Uṭaiyār Sri Sundara Cōḷa Pāṇḍya Dēva.	(10th) year	Tamil.	Registers a gift of 50 sheep for a lamp to the temple of Kanniyāpaṭāriyār at Kumari in Purattāyanāṭu, a sub division of Uttamacōḷavaḷanāṭu, which was a district of Rājarāja-Pāṇḍināṭu by a maid-servant of queen Mukkokiḻān Aṭikal. Mentions Uttungatungavalanāṭu. (T. A. S. Vol. VI. p. 150).
74	At the entrance into the *Karivēlam* in the same temple. (7/1095)	...	...	...	Do.	Contains the words Iravikēralanmaṇḍagam.
75	On the south wall of the same. (8/1095)	Cōḷa.	Rājarāja kēsarivanmar.	(20th year)	Do.	Unfinished. Begins with the historical introduction திருமகள் போல etc. (T. A. S. Vol. VI. p. 145)

76	On the east wall of the *maṇḍapa* in front of the same temple. (near the steps leading to the well) (9/1098 and 28/1087)	Do.	Parakēsarivarman *alias* Rajēndra Cōḷadēva.	5th year.	Do.	Gift of 25 sheep for a lamp to the temple of Kanniyāpaṭāriyār at Kumari, in Purattāyanāṭu, a sub division of Rājarāja-maṇḍalam, by a native of the Cōḷa country. (T. A. S. Vol. VI. p. 147)
77	On the same wall. (10/1095)	Do.	Sundara Cōḷa Pāṇḍya dēva.	18th year.	Do.	Fragment. (T. A. S. Vol. VI. p. 151 F. N.)
78	On a pillar of the *maṇḍapa* at the northern entrance into the second prākāra of the same temple. (11/1085 and 40/1085)	Travancore.	Sankaranārāyaṇa Venrumaṇkoṇḍa Bhūtala Vīra Udaiya mārttāṇḍavarman of Jayatunganāṭu.	Kollam 708, Mārkaḷi 21. ba. di. 8; Thursday, Hasta.	Do.	Registers a gift of land for offerings to the temple of Bhagavati Nācciyār at Kumari, on the occasion of the service called Vīramārttāṇḍan Sandhi. At the time of making the grant the king was encamped at Vīramārttāṇḍacaturvēdimangalam named after himself and situated in Kaḷakkāṭu *alias* Cōḷakuḷavallipuram, a village in Paccaṟuppōkku, a sub-division of Vānavan-nāṭu. Sections 2 and 4 are so engraved as to be read from bottom to top. (T. A. S. Vol. VI. p. 126)

Kanyākumāri. (*contd.*)

No.	Name of inscription.	Dynasty.	King.	Date.	Language and Alphabet.	Remarks
79	On six pillars in the maṇimaṇḍapa of the same temple. (12/1095, 42 to 47/1085 and 1 to 48/1092)	Cōḷa.	Rājakēsari varman *alias* Vīrarājēndradēva.	7th.	Grantha and Tamil.	Incomplete. Contains the genealogy of the Cōḷas and registers gift of the village of Narrarakkuṭi. (T. A. S. Vol. III. p. 87)
80	On a slab in Kumarimuṭṭam near Kanyākumāri. (50/1099 and 48/1085)	...	...	Ko. 669, Cittirai 15.	Tamil.	Registers a royal gift of certain taxes on fishing rights from the income from which a lamp was to be burnt in the paḷḷi at Kumarimuṭṭam. (T A. S. Vol. VI. p 179)
81	On another slab in the same. (51/1099 and 49/1085)	Travancore.	Ciraivāy Mūtta Tampirānār.	Ko. 701, Panguni 20.	Do.	Records certain exemption of taxes which the king was pleased to grant to Mūtta Kangan. (T A. S. Vol. VI. p. 181)
82	On a slab in the grave yard opposite to the same church. (52/1099)	...	...	A. D. 18	Do.	Records the death of a private individual. (T. A. S. Vol. VI. p. 181)

83	On a slab kept in the R. C. Church at Cape Comorin. (53/1099 and 33/1087)	...	...	A. D. 1763, March 13.	Dutch.	Records the death of Mr. Casper Coenrad Smith of Hamburg, Book-keeper and First Resident in charge of the Company's trade. (T. A. S. Vol. VI. p. 181)
84	On the wall of the namaskāramaṇḍapa in the Kanyābhagavati temple at Kanyākumāri. (38/1100)	Pāṇḍya.	Jaṭāvarmn alias Parān takadēva.	9th year.	Do.	Built in at the beginning and some what damaged. Refers to some gift of land for the conduct of worship to the goddess Kanyā-Bhagavati.
85	On a pillar in the north-west corner in the second prākāra in the same temple. (39/1100)	...	...	Kollam 745, Cittirai.	Do.	States that Periyanayanar-Mudaliar and others built the portion of the maṇḍapa.
86	On a pillar standing rightside of the Mukha-maṇḍapa in the northern entrance of the Kanyā-Bhagavati temple, Kanyākumāri. (9/1105)	...	...	Ko. 589 Āni 28.	Do.	States that Sandal paste weighing 3 palams be given to Kumari Bhāgāvati for Kārtikai by Peṟṟa Perumāl, the son of Tattan Tampi Katanallan, a devotee.

Kanyākumāri. (*contd.*)

No.	Place of inscription.	Dynasty.	King.	Date.	Language and Alphabet.	Remarks.
87	On the inner wall of the first Prākāra (back wall of the Srībalippura) in north-western corner of the same temple. (10/1105)	Pāṇḍya.	Ko. Jaṭaya Varma Tribhuvana Cakravarti Kulasēkharadēva.	9th year 1149 day year 943	Tamil.	Begins with the introduction பூகலைமடந்தை புகழுடன் மேவிய and registers that from the income derived from Kulasēkhara Caturvēdimangalam *alias* Kodalur in Melvembanaṭu which is a Devadanam 50 *Kasus* be utilised to feed Paradesis who come for Taipusa festival of Kumari Bhagavati. (see also 29/1087)
88	On the base of the Dvaja stambha of the Kanyā Bhagavati temple at Kanyākumāri. (14/1107 22/1087 and 1111)	Vijaya nagara.	...	...	Sanskrit Grantha.	Begins with the introduction नमस्तुंगशिर...... Mentions Vira Nrisimha, Acyuta Rāya Ranga Rāya, Krishna Rāya and Rāma Rāya. Damaged.
89	On the western wall of the second prākāra of the same. (15/1107)	Cōḷa.	Rājēndra Cōḷa.	...	Tamil.	Begins with the introduction [illegible].

90	On the left side post at the eastern entrance behind the dvajastambha in the same. (3/1111)	...	...	Ko. 740. Āṭi 10.	Tamil.	Damaged. Seems to register a gift and refers to Dēvi, daughter of Āṇḍicci Ammai of Isāntimangalam.
91	On the back of the western wall of the same. (4/1111)	Cōḷa.	Rājakēsari.	15th year.	Tamil in Vaṭṭeḻuttu.	The inscription is highly damaged. Seems to refer to the gift of 25 sheep for a lamp.
92	On a pillar just north of the Maṇi-Maṇḍapa in Ūtsavabēra Shrine, Kanyā Bhagavati temple, Cape Comorin. (1/1113)	Cōḷa.	Kulōttunga Cōḷa.	14th year.	Tamil.	Records the gift of some 'Kalams' for the feeding of Brahmins.
93	On a pillar on the left side of the northern entrance where the Police Guard is placed in the same temple, Cape Comorin. (2/1113)	Travancore.	King born in Trikkēṭṭa (Iravivarmar).	Ko 759. Arpasi	Do.	Damaged. Records the gift of 500 fanams.
94	On a stone south of the Roman Catholic Church, Cape Comorin. (17/1113)	...	...	...	Do.	Fragmentary. Mentions "Ancinān-pukaliṭam."

Karaikuḷam. (Neṭumaṅṅāṭu)

No.	Place of inscription.	Dynasty.	King.	Date.	Language and Alphabet.	Remarks.
1	On the lintel of the Tirumānūr Siva temple at Karaikuḷam. (35/1095)	...	...	...	Tamil in Vaṭṭeḻuttu.	Relates to repairs executed in the temple of the Mahādēva at Karaikuḷam. (T. A. S. Vol. VII. p. 96)
2	On the Yāḻi screen at the entrance into the Viṣṇu temple at Sanaccal near Karaikuḷam. (37/1095)	...	...	...	Do.	Records that Kāman Kunran of Mayilam built the temple and its entrance. (T. A. S. Vol. VII. p. 97)

Karakunnu (Mūvaṟṟupuḻa)

No.	Place of inscription.	Dynasty.	King.	Date.	Language and Alphabet.	Remarks.
1	On a tomb-stone in the door-way of the Syrian church at Karakkunnu. (94/1100)	...	...	A. D. 1670, Kollam 845, Mīnam 7, Monday.	Do.	States that Koreda-Accar died and went to (the abode of) god (tamburan). (T. A. S. Vol. VII. p. 142)

Kariyamanikkapuram. (Agastīsvaram)

1	On the east base of the *Mahāmaṇḍapa* of the Viṣṇu temple at Kariyamāṇikkapuram. (near Sucīndrum) (106/1099)	Travancore.	Kulasēkhara Nambiraṭṭiyār.	Kollam 643, Cittirai 30.	Tamil.	States that Kulasēkhara Nambirāṭṭiyār repaired the temple of Nayinār Kariyamāṇikka-Viṇṇakar Emperumān at Iṭarāyakkuṭi, built the *mahāmaṇḍapa* and the stepped porch (sōpānam) and had the consecration ceremony performed. (T. A. S. Vol. VI. p. 44)
2	On the east wall of the same *maṇḍapa*. (107/1099)	...	...	Kollam 734, Vaikāsi 15, Pancami, Friday, Makayiram.	Do.	Registers gift of land by Madisūdan of Mangalaccēri for thatching the *ambalam* attached to the temple with cadjan leaves, for supplying gruel every fortnight, and also for feeding *Brahmans* during newmoon days at Agastīsvaram. (T.A.S. Vol. VI. p. 47)
3	On the same wall. (108/1099)	Travancore.	Āditya Varman *alias* Ciravāy-mūtta.	Kollam 734, Āni 11.	Tamil.	Records that while the king was staying in the new palace at Vīrakēraḷēsvaram near Muttalaikkurucci, be exempted the lands set apart for the above charity, from the payment of several taxes. (T. A. S. Vol. VI. p. 48)

Kariyamāṇikkapuram. (*contd.*)

No.	Place of inscription.	Dynasty.	King.	Date.	Language and Alphabet	Remarks.
4	On the north base of the kitchen of the same temple. (109/1099)	...	...	Kollam 685, Avani 14, ba. 13, Monday, Pusyam.	Do:	Records gift of land by purchase by Arangan Peruman, Bhaatta-ariya of Tattaippattinam in Sembinadu for daily offerings, and supply of garlands to the god Kariyamanikka-Vinnagar Emberuman in Idarāyakkudi *alias* Raja-nārāyana-caturvedimangalam. (T. A. S. Vol. VI. p. 45)
	Kaṭhinamkuḷam. (Trivandrum)					
1	At the left of entrance into the Mahādēva temple at Kaṭhinamkuḷam. (31/1095)	Vēnāṭu.	Vīra Rāman Kēraḷa-varma Tiru-vaṭi.	Jupiter in Kumbham Kollam 389+1 Mīnam 18 Thursday Puṣya.	Tamil in Vaṭṭeḻuttu.	Mentions Sri Vīra Rāman Umaiyammai. (T. A. S. Vol. IV. p. 69.)
2	On the base of the west wall of the first *prākāra* of the same temple. (32/1095)	...	...	Kollam 492 Mēṣa 1.	Do.	Damaged. Registers gift of land and taxes for feeding 33 Brāhmans in the temple of Mahādeva at Kaṭhinamkuḷam *alias* Vīrakēraḷapuram.

Kaṭṭimānkōṭu. (Kalkulam)

1	On the four faces of a pillar set up in front of the Mahādēva temple Kaṭṭimāñkōṭu, Kalkulam Taluk. (8/1112)	...	...	S. 1775 () Ko. 849 A. D. 1674 Saturday.	Tamil.	Gift of land for the *Ucca* pūja and offerings by *Kanakku* Uṭayān Īccaran belonging to *Daivaputra* caste in Kaṭṭimānkōṭu.
2	On a pillar in the *maṇḍapa* of the same temple. (9/1112)	...	...	Ko. 47 (?)	Do. Vaṭṭeḻuttu.	Refers to the contribution of a pillar by Ādiccan Nārāyaṇan.

Kaviyūr. (Tiruvalla

1	On the base of the central shrine in the Siva temple at Kaviyūr. (16/1098 and 2/1087)	...	...	Kali 4051	Tamil in Vaṭṭeḻuttu.	Records gift of land by Dēvan Cēnnan of Makilañjēri for offerings, lamps, sandal and incense to the god at Kaviyūr. (T. A. S. Vol. V. p. 6 and Vol. I. p. 288)
2	On the same base. (17/1098 and 1/1087)	...	...	Kali 4052	Do.	Records gift of land by Nārāyaṇa Krṣṇan of Mangalam for lamps and offerings to the same god. (T. A. S. Vol. V. p. 7 and Vol. I. p. 289)

Kaviyūr (*contd.*)

o.	Place of inscription.	Dynasty.	King.	Date.	Language and Alphabet.	Remarks.
3	On a lamp-pillar outside the temple at the turning of the lane (18/1098)	...	...	...	Malayalam.	Records gift of a stone lampstand by Kadukkandi.
4	On a pillar in the Cuṟṟū-*maṇḍapa* of the Siva temple at Kaviyūr. (3/1087	...	..	...	Do.	Contains the words:—വൈ[illegible]ിപ്പട്ടതിരി പണിചയിപ്പി[illegible] [illegible]. (T. A. S. Vol. V. p. 7 F. N.
	Kēraḷapuram. (Kalkulam)					
1	On the south base of the central shrine of the Siva temple, Kēraḷapuram. (8/1086)	Travancore.	Vīra Udaya Mārttāṇḍa Varma Tiruvaṭi Vīra Paṇḍyadēva	Kollam 491	Tamil.	Grant of taxes to the temple of Vīrakeraḷēśvaram at Muttalakkuricci. (T. A. S. Vol. IV. p. 91)

2	On the west base of the same. (9/1086)	Do.	Vīra Ravi Ravivarman born in the Tirukkēṭṭai nakṣatrā, son of Umaiyammai who was born in the Rohini nakṣatra belonging to the Tiruppāppūr Svarūpam and Kīḻappērūr-illam	Kollam 4708 *Ravistudhanyaissaha* Kali day, Kollam 782, Cittirai 6 Friday, Svati, ka. 1.	Do.	Records that the king (with many praises) rebuilt the temple of Vīrakēraḷēśvaram in Muttalakkuricci in Ceṅgaḻunīr Vaḷanāṭu. (T. A. S. Vol. I. p. 179)
3	On the base of the maṇḍapa in front of the same. (54/1093)	...	...	Kollam 782 Cittirai 6, Jupiter in Mīnam	Tamil.	States that the individual Aiyyan Aiyyan of Parakkōṭṭu dēśam set up the two pillars containing the sculpture of Cēramān perumāl and Sundarapperumāl. (T. A. S. Vol. V. p. 94)
4	On the base of the *maṇḍapa* in front of the same. (55/1093)	..	...	Kollam 792 Cittirai 6	Do.	This is the *sadāsēvai* of two ladies who set up the pillar of Kulaśēkharapperumāl. (T. A. S. Vol. V. p. 95)

Kēraḷapuram, (*contd.*)

No.	Place of inscription.	Dynasty.	King.	Date.	Language and Alphabet.	Remarks.
5	On the base of the *maṇḍapa* in front of the same. (56/1093)	Cōḷa Pāṇḍya.	*Jaṭāvarman Sundara-Cōḷa Pāṇḍya.	27th year	Tamil Vaṭṭeḻuttu	Fragmentary. Mentions temple of Tiruvarangamuṭaiyār.
6	Do. Do. (57/1093)	...	...	Kollam 782 Cittirai 6	Tamil.	Records that the *sadāsēvai* of Nācciyār, the daughter of Nācciyār, to the shrine of Mahādēva of Kēraḷapuram. (T. A. S. Vol. V. p. 95)
7	On five pillars of the Cuṟṟu-maṇḍapa (back of the shrine) of the same (58/1093)	...	...	do.	do.	*Sadāsēvai* of Dēvan Tiruvikkiraman who presented the pillar. (T. A. S. Vol. V. p. 114)
8	do. do. (59/1093)	...	...	do.	do.	Records the name of the person who presented the pillar. (T. A. S. Vol. V. p. 115)

9	do. do. (60/1093)	...	...	do.	do.	Records that Tiruvālmārvan presented the pillar. (T. A. S. Vol. V. p. 115)
10	do. do. (61/1093)	...	...	do.	do.	Records the *sadāsēvai* of Iravi of Vilavūr who presented the pillar. (T. A. S. Vol. V. p. 115)
11	do. do. (62/1093)	...	...	do.	do.	Records that Pāppan Pāppan of Pālaikkōṭu presented the pillar. (T. A. S. Vol. V. p. 115)
12	On the base of the *Oṟṟaikkal* in front of the central shrine of the same. (63/1093)	...	...	do.	do.	Fragmentary. Relates to a gift of land whose details are given. Mentions Muttalakkuricci.
13	On the east, north and south walls of the maṇḍapa in front of the Kṛṣṇa temple at Kēraḷapuram. (64/1093)	...	...	Sa. 1631 Ko. 887 Āvaṇi 5 Monday uttiram. su. 3	do.	Refers to the gift of certain lands by Silaya Pillai Ariyakkuṭṭi to the temple in Ko. 838 when Ravi Ravi Varman Ciravaymūttatampirān was the reigning king and states that a stone was set up by the donor's son. (T. A. S. Vol. V. p. 116)

Kiḻimānūr. (Cirayinkīl.

No.	Place of inscription.	Dynasty.	King.	Date.	Language and Alphabet.	Remarks.
1	On a pillar in the Siva temple of Dēvēccuram near Kiḻimānūr. (115/1096)	...	...	...	Malayalam.	Contains the syllables '*Kaida Kondapp-Nayar Koṇakku*'. Probably this is the name of the person that presented the pillar. (T. A. S. Vol. VII. p. 105 F. N.).
2	On another pillar in the same temple. (116/1096)	...	...	...	Malayalam in Vaṭṭeḻuttu.	States that the pillar was presented by a certain Kēśavun. (T. A. S. Vol. p. 105 F. N.)
3	On a third pillar in the same temple. (117/1096)	...	...	...	Malayalam.	Another private individual presented this pillar. (T. A. S. Vol. VII. p. 105 F. N.)
4	On the south base of the Subrahmaṇya Shrine in the Ālattūrkāvu temple near Kiḻimānūr. (119/1096)	...	...	Koilam 616 Ṛṣabha.	Do. Vaṭṭeḻuttu.	Registers that Sankaran Akikkiraman of Vamanapalli and Narayanan Tiruvikkiraman of Pallimanram caused the temple to be built of stone and covered it with copper sheets. (T. A. S. Vol. VII. p. 105)

5	On a lamp-stand in front of the Māṭan shrine in the same place. (120/1096)	...	...	...	Malayalam.	States that a native of Vattamvilakam had it made. (T. A. S. Vol. VII. p. 105).
6	On the east base of the maṇḍapa in the temple at Kēśavapuram near the same village. (121/1096)	...	...	Kollam 746 Vṛscika 19.	Do.	Damaged. Records that the *maṇḍapa* was built by a native of Pallikkal. (T. A. S. Vol. VII. p. 100)
7	On the base of the *nālambalam* opposite the same maṇḍapa. (122/1096)	...	...	...	Do.	Unfinished. Mentions Kēśavapurattu-Mukkālvaṭṭam. (T. A. S. Vol. VII. p. 100 F. N.)
			Kiḷḷiyūr. (Viḷavankōṭu)			
1	On a stone pillar set up near a ruined Śiva temple at Kiḷḷiyūr. (44/1100)	Travancore.	Udaya-mārttāṇḍavarman.	Kollam 354, Vṛscika 8, Mūlam.	Tamil.	States that when the king was encamped in the flower-garden to the east of Tiruvāṭṭāru, he made a gift of land to Sēkharan-Kumāran of Vayakkalūr for the expenses of the temple of God Mahādēva of Pirāyīsvaram in Kiḷḷiyūr. (T. A. S. Vol. VII p. 25)

Kṛikkāṭu. (Kārttikappaḷḷi)

No.	Place of inscription.	Dynasty.	King.	Date.	Language and Alphabet.	Remarks.
1	On the four sides of the base of the platform built round a Pippala tree in Kṛikkāṭu near Kāyamkuḷam. (97/1092)	...	....	Ko. 1028 Iṭava, Karkaṭaka-Rāṣi, Paurṇima, Rōhiṇi.	Malayalam.	Records that the temple was consecrated on this day mentioned.

Kōtamaṅgalam. (Mūvāṟṟupuḻa.)

No.	Place of inscription.	Dynasty.	King.	Date.	Language and Alphabet.	Remarks.
1	On a bell kept above the altar in the Valiyapaḷḷi at Kōtamaṅgalam. (87/1100)	...	...	Kollam 905 Kanni 8.	Malayālam.	States that the bell was cast for the church on that day. (T. A. S. Vol. VII. p. 143)
2	On a tombstone kept in the same church. (88/1100)	...	...	Kollam 819, Vṛscika 13.	Tamil in Vaṭṭeḻuttu.	The name of the individual is not readable. (T. A. S. Vol. VII. p. 142)
3	On another tombstone. (89/1100)	...	...	Kollam 794, Mēṭam 30.	Do.	Records the death of Kuriyada Paṅiccar, the wife of Korada of Mudalakkodam. (T. A. S. Vol. VII. p. 142)

	Do. (90/1100)	....	...	Kollam 809, Kanni 18.	Do.	Records the death of Avirān Koratta of Mudalakkodam. (T. A. S. Vol. VII. p. 142)
5	On a tombstone in the Ceriyapaḷḷi at Kōtamaṅgalam. (91/1100.)	...	...	Kollam 775, Makaram 3, Saturday.	Do.	States that......ccar died. (T. A. S. Vol. VII. p. 143)
6	On another tombstone in the same church. (92/1100)	...	...	Kollam 774, Vṛscika 1 (9), Monday.	Tamil in Vaṭṭeḻuttu.	Records the death of Ittiyira of Mundekkal. (T. A. S. Vol. VII. p. 143)
7	Do. (93/1100)	...	...	Kollam 893, Makaram 3.	Do.	Records the death of Tomman Mattāyi. (T. A. S. Vol. VII. p. 143)

Kōticcanakaram. (Kō-ccaippiṭāram, Agastīṣvaram.)

1	On a slab set up in the compound of the Visṇu temple Kōticcanakaram near Nāgerkōil. (110/1099)	...	...	Kollam 669, Āvaṇi 20, su. 7, Tuesday, Anusham.	Tamil.	Registers the gift of money by Gaṅgādhara-Brahmacāri, a *Brahmin* of Āryadēṣam, Siṅgapperumāl of Toṇḍaimaṇḍalam, and Sokkiyār of Cōlamaṇḍalam, from the interest from which certain Brahmans were to be fed. (T. A. S. Vol. VI. p. 136)

Koṭumāḷūr. (Kōṭṭayam.)

No.	Place of inscription.	Dynasty.	King.	Date.	Language and Alphabet.	Remarks.
	On a stone built into the *gopura* of the Kṛṣṇa temple at Vāsudēvapuram in Koṭumāḷūr. (5/1091)	...	...	Kollam 878 Simha 7.	Malayalam.	Mentions a certain Unni of Kana.....................

Kōṭṭār. (Agastīṣvaram)

No.	Place of inscription.	Dynasty.	King.	Date.	Language and Alphabet.	Remarks.
1	On a slab embedded in a chapel in the R. C. Church at Kōṭṭār. (54/1099)	...	...	A. D. 1825.	Latin.	States that Rev. Alexio de Souza, the Bishop of Cochin, who died on the day mentioned, was buried in the church.
2	On the same slab. (55/1099).	...	...	A. D. 1823, Kārttikai 27.	Tamil.	Requests that a prayer be said for the repose of the soul of Padre Allesu De Souza, who has been buried in the grave.

3	On another slab near the same chapel. (56/1099)	...	...	A. D. 1823, Nov. 11.	English.	Records the death of Mary Truyens, wife of J. N. F. Everett.
4	On the same slab. (57/1099)	...	...	A. D. 1823, Nov. 11.	Tamil.	Records the same facts as the above.
5	On a stone in the Dēśivināyakar temple, Ceṭṭi Street, Kōṭṭār. (117/1099)	...	...	Śaka 1619, Kollam 872, Mārkaḻi 26, Friday, Rōhiṇi Su. 12 Pulikkaraṇam, Śubhayōgam.	Do.	States that Śeṭṭu Vendavalandān of the Nedunteruvu of Koṭṭaru probably built the shrine.
6	On a slab kept near the well called the *Maṅgammāl Kiṇaru* near Kōṭṭār. (118/1099.	Madura Nayaka.	Maṅgammāl.	Śaka 1619... śu. 2 Subhayōgam, Pannikaraṇam, Hasta.	Do.	Very much misspelt. Mentions Maṅgammāl, and the date of the record falls in the period of regency of the famous Maṅgammāl of Madura. The record presumably relates to the digging of the well. (T. A. S. Vol. V. p. 210)

Koṭṭārakkara.

No.	Place of inscription.	Dynasty.	King.	Date.	Language & Alphabet.	Remarks.
1	On the southern base of the central shrine in the temple at Koṭṭārakkara. (1/1088)	...	...	...	Malayalam Vaṭṭeḻuttu.	Fragmentary.
2	Do. (2/1088)	...	...	...	Do.	Do.
3	On a stone lying in the court-yard of the Nambūri's Maṭham situated on the south-east of the Gaṇapati temple at Koṭṭārakkara. (96/1092)	...	...	...	Do. (Archaic)	Fragment.

4	On the east base of the central shrine of the Viṣṇu temple at Kōṭṭattala near Koṭṭārakkara. (3/1094)	...	...	Kollam 410 Simha.	Tamil in Vaṭṭeḻuttu.	Records provisions made for feeding 15 persons by Tāyan Kēśavan of Mannilam for the merit of his dead father. 6 persons had to be fed on the day of Āśleṣa in the month of Simha, 6 persons on the day of Śatabhishaj in Mīna and 3 persons on the day of Punarvasu in Dhanus. (T. A. S. Vol. VII. p. 66)
5	On the balikkal of the Siva temple at Veṭṭikavila, Koṭṭārakkara Taluk. (3/1098)	...	...		Do.	Records that Dēvan-Nārāyaṇan and Nārāyaṇan-Keśavan set up the bali-stone. (T. A. S. Vol. VI. p. 140)
6	On the pedestal of the flagstaff of the same temple. (4/1098)	...	...	Kollam 923, Iṭavam 13.	Malayalam.	States that the flagstaff was erected on the day mentioned. (T. A. S. Vol. VI. p. 140)
7	On a stone lampstand outside the temple. (5/1098)	...	...	Kollam 925.	Malayalam.	States that the lampstand was the gift of Marttāṇḍan Śankaran of Kulikkāṭu. (T. A. S. Vol. VI. p. 140)

Koṭṭārakkara (*contd.*)

No.	Place of inscription.	Dynasty.	King.	Date.	Language & Alphabet.	Remarks.
8	On the balistone in the Kṛṣṇasvāmin temple. (6/1098)	...	...	Kollam 824, Makaram 18.	Tamil in Vaṭṭeḻuttu.	States that the balikkal was constructed by Kaṇḍan, the *kaṇakku* of Valakkunram. (T. A. S. Vol. VI p 141)
9	On the south side of the base of the central shrine in the Maṇikaṇṭheśvara temple at Koṭṭārakkara. (7/1098)	...	...	...	Do.	Mentions that the name of the temple is Maṇikaṇṭheśvaram. The inscription is much damaged.
10	On the same base. (8/1098)	...	...	...	Do.	Specifies certain restrictions on the residents of Kuṭṭanāṭu. The record is incomplete.
11	On several stones lying scattered on the tank-bund and in the maṭha. (9-13/1098 and 2/1104)	...	...	...	Tamil in Vaṭṭeḻuttu.	These fragments engraved in the same writing were copied with a view to connect them if possible, but they are separate fragments and some more pieces are missing. It is reported that they have been utilised in building the tank bund.

12	A few fragmentary inscriptions from the Gaṇapathi temple Koṭṭārakkara. (1/1104)	...	...	...	Do.	Fragmentary.
			Kōṭṭayam.			
1 to 21	On slabs built into the steps in front of the Valiapaḷḷi Church at Kōṭṭayam. (4 to 24/1096)	...	..	...	Malayalam Vaṭṭeḻuttu.	Records the names of deceased persons and the dates on which they died. (T. A. S. Vol. IV. 166.)
22	On a stone in the flooring in the Viṣṇu temple at Muṭṭambalam near Kōṭṭayam. (66/1100)	...	...	...	Malayalam.	The writing is much damaged on account of exposure. Mentions Dāmōdara-Kṛṣṇan and Nārāyaṇan, who probably got the flooring paved.
23	On the base of the pial in the Balikkalpurai of the Śiva temple at Tirunakkara. (88/1087)	...	...	212 plus 1st year after the appearance of Iravipuram.	Tamil in Vaṭṭeḻuttu.	Records that when Iravi Kēraḷar was staying in the Vātilmāṭam of Tirunakkarai, certain provisions of rice and money were made to the temple.

Kṛṣṇankōvil. (Vaṭaśēri, Agastīśvaram.)

No.	Place of inscription.	Dynasty.	King.	Date.	Language & Alphabet.	Remarks.
1	On the four faces of the stone lying on the south side of the second prākāra of the Kṛṣṇasvāmi temple at Kṛṣṇankōvil near Nāgerkōil. (66/1084)	...	...	Ko. 639.	Tamil.	Gift of ... ...to the God Rūpanārāyaṇa of Vaṭaśēri *alias* Ādityavarma-Caturvēdimaṅgalam. (T. A. S. Vol. V p. 125.)
2	On a stone built into the east wall of the first prākāra of the same. (67/1084)	...	...	Ko. 548.	Do.	Fragmentary. (T. A. S. Vol. V. p. 127)
3	On the east base of the flag staff in front of the same. (68/1084)	...	..	Ko. 945.	Do.	Records the setting up of the flag-staff. (T. A. S. Vol. V. p. 127)
4	On the west base of the *maṇḍapa* in front of the north gate leading into the first prākāra of the same. (69/1084)	...	...	Vikṛti.	Do.	Fragmentary.

5	On the east base of the same. (70/1084)	...	...	Ko. (608)	Tamil.	Do. (T. A. S. Vol. V. p. 127)
6	On the east base of the *maṇḍapa* in front of the central shrine of the same. (71/1084)	Travancore.	(Sarvāṅganātha) Ādityavarman.	...	Sanskrit in Grantha.	Praises of the King. (T. A. S. Vol. I. p. 172)
7	On the north base (outside) of the *maṇḍapa* in front of the central shrine of the Kṛṣṇasvāmi temple, Kṛṣṇankōvil. (Vaṭaśēri) (1 /1086)	Do.	...	Ko. 839	Tamil.	Damaged.
8	On the south wall of the *maṇḍapa* in the Taḷiyil Mahādēvar temple at Vaṭaśēri. (111/1099)	Travancore.	Jayatuṅganāṭṭu Śaṅkara-Nārāyaṇa Venṟumaṇkoṇṭa Bhūtalavīra Vīra Udaya mārttāṇḍavarman Tiruppāppūr, Mūttavar.	Kollam 708, Kārttikai 12, su. 13 Sunday, Aśvati.	Tamil.	Registers that when the King was staying in his new palace at Vīra [illegible]ārttāṇḍa-caturvēdimaṅgalam in Kalakkāṭu *alias* Cōḷakulavallipuram, he appointed Ariyan Cokkapperumāl Mārtāṇḍa-brahmādarāyan, of the *Kōtukulasabha* at Suchindram, as the accountant of the temple of Nanatisvaramuṭaiya-Nayinār at Vaṭaśēri, with the perquisites appertaining to that Office. (T. A. S. Vol. VI. p. 130)

Kṛṣṇankōvil. (*contd.*)

No.	Place of inscription.	Dynasty.	King.	Date.	Language & Alphabet.	Remarks.
9	On a slab set up in the roadside near the same temple. (112/1109)	...	...	Kollam 873 Kārttikai 4.	Tamil.	Registers the resolutions decided on by the ryots of Nānjināṭu in regard to the stoppage of certain taxes which they were unable to pay on account of the disordered state of the country consequent on the Nāyaka invasions from Kollam 852. The record states that this stone was engraved in accordance with the resolution of 13th Vaikāsi 871, and that copies of it were set up at two other places. (T. A. S. Vol. V. p. 210)

10	On a slab set up in the Kommanḍaiamman temple at the same place. (113/1099)	Cōḷa.	Rājarāja I.	18th year.	Tamil.	First two lines broken off. Registers the gift of land by purchase from the *Ūrār* of Tirukkōṭṭāru by Kōn-Koṟṟan *alias* Nēriyamūvēntavēḷār of Cirnasur in Ārkāṭṭukkūṟṟam, a division of Conadu, for the expenses of providing offerings to Piṭāriyār Kommanḍainangai of Vaṭaśēri, a suburb of Tirukkōṭṭāru in Nānjināṭu, which was a subdivision of Rajaraja-vaḷanāṭu. (T. A. S. Vol. VI. p. 143)
11	On the wall of the Madhavamaṭham near the same temple. (114/1099)	...	...	Śaka 1615, Kollam 870, Tai 29, ba. Saptami, Sunday, viruttiyōgam, Cingakkaraṇam, Svāti.	Tamil.	Damaged at the end. Registers the gift of land by Mayilērumperumāl Kumārasvāmi of Vaṭaśēri, a suburb of Tirukkōṭṭāru *alias* Mumuṭiccōḷapuram for the maintenance of the *panḍāram* staying in the *maṭham* built by the donor's father-in-law Māṭan-Mādhavan, and for the worship of the Piḷḷaiyār set up therein.

Kṛṣṇankōvil. (*contd.*)

No.	Place of inscription.	Dynasty.	King.	Date.	Language & Alphabet.	Remarks.
12	On the slab set up in the compound of a Vināyaka temple near the Government Satram, Vaṭaśēri. (115/1099 s. a. 11/1112.).	Travancore.	Jayatunganāṭṭu mūttavar and Ciravāy mūttavar.	Kollam 682, Āni 15. Ēkādaśi, Saturday, Asvati.	Tamil.	Registers certain tax-exemptions which were claimed by the Nāṭāḻvārs of the country lying between Tōvāḷai, Paraḷi and the hills on the east and west in accordance with the royal writs granted by Jayatunganāṭṭu-Mūttatiruvaṭi and Ciravāy-Mūttatiruvaṭi.
13	On a stone near the well inside the Kṛṣṇasvāmin temple, Kṛṣṇankōvil. (116/1099)	Travancore.	Cenpaka-Ādityavarman Ciravāy-mūttatu.	Kollam 639, Panguni 13.	Tamil.	States that the stone work of the well was finished on Vaikāśi 10, Kollam 640.

Kuḷattummēl. (Neṭumaṅgāṭu).

1	On the north base of the *maṇḍapa* in front of the Muliyur temple at Kuḷattummēl.(45/1095).	...	...	Kollam 773, Vṛscika (10).	Tamil in Vaṭṭeḻuttu.	Fragment, Mentions two private individuals of Kīc-cēri. (T. A. S. Vol. VII. p. 97.)

Kuḻikkōṭu. (Kalkulam)

1	On a boulder on the bund of a tank at Kuḻikkōṭu. (45/1100).	...	...	Jupiter in Tulām Panguni 1.	Tamil Vaṭṭeḻuttu.	The inscription is much damaged. The alphabet may belong to the 12th or the 13th century A. D. The name Jayankoṇḍacōḷapuram is traceable.
2	On a slab standing in a field in the same village. (46/1100).	...	...	Śaka 1704, Saturn in Dhanus Jupiter in Dhanus, Kollam 957, Subhakṛt, Cittirai, 8, Wednesday Makayiram.	Tamil.	Incomplete. Referes to the gift of some land by Māti-kkuṭṭi of Paḷḷiccavīṭu in Kaviyallūr-mēccēri to Brahmans of various gōtras as a *nānāgōtradāna*. (T. A. S. Vol. VII. p. 38.)

Kuḻitturai. (Viḻavankōṭu)

No.	Place of inscription.	Dynasty.	King.	Date.	Language and Alphabet.	Remarks.
1	On a rock in the north side of the Śiva temple at Kuḻitturai. (25/1096 and 76/1087.)	...	..	...	Tamil Vaṭṭeḻuttu.	Registers gift of lands made for offerings, worship, feeding *Brahmins*, *Sivārātri* expenses, lamps etc. in the shrines of Naṭuvattudēvar and Tekkindēvar. Mentions Pākōṭu.
2	On the same rock. (26/1096 and 77/1087.)	...	...	...	Do.	Records gift of lands for feeding *Brahmins* on *Amāvāsya* days, and for various other requirements in the shrines of Vaṭakkindēvar and Tekkindēvar. Mentions Dēvan Dēvan of Nanga-maṅgalam, Vikkiraman Dēvan of Ayiramarram, Pākōṭu etc. Below this is a much damaged later inscription in Vaṭṭeḻuttu dated in the year when Jupiter was in Vṛscika, recording a gift of

						money and mentioning Tirukkaṇḍiyūr Mahādēvar and Tiruvitāmkōṭu. (T. A. S. Vol. V. p. 160.)
3	On the same rock. (27/1096.)	...	...	Jupiter in Vṛschika, Kollam 423, Ṛṣabha 25, Rēvati.	Tamil in Vaṭṭeḻutu.	Damaged. Gift of land for offerings and feeding 12 Brahmins on the New Moon days. Mentions Tirukkaṟṟuraiambalam.
4	On the yāḻi screen at the side of the steps in the same temple. (28/1096.)	...	...	...	Do.	Damaged. Records provisions made for offerings, to the shrine of Tekkin-mahādēva at Tirukkaṟṟurai.
			Kumāramaṅgalam. (Toṭupuḻa.)			
1	On a bell kept in the Syrian Church at Kumāramaṅgalam. (85/1100.)	...	...	A. D. 1606 Mīnam 5	Do.	States that on this day the bell was given to the Mār Thōmmāppaḷḷi at Mayilakkombu.
2	On a stone set in the stair case of the priest's quarters in the same Church. (86/1100.)	...	...	Kollam...	Do.	Much damaged. This appears to be a tombstone.

Kumāranallūr. (Kōṭṭayam.)

No.	Place of inscription.	Dynasty.	King.	Date.	Language and Alphabet.	Remarks.
1	On a stone built into the floor in front of the kitchen of the Bhagavati temple at Kumāranallūr. (6/1091.)	...	...	...	Tamil in Vaṭṭeḻuttu.	Much damaged. Only the following is traceable:—குமாரநல்லூர்படாரி கோயில்க் கா,......
2	On the wall of the north portion of the Bhagavati temple at Kumāranallūr. (7/1091.)	...	...	...	Do.	Records certain rules and regulations made in respect of criminal offences such as meddling with the constitutions of the assembly of ūrār unlawful entry into private properties etc. (T. A. S. Vol. IV. p. 191.)

Kunnūrśālai. (Neṭumaṅgāṭu.)

No.	Place of inscription.	Dynasty.	King.	Date.	Language and Alphabet.	Remarks.
1	At the right of entrance into the Subrahmaṇya temple at Kunnūrśālai. (36/1905.)	...	....	...	Do.	Records that Cāttan Gōvindan and Kaṇṭan Cāttan of Naṟaikkāttūr built the temple. (T. A. S. Vol. VII. p. 99.)

	Kuṟattiyaṟa. (Tōvāḷa.)					
1	On a rock lying in Kuṟavantaṭṭuviḷa, Kuṟattiyaṟa. (16/1107.)	Cōḷa.	Parakēsari varma.	....	Tamil in Vaṭṭeḻuttu.	Damaged.
	Kuṟavalaṅgāṭu. (Kōṭṭayam.)					
1	On a bell in the tower of the R. C. Church at Kuṟavalaṅgāṭu (67/1100)	...	....	...	Greek?	On a line of writing on the rim of the bell in unknown characters.
2	On another bell within the church. (68/1100.)	....	...	A. D. 1581	Syriac.	Said to record the gift of the bell to the Church of the Holy Mary at Kuṟavalaṅgāṭu.
3	On three other bells in a separate out house in the same church compound. (69/1100)	...	...	A. D. 1910	Latin.	States that these bells were cast for the Kuṟavalaṅgāṭu Church in A. D. 1910 and were dedicated to S. Maria, S. Joseph and Emmanuel.
4	On a tomb stone in the sanctum of the same church. (70/1100.)	...	...	A. D. 1687	Syriac and Malayalam.	States that the tomb stone recording the death of Mar. Alexandrius the Metrappolitta of Malangara, on Thursday and his buriel on Friday, Dhanu 24. A. D. 1687 in the Sanctum of the Church, was set up by Varkki-Kattanar.

Kuṟicci. (Canganāśēri.)

No.	Place of inscription.	Dynasty.	King.	Date.	Language and Alphabet.	Remarks.
1	On the south base of the Mahādēva temple at Kuṟicci, Canganāśēri. (34/1098.)	...	...	Ko. 595 Mēṭam.	Malayalam.	States that Kumāran covered the roof with copper and had the purification ceremoney performed in Mēṭam. (T. A. S Vol. VII. p. 137.)
2	On the same base.	...	...	...	Do.	Damaged. Records that the basement of the temple was finished in some year which is illegible.

Kūvappaḷḷi. (Canganāśēri.)

No.	Place of inscription.	Dynasty.	King.	Date.	Language and Alphabet.	Remarks.
1	On a fragment of a cross set up on a hill at Kūvappaḷḷi near Kāñjirappaḷḷi. (10/1100)	...	...	...	...	The writing which is supposed to be Greek is extremely damaged.

Maṭavūr. (Cirayinkīl).

1	On a pillar in the *Namaskāramaṇḍapam* in the temple at Maṭavūr. (118/1096).	...	...	...	Tamil in Vaṭṭeḻuttu.	Contains the name Sātta-Nārāyanau of Kulikkāṭu.

Malayāṟṟūr. (Kunnattunāṭu).

1	On the open-air cross in front of the R. C. Church at Malayāṟṟūr. (101/1100)	...	...	Kollam 913 Mithunam 24	Tamil in Vaṭṭeḻuttu.	Refers to the freshes (?) that came (in the river ?) on the particular day ; but the rest of the inscription is not decipherable.

Maṇalikkara. (Kalkulam).

1	On a pillar set up in the compound of the Āḻvārkōvil, Maṇalik-karai.	Travan-core.	Vīra Ravi Kēraḷavar-man	Ko. 410	Tamil in V tu.	The object of the inscription is to fix the amount of taxes to be paid on the lands in the possesions of the members of the Assembly and the *ūrār* of Kōtanallūr. Mentions *Sabhaiyār*, *Ūrār*, *Teruvu* etc. (T. A. S. Vol. III. p. 59.)

Maṇalikkara. (contd.)

No.	Place of inscription.	Dynasty.	King.	Date.	Language and Alphabet.	Remarks.
2	On a pillar set up in the Siva temple at Pannippākam near Maṇalikkarai.	...	...	...	Tamil.	Records the gift of twenty old *Kāśu* for maintaining a perpetual lamp by Kaccetti Vikalankan. (T. A. S. Vol. III. p. 65.)
3	On the granite pedestal of Nandikēśvara in the same temple.	...	...	Ko. 735	Do.	Registers a gift of land and made to a certain Ayyikutti for playing on the flute in the temple. (T. A. S. Vol. III. p. 66.)

Maṇalttiṭṭai. (Tōvāḷa).

No.	Place of inscription.	Dynasty.	King.	Date.	Language and Alphabet.	Remarks.
	On a rock at Maṇalttiṭṭai. (85/1099)	...	...	Kollam 722, Tai 11.	Tamil.	Contains some regulations as to the manner in which the *mēlvāram* on the land belonging to the temples of Śrī Padmanābhapperumāl, Ādikēśavapperumāl, Aḻakiyanambi at Tērūr, Śucīndiramuṭaiyar and Bhūtappāṇḍīśvaram uṭaiyār were measured. (T. A. S. Vol. VII, p. 36.)

			Mañcappurai. (Kunnattunāṭu.)			
1	On the south side to the entrance of the Kṛṣṇankōvil of Mañcappurai. (82/1085).	...	...	...	Malayalam in Vaṭṭeḻuttu.	Records that temple was built by the Nāyar of Illavīdu of Caṅṅaramangalam.
			Maṇṇañcēri. (Ambalappuḻa).			
1	On a pillar in the *maṇḍapa* in the Siva temple at Maṇṇañcēri. (17/1100).	...	...	Kollam 878, Karkaṭakam	Tamil in Vaṭṭeḻuttu.	States that Ceruvelli Iṭṭiṇṇān contributed some portion of the stonework to the temple.
2	On the other side of the same pillar. (18/1100).	...	...	Kollam 872	Do.	Records that the southern block was built by the same individual.
3	On another pillar in the same temple. (19/1100)	...	...	Kollam 878, Karkaṭakam, 18	Do.	Illegible. Refers to the completion of some stone works in the same temple.
			Māṇṇār. (Tiruvalla).			
1	On the base of the *maṇḍapa* in front of the Siva temple at Panayannārkāvu Bhagavati temple at Māṇṇār. (75/1092).	...	...	Ko. 771.	Tamil in Vaṭṭeḻuttu.	Seems to provide for the bathing of the image with (cocoanut) oil.

Mānnār. *(contd.)*

No.	Place of inscription.	Dynasty.	King.	Date.	Language and Alphabet.	Remarks.
2 & 3	On two pillars in the Bhagavati temple at the same. (77/1092 and 77/1092).	...	...	...	Malayalam.	Contains the names *Murikkoli Uṇikkuññar* and *Kāvuṅgal Maṇiyan.*
4 & 5	On two pillars in the *Vaḻiambalam* of the Śiva temple at Kuraṭṭi, Mānnār. (78 & 79/1092).	...	...	Ko. 818 Ṛṣabha.	Tamil in Vaṭṭeḻuttu.	Damaged.
6 to 10	On a number of pillars in the *Vaḻiambalam* of the Śiva temple at Kuraṭṭi, Mānnār. (80 to 84/1092).	...	...	...	Do.	Damaged. One of the pieces contains the word "*Āṟṟiṅgal*".

11	On a stone built into the floor in front of the Śiva shrine in the Panayannārkāvu Bhagavati temple at Mānnār. (85/1092).	...	...	Jupiter in Kanni, Karkaṭakam.	Tamil in Vaṭṭeḻuttu.	Records gift by Nārāyaṇan dēvan of Kurumūr of 28 *accu* which was the income on Tamaraicceri-puraiyiṭam and Pallam for bathing the Tirumaramaṅgalattu-Bhaṭṭārakar with ghee. The name of the engraver is given as Kunrappoḻan Rāman.
12	On the east base proper left of the *Vaḻiambalam* of the Śiva temple at Kuraṭṭi, Mānnār. (86/1092).	...	...	Jupiter in Kumbham, Tulām, 12.	Do.	Jñānādhyakṣa-Paḻarar-Tiruvaṭi, his disciple, the people of the village and the Svāmi having met together in the *Vātilmāṭam* of Kuraṭṭi unanimously decided that Kumāran Rāman, his younger brothers and nephews should not be made Potuvāls for certain offences.
13	On the east base proper right of the entrance of the same. (87/1092).	...	...	Jupiter in Kanni, Makara	Tamil in Vaṭṭeḻuttu.	Registers an order prohibiting the issuing of loans to the *Samudāya* of Tirukkuraṭṭidēva and fixes the fines and penalties to be imposed on those who did so.

Mannār. (*contd.*)

No.	Place of inscription.	Dynasty.	King.	Date.	Language and Alphabet.	Remarks.
14	On the stone lying in the yard near the well of the Śiva temple at Kuraṭṭi, Mānnār. (88/1092).	...	...	Kollam (8) 35	Do.	Consists of two lines of damaged writing.
15	On the base of a ruined temple of Subrahmaṇya near Mānnār. (3/1100).	...	...	Jupiter in Simha.	Do.	Much obliterated. Seems to refer to a gift of lands for the temple.
16	On the base of the *maṇḍapa* in front of the Panayannārkāvu Bhagavati temple at Mānnār. (4/1100).	...	...	Kollam 771	Tamil in Vaṭṭeḻuttu.	Damaged. Mentions the name Īccaran.
17	On a stone in the flooring of the same temple. (5/1100).	...	...	Jupiter in Kanni, Karkaṭakam.	Do.	Registers a gift of the income from a piece of land belonging to Nārāyaṇan-Devan for conducting the bath of God Bhaṭṭāraka at Tirumāramaṅgalam.

No.						
			Maruṅgūr. (Agastīśvaram)			
1	On a slab set up at a street crossing at Maruṅgūr. (50/1100)	...	...	Kollam 670 Tai 12.	Tamil.	States that certain tenants were permitted to colonise the precincts of the Akattaṭi-Piḷḷaiyār temple at Maruṅgūr.
			Māvēlikkarai.			
1	On the lower sill of the door-way of the central shrine of the Siva temple at Cunakkara near Māvēlikkarai. (1/1093)	...	...	967 Mīnam 20.	Malayalam.	Mentions a certain Karuṇākara Bhiṣāravaṭi.
			Mēlila. (Koṭṭārakkara)			
1	On the pillar in the Śāsta temple at Mēlila. (14/1098)	...	...	...	Malayalam.	States that the entrance was erected by Nārāyaṇan. (T. A. S. Vol. VI. p. 140)
2	On another pillar in the same place. (15/1098)	...	...	...	Malayalam in Vaṭṭeḻuttu.	States that the pillar was the gift of Kaṇḍan Kunnu Kaṇḍacca Nair. (T. A. S. Vol. VI. p. 140).

Mutukuḷam. (Kārttikappaḷḷi)

No.	Place of inscription.	Dynasty.	King.	Date.	Language and Alphabet.	Remarks.
1	On one face of the north east pillar in the *namaskāra* maṇḍapa in front of the central shrine of the Pāṇḍavarkāvu Bhagavati temple in Mutukuḷam. (98/1099)	...	...	...	Malayalam in Vaṭṭeḻuttu.	Maṅgalattu Devan Nārāyaṇan presented the pillars. (T. A. S. Vol. VII. p. 108)
2	On the four sides of the base of the bali-pīṭha in front of the same. (99/1092)	...	—	...	Do.	Refers to Allankari-illam. Mentions Śankaramūrti. (T. A. S. Vol. VII. p. 108)

Muḻikkaḷam. (Parur)

No.	Place of inscription.	Dynasty.	King.	Date.	Language and Alphabet.	Remarks.
1	On the north base of the central shrine of the Viṣṇu temple at Muḻikkaḷam. (87/1084)	... ...	...	...	Malayalam and Tamil.	Damaged. Contains a few meaningless syllables.

2	Do. Do. (88/1084)	...	...	Kali day expressed by Ramānujōhivandyah.	Do.	It records that something was done on this day, perhaps the building of the temple. The date corresponds to nearly 148th year of the Kollam era. (T. A. S. Vol. VII. p. 138)
3	On a stone built into floor east of the well in the same. (89/1084)	...	...	Ko (6) 4. *	Tamil.	Damaged. Mentions some boundaries of land and Nēriyamaṅgalam. (T. A. S. Vol. VII. p. 138)
4	Near No. 89. (90/1084)	...	...	...	Tamil in Vaṭṭeḻuttu.	Registers a gift of 350 Putuppaṇam. (T. A. S. Vol. VII. p. 138)
5	On a stone built into the floor west of the Central shrine of the same. (91/1084)	...	...	...	Tamil and Grantha.	Gift of 40 *paṇam* for the purchase of stones by one. Karambiceṭṭu Nārāyaṇabhaṭṭan. (T. A. S. Vol. VII. p. 138).
6	On another stone near the one mentioned by the side of a prostrate figure of a man in the same. (92/1084)	...	...	Ko. 640.	Tamil in Vaṭṭeḻuttu.	Mentions simply the name Karaṇatta Kaṇḍan Kumāran perhaps the name of the person whom the figure represents. (T. A. S. Vol. VII. p. 138.)

Muḻikkalam. (*Contd*)

No.	Place of inscription.	Dynasty.	King.	Date.	Language and Alphabet.	Remarks.
7	On the east base of the Cuṟṟumaṇḍapa inside the same·(93/1084)	Cēra ...	Bhāskara Ravi. ...	Year opposite. 48. ...	Do.	Records the gift of land by Manukulādityan. (T. A. S. Vol. II. p. 46)
8	On the east base of the same (outside) in the same place. (94/1084)	...	Kōv-Indu Kōtai.	5th and 1st.	Do	Records the arrangements made re the times of offerings during the course of the day. (T. A. S. Vol. III. p. 189)
9	On a stare built into the floor of these *prākāra* in front of the Viṣṇu temple at Mūḻikkaḷam. (6/1090)	...	...	...	Vaṭṭeḻuttu (old characters.)	Fragment. Seems to provoide land for feeding. Mentions Tirumūḻikkaḷam.

Muṇḍankāvupaḷḷi. (Tiruvalla)

No.	Place of inscription.	Dynasty.	King.	Date.	Language and Alphabet.	Remarks.
1	On a slab in the Muṇdan kāvupaḷḷi. (3/1097)	...	...	Ko 841 Makaram 9 Sunday.	Malayalam Vaṭṭeḻuttu.	The Kaiyi (*i. e.* the Cross) was made by Chackko Ayippe of Muṇḍankāvu. (T. A. S. Vol. VII. p. 147)

2	On other slab in the same Church. (4/1097)	...	...	Ko 909 Tulām 1 Sunday.	Do.	Records the death of Alamma.......(T. A. S. Vol. VII. p. 147)
3	Do. (5/1097)	...	...	845, Dhanus 2.	Do.	Records the death of Thomman.... (T. A. S. Vol. VII. p. 147)
4	Do. (6/1097)	...	...	Vṛścika 9.	Do.	Refers to the baptism of a private individual. (T.A.S. Vol. VII. p. 147)
5	On a pillar in the same church. (7/1097)	...	...	...	Do.	Mentions Kora-Tomman. (T.A.S. Vol. VII. p. 147)
6	At the left of entrance into the central shrine in the Umaiyāṟṟubhagavati temple near the same village. (8/1097)	...	...	...	Do.	Records that a certain Nāgaramman of Veṇmaṇi renewed the *śrīpīṭha* the stone pavement and the central shrine and obtained *Viṣṇulōka*. Rest of the work was finished by the residents of Akacceri.
7	On a pillar in the front *maṇḍapa* of the same temple. (9/1097)	...	...	Kōlambha year expressed by the chronogram *Sikhirajīvarana* ?	Malayalam.	Gives only the details of the date.

Muṇḍankāvupaḷḷi. (*contd.*)

No.	Place of inscription.	Dynasty.	King.	Date.	Language and Alphabet.	Remarks.
8	On the base of the *dvajastambha* outside the same temple. (10/1097)	...	....	Ko 1054 Iṭavam 8 Ciṅga-Rāśi.	Do.	On this day the flag staff was set up.

Muncirai. (Viḷavankōṭu)

No.	Place of inscription.	Dynasty.	King.	Date.	Language and Alphabet.	Remarks.
1	On a slab built into the floor near the Viṣṇu shrine in the Tirumalai temple at Muncirai. (52/1096 and 1/1084)	Travan-core.	Śrīvīrakēraḷa Mārttāṇḍavarman of Kīḷappērūr.	Ko. 610, Karkaṭaka, su. di., Friday.	Tamil in Vaṭṭeḻuttu.	Much damaged. Seems to provide for offerings to the temple of Tirumalai Mahādēva at Muñcirai. (T. A. S. Vol. VII. p. 22)
2	On the *mālaikaṭṭi* stone in the same temple. (53/1096)	...	...	...	Do.	States that, a certain (Adi?) Nārāyaṇan Suvaran presented the (stone for making flower garlands). (T. A. S. Vol. VII. p. 22)

3	On a pillar in the outer *maṇḍapa* of the same temple. (54/1096)	...	...	Ko. 1007, Tai 1.	Tamil.	Contains the name of the temple accountant Karumbanavil Koocam-pillai who probably presented the pillar. (T. A. S. Vol. VII. p. 22)
4	One another pillar in the same maṇḍapa. (55/1096)	...	...	...	Do.	Contains the name Īccuvaramūrtti Tāṇuvan, one of the *Cettis* living in the street called Cenpakarāman-pututteru at Kunnattūr. (T. A. S. Vol. VII. p. 23)
5	On another pillar in the same *maṇḍapa*. (56/1096)	...	...	Ko. 1005, Āvaṇi 1.	Do.	Contains the name Tandala Kumaran Palppanapan of Tirumalai. (T. A. S. Vol. VII. p. 23)
6	Do. (57/1096)	...	...	Ko. 1007, Kārttikai 28.	Do.	Records that Pullali Ādiccan Iśakki living in Cenpakarāmanpututteru at Kunnattūr presented the pillar. (T. A. S. Vol. VII. p. 23)

Muncirai. *(contd.)*

No.	Place of inscription.	Dynasty.	King.	Date.	Language and Alphabet.	Remarks.
7	On another pillar in the same *Maṇḍapa.* (58/1096)	...	...	Ko. 1005, Māsi 18.	Tamil.	Records that Kalluvalvicca Mādēvan presented this stone pillar (T. A. S. Vol. VII. p. 23)
8	Do. (59/1096)	...	...	...	Do.	Contains the donor's name Nīlakaṇṭha-Pillai of Ramacca-viḷākam in Pārthivaśēkhara-puram. (T. A. S. Vol. VII. p. 13)
9	Do (60/1096)	...	...	Ko. 83, Āni 7.	Tamil in Vaṭṭeḻuttu.	States that the work of the western hall was finished on this day. (T. A. S. Vol. VII. p 23)
10	On the rock to the west of the same temple. (61/1096)	...	...	Jupiter in Vṛscikam, Vṛscikam (1) 5.	Do.	Much damaged. Mentions Cēnnan Caṅkaran. (T. A. S. Vol. VII. p. 20)

11	On the same rock (near the tank). (62/1096)	...	...	Jupiter in Vṛścika, Kumbham.	Do.	Damaged. Registers a gift for the maintenance of Vṛścika lamps in the temple of the Bhaṭṭāraka on the Tirumalai hill at Muncirai. (T. A. S. Vol. VII. p. 21)
12	Do. (62-a-/1096 and 83/1087)	Cōḷa.	Parakēsarivarman alias Rājēndra Cōḷa.	7th year.	Do.	Contains the introduction commencing with the words திருமன்னிவளர. (T. A. S. Vol. VI. p. 148)
13	Do (63/1096 and 86/1087)	...	....	Jupiter in Mīnam 9th year.	Do.	Damaged. Registers gift of gold for a lamp to the same temple and mentions the assembly of Muñcirai. (T. A. S. Vol. VII. p. 21)
14	Do (64/1096 and 84/1087)	....	...	...	Do.	Damaged and partly built in. Seems to record that Kāman Sattan of Murukkamaṉ and Naranan Kaman of Alappulai built a shrine in the temple of Muncirai. (T. A. S. Vol. VII. p. 21)

Muṭṭucira. (Vaikam)

No.	Place of inscription.	Dynasty.	King.	Date.	Language and Alphabet.	Remarks.
1	On a mutilated Cross in the R. C. Church at Muṭṭucira. (71/1100)	..	..	...	Pahlavi.	Contains a few letters on the left limb resembling the writing on the Kōṭṭayam Cross and another line contains some more letters of Pahlavi.
2	On an open-air cross in the same Church compound. (72/1100)	...	...	A. D. 1624, Ko. 799 Kanni.	Malayalam in Vaṭṭeḻuttu	Damaged at the end. Appears to state that the stone cross was set up by a private individual named Mattu of Kallarve....... (T. A. S. Vol. VII. p. 78)
3	On a stone lying in the same compound. (73/1800)	...	...	A. D. 1528, A. D. 1580, Kanni 13; A. D. 1581, Mīnam 29.	Do.	States that a *karingal-kurisu* (stone cross) was set up in the time of Mar Simeon and Jacob-Patiri in place of an older wooden (?) cross. The inscription also mentions Mar Denha and Mar George who were the previous Metrans. (T.A.S. Vol. VII. p. 77)

4	On another tomb-stone. (74/1100)	...	...	Ko. 812, Mithunam 1 (4), Friday.	Do.	Records the death of Kuriyan-Avuran. (T. A. S. Vol. VII. p. 78 F. N.)
5	On another stone slab. (75/1100)	...	...	Ko. 806, Cingam 24.	Do.	States that Alamma of Mattuven Kuriyada Kallar-veli died. (T. A. S. Vol. VII. p. 78)
6	Do. (76/1100)	...	...	Ko. 810, Mithunam 24.	Do.	States that Audeppu-Kuri-yada of Konnapele died. (T. A. S. Vol. VII. p. 78)
7	Do. (77/1100)	...	...	Kumbha.	Do.	Records the death of Alamma of Tarida-Mariam. (T. A. S. Vol. VII. p. 78)
8	Do. (78/1100)	...	...	Ko. *42, Makaram 8.	Do.	Records the death of Alamma of Mattayi-Ayippu. (T. A. S. Vol. VII. p. 78)
9	On two broken slabs in the same compound. (79/1100)	...	...	Ko. 875, MTnam 26, Saturday.	Do.	Records that Elisa-An-amma of Kadappiram died. (T. A. S. Vol. VII. p. 78)

Nāgarkōvil (*Agastīśvaram*)

No.	Place of inscription.	Dynasty.	King.	Date.	Language and Alphabet.	Remarks.
1	On a stone set up on the proper right of the entrance into the central shrine of the Nāgarāja temple at Nāgarkōvil. (55/1084)	Travancore.	Śaṅkaranārāyaṇa Venrumaṇkoṇḍa Bhūtala Vīra Śrī Udaya-mārttāṇḍa Varma, Ciravāy mūttatu, of Jayatunga-nāṭu.	Ko. 692	Tamil.	The king, while he was camping in the house of Śiṅgaperumāl in Seval, granted lands for the *pūja* of Nāgarāja. Mentions Guṇavīra Paṇḍitan and Jīvakaruṭaiyān Kamalavāhana Paṇḍitan. (T. A. S. Vol. VI. p. 160)
2	On the same. (56/1084)	Do.	Do.	Ko. 694	Do.	When the king was sojourning at Śucīndram, granted lands for the same temple for the night *puja*. (T. A. S. Vol. VI. p. 161)
3	On a second stone in the same. (57/1084)	Do.	Do.	Ko. 697	Do.	Grant of lands for *Prāyaścittam.* (T. A. S. Vol. VI. p. 165)

4	On the same. (58/1084)	Do.	Do.	Do.	Do.	Grant of land in the Mulaiyanur-paṟṟu for offerings in the morning. The king was camping at Śrīvallavan-maṅgalam. (T. A. S. Vol. VI. p. 156)
5	On a third stone in the same. (59/1084)	Do.	Do.	Ko. 696	Do.	Grant of land in Kōṭṭāru. The king was staying in the house of Śenbagavan-perumāl in the *agrahāram* of Cendanśeri on the bank of Ciṟṟāru. (T. A. S. Vol. VI. p. 164)
6	On a fourth stone set up near the entrance into the central shrine of the same. (60/1084)	Do.	Do.	Ko. 692	Do.	Grant of land for *uṣa pūja* while the king was residing in the new palace belonging to Adityavarman-aṇṇan in Ayappillaiputtur near Vīraśēkharanallūr. (T. A. S. Vol. VI. p. 159)
7	On a stone set up on the east side of the *prākāra* of the same.	...	...	Ko. 820* S. 1567.	Do.	Registers that Maluvanampiyar Maluvanambi and Tampirankutti caṭaiyan collected money from several men and cast a makaratorana lamp and made provision for lighting.

Nāgarkōvil. (*contd.*)

No.	Place of inscription.	Dynasty.	King.	Date.	Language and Alphabet.	Remarks.
8	On the west wall of the central shrine of the the Kṛṣṇa shrine in the same. (62/1084)	....	..	Ko. 764*	Tamil	States that Nāgar Tiruvanantāḷvār was set up by Tirukkurukaiperumāl of Kumbikulam in the Karungula-vaḷanāṭu and registers a gift of money for offerings. (T. A. S. Vol. VI. p. 166)
9	On the east wall of the Kṛṣṇa shrine within the Nāgarāja temple at Nāgarkovil. (49/1100)	...	...	Ko. 819, Kārttikai 3	Do.	Mentions Śrīkṛṣṇan-kōyil and the date. (T. A. S. Vol. VI. p. 166)

Nallūr. (*Agastīśvaram*)

No.	Place of inscription.	Dynasty.	King.	Date.	Language and Alphabet.	Remarks.
1	On a slab of stone set up near the Vināyāka temple at Nallūr. (51/1100 and 9/1113.)	...	...	Śaka 1648. Kollam 902., Arpaśi 7.	Tamil.	The pillar is in the midst of a cactus bush. Registers the gift of land by Tānuvan for conducting worship in the temple.

			Naṭṭālam. (Viḷavankōṭu.)			
1	On a rock in front of the Siva temple at Naṭṭālam. (32/1096)	...	...	...	Tamil in Vaṭṭeḻuttu.	Damaged. Registers a gift of land in Kōtanallūr, to the temple of the Āḻvār at......napuram. (T. A. S. Vol. VII p. 17.)
2	On a pillar in an *ambalam* (stone-shed) near the same village. (33/1096)	....	...	Ko. 840 Āṭi 15.	Do.	Registers gift of land and house site to the person conducting charities in the *ambalam*, built by Tiruvikkiraman Ravi of Naṭṭālam. (T. A. S. VII. p. 16.)
			Nāvāyikkuḷam. (Cirayinkīl)			
1	On the front base of the central shrine of the Saṅkaranārāyaṇa temple (proper right of the entrance) at Nāvāyikkuḷam. (6/1085)	Travancore.	Rāma Mārttāṇḍan *alias* Jayatuṅganāṭṭu Mūtta Tiruvaṭi of the Kīḻappērūr illam.	Ko. 614.	Tamil in Vaṭṭeḻuttu.	Records that the temple and the *maṇḍapa* were rebuilt of stone, the central shrine covered with copper-plate and the *Kumbhābhiṣēka* was celebrated by the king Sri Vīra Rāma Marttāṇḍavarman Tiruvaṭi of Jayatunganāṭṭu and Kīḻappērūr illam. (T. A. S. Vol. I. p. 299.)

Nāvāyikkuḷam.—(*contd.*)

No.	Place of inscription.	Dynasty.	King.	Date.	Language and Alphabet.	Remarks.
2	On the *balikkal* of the Saptamatṛkas in the temple of Śaṇkaranārāyaṇa at Nāvāyikkuḷam. (7/1085.)	...	...	...	Malayalam in Kōḷeḻuttu.	Mentions one Mādhavan Śaṅkaran. (T. A. S. Vol. VI. p. 83.)
3	On the *balikkal* in front of the same. (8/1085.)	...	...	Ko. 782	Tamil in Vaṭṭeḻuttu.	Damaged. (T. A. S. Vol. VI. p. 83.)
4	On two sides of a stone set up in front of the same. (9/1085)	...	...	...	Do.	Gift of gold for a lamp by a private individual of Eranaṭu- *Mūlikkalakkaccam* occurs.(T. A. S. Vol. VI.p.83.)
	Neṭuvangāṭu.					
	On a stone built at the entrance into the tank in front of the Tiruccitṭai temple near Neṭuvangāṭu. (40/1095.)	...	...	Kollam 1066, Avaṇi 23	Tamil.	Records that a native of Kuḻiviḷākam constructed the tank. (T. A. S. Vol. VII. p. 99.)

			Nelvēli (Viḷavankōṭu)			
1	On the south wall of the central shrine in the śiva temple at Nelvēli. (40/1096.)	...	...	...	Tamil in Vaṭṭeḻuttu.	Much damaged. Seems to register a gift of land to the temple of Saniccericcvaram. (T. A. S. Vol. VII. p. 96.)
2	On the west wall of the Viṣṇu shrine in the same temple. (41/1096.)	...	...	...	Tamil. (Archaic.)	Damaged and portions lost. Mentions a number of persons. (T. A. S. Vol. VII. p. 96.)
			Nīramaṅgalam (Neyyāṟṟinkara.)			
1	Right of entrance into the śiva temple at Nīramaṅgalam. (13/1095.)	...	...	Jupiter in Mithuna, Simha 4, Friday, Uttiram	Tamil in Vaṭṭeḻuttu.	Unfinished. Seems to register gift of land in Cempakacēri in Iravimaṅgalam and Karippuram.
			Niraṇam. (Tiruvalla.)			
1	On a slab in the courtyard of the church at Niraṇam. (13/1097.)	...	...	Kollam 792, Mēṭam 9.	Malayalam in Vaṭṭeḻuttu.	Mentions Tomman Chandi. (T. A. S. Vol. VII. p. 144.)

Okkal. (Kunnattunāṭu.)

No.	Place of inscription.	Dynasty.	King.	Date.	Language. and Alphabet.	Remarks.
1	On the east side of the north *prākāra* of the Viṣṇu temple at Okkal near Kālaṭi. (84/1085).	...	...	...	Tamil in Vaṭṭeḻuttu.	Fragmentary.
	Ōmallūr (Pattanamtiṭṭa.)					
1	On the west base proper left of the entrance of the *gōpura* of the temple of the Śāsta named Arattakaṇḍan in Ōmallūr. (89/1092.)	...	...	Kollam 936 Makaram 1.	Malayalam.	Records a gift for the conduct of worship in the temple of Arattakaṇḍan. Mentions Ceruppaḷḷi and Parur. (T. A. S. Vol. VII. p. 131.)
2	On a stone built into the floor near the *dhvajastambha* of the same. (90/1092.)	...	...	...	...	

Omallūr.—(*contd.*)

3	On the same. (91/1092.)	...	...	...	Malayalam.	Damaged. Only a few letters are seen.
4	Do. (92/1092.)	...	...	...	Do.	Mentions Iṭaippalli Panikkar and Venkaṭa Krishnan.
5	Do. (93/1092.)	...	...	...	Telugu.	Do.
6	On a stone built into the floor of the Maṇḍapa in front of the gōpura of the same. (94/1092.)	...	...	...	Tamil.	Contains some syllables.

Padmanābhapuram. (*Kalkulam*).

1	On a stone set up in front of the Kulaśēkhara Piḷḷaiyār shrine in the south street, Fort, Padmanābhapuram. (41/1093).	Travancore.	Iravivarma Ciravāy-mūtta tampirān.	Ko. 7 (9) 8 Thursday, su. 5.	Tamil.	Fragmentary. Seems to record the consecration of God Kulaśēkhara Piḷḷaiyār (T. A. S. Vol. VII. p.219).
2	On the base of the south wall of the central shrine in the Nīlakaṇṭhasvāmin temple at Padmanābhapuram. (46/1095).	Vēṇāṭu.	Vīra Ravi Kēraḷa Varman.	Kollam 41 (2) Kumbham.	Tamil in Vaṭṭeḻuttu.	Damaged. Provides for offerings to the temple of Iraṇasiññeccorattu Mahādēva. In some respects this inscription is similar to the Maṇalikkarai record of the same king. (T. A. S. Vol. VII. p. 127).

Padmanābhapuram—(*contd.*)

No.	Place of inscription.	Dynasty.	King.	Date.	Language and Alphabet.	Remarks.
3	On the west base of the *maṇḍapa* in front of the same shrine. (47/1095)	...	...	Kollam 753, Arpaśi 9, Wednesday, Uttaram, ba. di. 13.	Tamil.	Registers that the paving of the inner *prākāra* with stone, the opening of a drain, the construction of the *maṇḍapa*, on both sides of the east entrance with *Vanam Jagati*, *Kadam* and *Pattikai*, were made in the temple of Mahādēva at Kalkulam in Kollam 753. (T. A. S. Vol. VII. p. 127).
4	On a slab in the *Pūjappura* of the place in the same village. (48/1095)	...	...	Jupiter in Makaram, Kollam 840, Māśi 4, ba. di. 11 Tuesday, Mūlam.	Tamil.	Incomplete. Provides for the expenses of a festival (*Panguni Uttiram*) in the temple of the Mahādēva at Kalkuḷam, by the Tampi of Tiruvāṭṭārudēśam, *i. e.*, Iravi-Iravi who had built the *kalmaṭham*, *i. e.*, a *maṇḍapa*, on the north side of the north street within the fort. (T. A. S. Vol. VII. p. 128).

5	On another slab in the same place. (49/1095).	...	...	Jupiter in Iṭavam, Kollam 856, Āvaṇi 30, Monday Uttiraṭṭāṭi.	Do.	Registers, gift of lands for worship to the Mahēśvara in the same *maṇḍapa*. Mentions Iravimakkuṭṭi-Padmanābhakutti and Tampi Iravi Padmanābhan of Tiruvaṭṭāru. (T. A. S. Vol. VII. p. 128).
6	On a pillar set up in the Subrahmaṇya temple at Kumārakōyil near Padmanābhapuram. (36/1098).	...	...	Śaka 1655, Jupiter in Tulām, Kollam 909, Āvaṇi 29, Thursday, Hasta, su. 2.	Do.	Records gift of lands by Perumāl-Cempakarāman of Maṇavāḷakkuricci near Kaṭikaippaṭṭinam, a village in Rājarāja-tennāṭu for offering and worship of the God Vēlāyudha Perumāl (Subrahmaṇya) of Vēḷvimalai.
7	On another pillar in the same temple. (37/1098).	...	...	Kollam (8) 54, Citrai 12	Tamil.	Records gift of lands by Ayyappan Ayyappan of Kuḻikkōṭudēśam for worship and supply of garlands to the God Vēlāyudha-Perumaḷ.
8	On the south wall of the first *prākāra* of the same temple. (38/1098)	...	...	Śaka 1650, Kollam 904, Arpaśi 22, Wednesday, Anuṣa, su. 3.	Do.	Records that Perumāḷ of Bhūtappāṇḍi gave 40 *paṇam* to the treasury of the Vēlāyudha-Perumāḷ temple.

Padmanābhapuram—(*contd.*)

No.	Place of inscription.	Dynasty.	King.	Date.	Language and Alphabet.	Remarks.
9	On the same wall. (39/1098).	...	...	Jupiter in Vṛścika, Kollam 897, Karttikai 17, Friday, Uttiraṭṭāti, su. 10.	Do.	Registers gift of lands by ......Ilappillaiyan — Alagiyan for festivals, worship and offerings to God-Vēlāyudha-Perumāḷ of Vēlvimalai near Brahmapuram.
10	On a pillar set up in the same wall. (40/1098)	...	...	Kollam 910, Citrai 19.	Do.	Damaged. Seems to register some gift of land made by Ādiccan-Dēvan of Sevvalai.
11	On a stone lying outside the Lāṭankōyil at Brahmapuram near Padmanābhapuram. (41/1098).	...	...	...	Tamil in Vaṭṭeḻuttu.	Records gift of a bell weighing 50 *palam* by Arunūṟṟuvan-Mādavan, a merchant of Kannannūr in Kīḻvēmba-nāṭu on behalf of his son Saṅkaran.

12	On another stone. (42/1098)	...	...	Jupiter in Mīnam, Mārkaḻi, Tiruvātirai.	Tamil Vaṭṭeḻuttu.	Incomplete. Records that Sottaiyyan, the brother of Perumānadi - Gamindan of Kuṭakunāṭu in Gangaimaṇḍalam, gave 30 *iḻakkāśu* for feeding a Brahman in the Peruntirukkōyil of Brahmapuram for the merit of his mother Joti-abbai.
13	On two other stones. (43/1098).	...	...	...	Do.	Fragmentary. One of them mentions the *anjukuai* and is the final portion of an inscription, the previous stones of which are not now traceable.
14	On the top of the door at the entrance to the Garbhagṛha of Ānaivaravēṟṟa Arattakaṇḍan Śāsta temple, Cārōṭu, near Padmanābhapuram. (11/1105).	...	...	Ko. 8 (7) 3 Alpaśi 30. Saturday.	Tamil.	Partly damaged. Seems to refer to the construction of *prākāra* and *mullappandal*.

Padmanābhapuram (*contd.*).

No.	Place of inscription.	Dynasty.	King.	Date.	Language and Alphabet.	Remarks.
15	On a stone discoverred at Viḻiññam. (Now at Padmanābhapuram) (10/1113).	...	...		Tamil in Vaṭṭeḻuttu.	Damaged. Mentions Viḻiññam. Seems to refer to the erection of a stone in honour of a warrior who fell in battle. The figure of the hero is also engraved on the back.
16	On a standing stone put up at Parasurāmanperunteru at Iṭalākkuṭi near Nāgerkōil. (Now at Padmanabhapuram Museum) 11/1113).	Travancore.	Jayasimha of Jayatunganāṭu.	Ko. 661 Cittirai 1.	Tamil.	States that Paṭṭāṭaikkuṭi makkaḷ who migrated to Paraśuramanperunteru *alias* Iṭarāyakkuṭi were given some concession in the payment of taxes such as *paṭaippaṇam*, etc, excluding *añcirai*. Mentions *Añcinānpukaliṭam*."

17	One pillar at Nāvalaṭipparru at Iraviputtūr (Now at Padmanābhapuram Museum). (12/1113).	Travancore.	Udayamārttāṇḍatṛbhuvanadēvi.	...	Tamil.	Records the construction of *Udayamārttāṇḍa Maṇḍapa*. Mention has been made of Udayamārttāṇḍa Tṛbhuvana Dēvi and Sri Vallabhaperumāḷ.
18	On a stone tub found lying near the Ūṭṭupura (feeding house) at Padmanābhapuram. (Now at Padmanābhapuram Museum). (13/1113).	Do.	Kēraḷavarma, Senior King of Ciravāy.	Ko. 871 Puraṭṭāsi 27.	Do.	States that a stone tub was placed at the entrance of the Ūṭṭupura (feeding hall) Padmanābhapuram for providing drinking water to cows.
19	On a standing stone at Rāmavarmapuram near the S. L. B. English High School. Nāgerkōil (Now at Padmanabhapuram Museum) (14/1113).	Do.	...	Śaka 1619 Kollam 8**Tai 13 Sun. 14 Thursday Mṛgasira.	Do.	Damaged. Registers the gift of paddy fields for a way side charitable institution.
20	On a standing stone at Cārōṭu near Padmanābhapuram (Now at Padmanābhapuram Museum). (15/1113).	Do.	Rāmavarma Ciravāy Mūttavar.	Kollam 798 Arpasi 1. (1)	Do.	Damaged. Seems to refer to the gift of *Tirumukha* by the king to Tampi Śrī-Padmanabhan of Ponnāyikkuṭi in Tenkarainātu.

Padmanābhapuram (*contd.*)

No.	Place of inscription.	Dynasty.	King.	Date.	Language and Alphabet.	Remarks.
21	On a stone now kept at Padmanābhapuram Museum. (16/1113).	Travancore.	...	Kollam 862 Āni 32.	Tamil.	Registers a gift of land for worship in the temple of the north street at Kalkulam by Tampi Iravi Sri Padmanābhan of Tiruvāṭṭār.
	Pākōṭu. (Vilavankōṭu).					
1	On the *bali-pīṭha* of the Siva temple at Pākōṭu. (36/1096).	...	...	Kali day expressed by the word Dharmasindhorjibharshya (: 1489, 759) (A.D. 977 Sept.).	Sanskrit & Tamil in Vaṭṭeḻuttu & Grantha.	Records that Kunran Gopan of Pākōṭu made of stone a *bali-pīṭha* to God Siva (Candrārdhamauli). (T.A.S. Vol. IV. p. 142.)
2	On the pedestal of the Nandi in the same temple. (37/1096.)	...	...	...	Tamil.	Records that Aruvalli Gōvindan Gōvindan caused to be made the Ṛṣabha. (T. A. S. Vol. VII. p. 105.)
3	At the base of the *Dvārastha* in the same temple. (38/1096)	...	...	...	Do.	Records that Mugadi Śankaran Rāman caused to be made the Dvārastha. (T.A.S. Vol. VII. p. 106).

No.	Description			Date	Language	Remarks
4	On a slab at the outer entrance into the same temple. (39/1096)	...	...	Kollam 7 (6)3, Mīnam 15, Friday, Rōhiṇi su. di. 5.	Malayalam.	Records that the flag-staff of Mahēscaramangalam in Pākōṭu was planted on this day and that repairs were executed in the temple, by a certain Purusō (ttaman). (T. A. S. Vol. VII. p 106).
	Paḷḷipuram. (Cērttala.)					
1	On the base of the Sāsta temple at Paḷḷippuram near Vaikkam. (4/1099)	...	...	Ko. 948, Mēṭam 29.	Malayalam.	States that the *Srīkōvil* was completed on that day by Pottayil Iṭṭiyaccappaṇikkar. (T. A. S. Vol. VII. p. 140).
2	On a tombstone in the R. C. Church at Paḷḷippuram near Vaikkam. (11/1100).	...	...	Ko. 809, Mīnam 9.	Malayalam in Vaṭṭeluttu.	Refers to the death of Narekkel Ciruta Koreda. (T. A. S. Vol. VII. p. 141).
3	On another tombstone in the same church. ([illegible]/1100)	...	...	Ko. 804, Vṛscikam 2.	Do.	Records the death of Eleccar. (T. A. S. Vol. VII). p. 141).
	(100)	...	...	A. D. 1653, Ko. 828, Kumbham 29, Thursday.	Do.	Records the death of ...... Chakko-Māppilla of Valakkadavu. (T. A. S. Vol. VII. p. 141).

Pallipuram. *(contd.)*

No.	Place of inscription.	Dynasty.	King.	Date.	Language and Alphabet.	Remarks.
5	On another tombstone in the same church. (14/1100).	...	...	Ko. 88*	Malayalam in Vaṭṭeḻuttu.	The portion containing the name of the individual is highly damaged. (T. A. S. Vol. VII. p. 141).
6	Do. (15/1100).	...	...	Ko. 884, Ciṅṅam 9.	Do.	Damaged. The name is not decipherable. (T. A. S. Vol. VII. p. 141).
7	Do. (16/1100).	...	...	Ko. 792, Makaram 29.	Do.	Records the death of Avuraṉ-Kuriyada. (T. A. S. Vol. VII. p. 141).
	Palūr. (Mūvāṟṟupuḻa)					
1	On the east base (proper right of the flight of steps leading to the central shrine) of the Śiva temple at Palūr. (87/1087)	...	...	Jupiter in Kanni, Māsa Month.	Tamil in Vaṭṭeḻuttu.	Mentions Puruṣōttaman Suvaran of Venkinkōṭu who probably constructed the temple.

Parakkai (Agastīśvaram).

1	On the east wall of the Madusūdanasvāmin temple at Parakkai. (46/1090.)	...	...	...	Tamil.	Very much damaged. Seems to register a gift of land by a certain Madusūdan Madusūdan.
2	On the east wall north of the entrance of the entrance of the Madusūdanasvāmin temple at Parakkai. (47/1090)	...	...	Ko. 749, Āṭi 1, Wednesday, Anuṣam su. 12.	Do.	Records that a certain Ādiccan Ādiccan was appointed accountant in the temple of Nayinār-Mudusūdanaviṇṇakar-Emberumān at Kīlāramangalam in Nāñjināṭu in place of Iccuran Amaraperumāḷ. (T. A. S. Vol. 6, D. 117.)
3	Do. (48/1090.)	...	...	Ko. 720, Tai 26, su. di. 12, Friday, Mrigaśīrṣa.	Do.	Registers a gift of land as *śirpavirtti* to Konmandai Nayinan mudaḷi *alias* Sirpapurandaran of Kōṭṭāru *alias* Mummuṭiccōlapuram. Signed by Ayyappan Mārttāṇḍan. (T. A. S. Vol. VI. p. 1114.)

Parakkai (*contd.*)

No.	Place of inscription.	Dynasty.	King.	Date.	Language and Alphabet.	Remarks.
4	Do. (49/1090)	...	...	Ko. 685 Arpaśi 16, ba. di. 8, Friday, Punarvasu.	Do.	Registers gift of 400 *Nenmēni Kaliyugarāmanpaṇam* for lamps to the temple of Nāyinar-Madusūdanaviṇṇagar Emberuman at Kiḻār-mangalam *alias* Abhimāna-mēru-caturvēdi-mangalam in Nānjināṭu by Sempalli Harisvamibhaṭṭan of Perunallur *alias* Sundara-Pāṇḍya caturvēdimangalam a *Brahmadēya* in Ādi-nāṭu (T.A.S. Vol. VI. p. 111.)
5	On the east wall, south of the entrance of the same No. (50/1090 125 same as of 1099.)	...	...	Ko. 786, Vaikāśi 8, Paurṇima, Thursday, Anuṣam.	Do.	Damaged and fragmentary. (T. A. S. Vol. VI. p. 120)
6	Do. (51/1090) 126 (same as of 1099.)	...	...	Ko, 786, Āni, Wednesday.	Do.	Do. Do. Mentions Kilarmangalam. (T. A. S. Vol. VI. p. 121)

7	On the door-posts of the entrance into the inner maṇḍapa which is in front of the central shrine of the same. (52/1090)	Travancore.	Śaṅkara-nārāyaṇa Venrumaṇ koṇḍa Bhūtalavīra Rāmavarman ciraivāymūttavar of Jayatuṅganāṭu born in the asterism Kārtikai.	Śaka 1508, Ko. 762, Puraṭṭāśi 23, su. di. 12, Tuesday, Tiruvōṇam.	Do.	Records a gift of land to Deviyar, the daughter of Āṇḍukoṇḍa-nāeciyār for supply of paddy for the early morning service of Cenpakarāman, instituted in the name of the king in the temple Nayinār Madusūdana Viṇṇakar-Emperuman at Kilaramangalam. (T. A. S. Vol. VI. p. 119.)
8	On the base of the *balikkal* in the first *prākāra* of the Madusūdana-viṇṇakar Emperumān temple at Parakkai. (119/1099.)	Pāṇḍya.	Caṭaiya-māran.	2nd + 5th year.	Tamil in Vaṭṭeluttu.	Broken at the beginning and incomplete. Seems to record purchase of lands made by the *sabha* of Kilaramangalam, a *Brahmadeya* in Nāñjināṭu for the expenses of conducting worship in the temple of Madusūdana-viṇṇakar-Emperumān. (T. A. S. Vol. VI. p. 108.)

Parakkai—(contd.)

No.	Place of inscription.	Dynasty.	King.	Date.	Language and Alphabet.	Remarks.
9	On two slabs in the pavement round the central shrine in the same temple. (120/1099.)	Travancore.	Vīra Ravi-Ravivarman of Kilappārūr, Tiruppappur Muttatiruvaṭi.	Ko. 640, Panguni 12 su. 11, Friday, Puṣya.	Tamil.	Incomplete. Seems to record some provision made for the conduct of the *pandiradi* worship and for feeding *Brahmans* in the temple of Madusūdana-viṇṇakar-Emperumān of Kilaramangalam *alias* Abhimānamēru-caturvēdimangalam in Nānjināṭu. (T. A. S. Vol. VI. p. 110.)
10	On a stone pillar set up in the western verandah round the same central shrine. (121/1099.)	...	...	Ko. 627, Vaikāśi 24.	Do.	Records that some lands were given by Periyanayinar Mavilērumperumāḷ for conducting worship to the God and that the donor promised to cultivate the lands and measure paddy to Sangattalakar of Tirukkottiyūr *alias* Tirunārāyaṇa-caturvēdimangalam for the several items of worship. (T. A. S. Vol. VI. p. 109)

11	On the wall of *balikkal purai*, left entrance into temple. (122/1099)	...	...	Saka 1611, Ko. 865, Āvaṇi 23, ba. 5, saturday, Dhruva yōgam, Varāhakaraṇam, Aśvati.	Tamil.	Records gift of lands by Deyvangaladiyan Tānuvan of Paśumpiram, a suburb of Sūcindrum in Nanjināṭu, for providing offerings to the God Madusūdana-viṇṇakar-Emperumān at Kilarmangalam for feeding *Brahmans*. (T. A. S. Vol. VI. p. 122.)
12	On the same wall. (123/1099)	...	...	Śaka 171 , Jupiter in Karkaṭakam Ko. 870, Āvaṇi 1?, Tṛtīya Monday, Hasta.	Do.	Records the gift of land by Kumārasvāmi, son of Aṇaiñcaperumāl of Parakkai in Nanjināṭu for feeding *Brahmans* daily. (T. A. S. Vol. VI. p. 123.)
13	On the wall, right of entrance. (124/1099)	...	...	Ko. 670, Āṭi 5 ba. 8. Wednesday, Aśvati.	Do.	Records gift of 400 *paṇam* by Sankaran-Parameśvaran of Mangalacceri, a suburb of Kilārmangalam for burning a perpetual lamp in the temple of Madusūdana-viṇṇakar. Emperumān. (T. A. S. VI. p. 113.)

Parakkai.—(contd.)

No.	Place of inscription.	Dynasty.	King.	Date.	Language and Alphabet.	Remarks.
14	On the same wall, (50 of 1090 same as (125/1099)	...	...	Ko. 786 Vaikasi 8, purnai, Thursday, Aunsham.	Do.	Incomplete. Records gift of money by Ammai, the daughter of a member of the *sabha* of the temple, for the conduct of certain festivals to the God. It also states that the Kṛṣṇa image was made by the same individual. (T. A. S. Vol. VI. p. 120.)
15	Do. (126/1099 s. a 51/1090)	...	...	Ko. 786 Ani, 21, Pancami, Wednesday, Catayam.	Do.	Records gift of 50 *paṇam* by Sucīndravāsi, a member of the *Sucīndram-sabha* for the supply of one garland daily to the God. (T. A. S. Vol. VI. p. 121)
16	On the lintel of the doorway of the Akkarai-Mahādēva temple in the same village. (127/1599).	...	...	...	Tamil in Vaṭṭeḻuttu.	Fragmentary, contains the syllables, அ[illegible]கிரஹிக்க வரந்தர வேணு மேன்[illegible] (T. A. S. Vol. VI. p. 107.)

17	On a stone slab set up in front of a maṭham in the same village. (128/1099)	Travancore.	Śankaranārāyaṇa-Venrumankoṇḍa Bhūtalavira Sri Vira Keralan Ciravaymūttatu.	Ko. 733, Tai 16, Tamil su. pancami, Friday, Rōhiṇi, Subhayōgam.	Tamil.	Records that a *kaikkōla* named Perumal Ponnan made some donation of land named Chidambaranathar for maintaining a water-booth, and the king, while staying in the Karungaiyil Bhagavati temple at Parakkai, exempted it from certain taxes. 736 Mārkaḷi 6, is also mentioned in the record. (T. A. S. Vol. VI. p. 115).
			Parappankōṭu. (Neṭuvangāṭu)			
1	On the base of the east wall of the central shrine in the Viṣṇu temple at Parappankōṭu. (41/1095)	...	...	...	Malayalam in Vaṭṭeḷuttu.	Damaged and portion missing. Seems to register a gift of land for offerings to the temple of Parappankōṭu. Mentions Suvaran Suvaran of.........kōṭu...... (T. A. S. Vol. VII. p 99 F. NS.)

Parappankōṭṭu—(contd.)

No.	Place of inscription.	Dynasty.	King.	Date.	Language and Alphabet.	Remarks.
2	On the pillars of the *maṇḍapa* in the *Cuṟṟu-maṇḍapa* of the same temple. (42/1095)	...	...	...	Malayalam.	Mentions Karikkattu Narasimhan Govindan, Kaikarai Ayyappan Kaliyampi and Pirappankōṭṭu Alakan Karuṇākaran. (T. A. S. Vol. VII. p. 100 F. N.)
3	At the left of the western entrance into the *prākāra* of the same temple. (43/1095)	...	...	Kollam 800.	Do.	Records that Isvara Narayanan of Karekkadu executed certain repairs in the temple. (T. A. S. Vol. VII. p. 100.)

Pārthivapuram. (*Viḷavankōṭu*)

1	On the west base of the *cuṟṟumaṇḍapa* outside, of the Viṣṇu temple at Pārthivapuram. (20/1084 s. a. 82/1087)	...	...	...	Tamil in Vaṭṭeḻuttu.	Grant of land to one Kēraḷan Ādiccavarman *alias* Rājādhirāja Vaḷḷuvanāṭāḻvān of Karitturai. (T. A. S. Vol. III. p. 52)
2	On the proper right verandah near the entrance into the *cuṟṟumaṇḍapa* of the same. (21/1084)	...	...	Ko. 98.	Sanskrit & Tamil in Grantha and Vaṭṭeḻuttu.	Gift of gold for lamps by Kumaran Narayanan *alias* Pancavan Brahmādirajan of Idaikulattur in the Tumanāṭu. (T. A. S. Vol. I. p. 287)
3	On the base of the *cuṟṟu-maṇḍapa* (outside) proper left of the entrance into the Viṣṇu temple at Pārthivapuram. (78/1087)	...	...	Jupiter in Ṛṣabha.	Tamil in Vaṭṭeḻuttu.	Records gift of lands by Kaman Tadakkan of Kunrattūr for Viruccika lamps to the temple of Pārthivaśekharattu-deva. (T. A. S. Vol. V. p. 171)
4	On a stone lying in the north side of the yard of the Viṣṇu temple at Pārthivapuram. (79/1087)	Cōḷa.	Vīra Cōḷapperumal	...	Tamil.	Damaged. States that Sankaran Ranasingan set up a silver image in the temple. (T. A. S. Vol. I. p. 295—6).

Pārvathipuram—(contd.)

No.	Place of inscription.	Dynasty.	King.	Date.	Language and Alphabet.	Remarks.
5	On the south base of the Visnu temple at Pārthivapuram (42/1100)	Cōla-Pāndya.	Sundaracōla Pāndya.	...	Tamil in Vatteluttu.	Built in stone steps. Refers to a gift of a perpetual lamp.
6	On a slab set up in a certain well in the same village. (43/1100)	...	...	Ko. 616, Tai 25.	Do.	Incomplete. Seems to refer to an order issued by the king (unnamed) while staying in the house of Krsnan-Acyutan of Kalcirai, that the *Taccar*, *Kollar* *Kolaccar* etc., living between Poykai and Tovalai shall not enjoy the privileges of throwing stones or knocking at doors.

Parur.

1	Round the margin of the stone water basin (Fountain) in the Jacobite church, N. Parur. (78/1086)	...	...	A. D. 1625.	Malayalam in Vaṭṭeḻuttu.	Records the dedication of a stone fountain by one Abraham Mappilla. (T. A. S. Vol. I. p. 107 & Vol. VII. p. 143)
2	On a slab built into the entrance of the R. C. Church at Parur. (31/1099)	...	...	A. D. 1729 Mithunam 3	Do.	Mentions Chakko Ceriyada Kattanar and Mattayi. (T. A. S. Vol. VII. p. 144)
3	On a slab set up in the wall of the Syrian church in the same village. (32/1099)	...	...	Ko. 1018.	Syriac.	Records the date of construction of the church.
4	On a slab built in the wall of the R. C. Church at N. Parur. (35/1099 s. a. 76/1086)	...	...	A. D. 1624, Ko. 799. Kumbham 8.	Malayalam in Vaṭṭeḻuttu.	Records the death of Mar Francisco Metran, the Bishop of the St. Thomas' Christians of Malangara. (T. A. S. Vol. I. p. 300 and Vol. VII. p. 146)
5	On a slab built into the wall of the Jacobite church in the same village. (36/1099 s. a. 75/1086)	...	...	A. D. 1566, Ko. 742. Vṛscika 6	Do.	States that Mar Joseph Metran built the church of St. Thomas in Pattamanai. Paravur and set up the cross. (T. A. S. Vol. VII. p. 144)

Parur (*contd.*)

No.	Place of inscription.	Dynasty.	King.	Date.	Language and Alphabet.	Remarks.
6	On a stone slab set up in front of the Jewish synagogue at Parur. (95/1100 s. a. 77/1086)	...	...	5376 years after the world was created.	Hebrew.	Said to record the construction of the synagogue by David, son of Jacob Caestilla.
7	On a tombstone lying in the compound. (96/1100)	...	...	...	Do.	Top broken. Said to refer to the death of Saddiya, son of Saddiya.
8	On another tombstone. (97/1100)	...	...	5368 years after the creation of the world.	Do.	Said to record the death of Moses, on of Elia.
9	Do. (96/1100)	...	...	5378 years after the world was created.	Do.	Said to refer to the death of Benay, son of Elia.
10	On the base of the [illegible] of the Siva temple at Peruvaram, Parur. (97/1100)	...	...	Ko. 1069, Mithunam 2	Malayalam.	Refers to the renovation of the temple in that year.

			Payaṇam (*Viḷavankōṭu*)			
1	On three faces of a *dīpastambha* in front of the Karippāra Bhagavati shrine at Payaṇam. (71/1087)	...	...	Ko. 840, Ani. 25.	Tamil in Later Vaṭṭeḻuttu.	Mentions *Kakkāṭṭu-Kirāmam* and refers to the execution of repairs in the temple.
			Perumpaḻutūr (*Neyyāṟṟinkara*)			
1	On the side base of the ruined *balipīṭha* in the Viṣṇu temple unearthed at Nārāṇattukāvu near Perumpaḻutūr. (1/1111)	Ay.	Ko. Karunandadakkan.	10th year Kanni Jupiter in Karkaṭaka.	Tamil in Vaṭṭeḻuttu.	Damaged at the end. The record refers to the construction of the *balipīṭha* and offering rice on it.
			Perunayil (*Canganāssēri*)			
1	On the south base of the central shrine of the Viṣṇu temple at Perunayil. (near Canganāssēri) (84/1086)	...	Ko- Nerinmaikoṇḍān Kō-Srī Pākkaran Iravivarma Tiravaṭi.	2nd + 3rd	Tamil in Vaṭṭeḻuttu.	Records an order of the king that 80 *kalams* of paddy be given by the Nanrūlaināṭu people. The name of the place where the temple is called Perunayil. Mentions the Koyiladikārikal, Coravellur Iravi Kanni and Kulamangalattu Sri Kumara Naryanan. (T. A. S. Vol. II. p. 44)

Perunayil *(contd)*

No	Place of inscription.	Dynasty.	King.	Date.	Language and Alphabet.	Remarks.
2	On the south and west bases of the same. (86/1086)	...	...	2nd + 12th.	Do.	Incomplete. Mentions Peruneydal, Kilakkulangarai, Pandavur, and the Chief of Vēṇāṭu ruling over Nanru (lanāṭu). (T. A. S. Vol. II p. 34)
3	On the south base of the central shrine of the temple at Perunayil. (14/1097 and 85/1086)	...	...	Jupiter in Kanni, Kanni Aśvati, Sunday	Do.	Registers a gift made for feeding 1000 *Brahmanas* at the rate of 100 persons for each day during the 10 days festival commencing from Kanni ba. 5 of each year. Mentions the chief Adiccan Kōdai of Muññināṭu and EdiranKaviran of Kavalakāṭu. In case of failure fine had to be paid to *Koyiladhikari*, Vaduvalumavan and Valkkaivalumavar. (T. A. S. Vol. V. p. 35)

4	On a slab on the west side of the same temple. (15/1097 and 87/1086)	...	Kulaśekhara Kōyiladhikārikal.	2 + 8th year Jupiter in Karkaṭaka Vṛścika	Tamil in Vaṭṭeḻuttu.	Records that the king took four *tali* Tirukkunrappolai and was the Nediyali when he made a gift of all the incomes of the year from Peruneydal to that temple. (T. A. S. Vol. V. p. 38)
			Podiyal (*Kunnattunāṭu*)			
1	On the north base of the central shrine of the Kṛṣṇankōyil of Podiyal near Aghōramanaikkal. (83/1085)	...	...	Ko. 635, Jupiter in Tulam, Mēṭam	Tamil in Vaṭṭeḻuttu.	Records the building of the shrine with stone.
			Poḻikkarai (*Quilon.*)			
1	On a slab in the Siva temple at Poḻikkarai. (113/1096)	...	...	...	Tamil in Vaṭṭeḻuttu.	Registers a gift of land by a native of Paravūr to the temple of Poḻikkarai-Bhaṭṭāraka, for offering and lamps. Mentions Veṇāṭṭumunnūṟṟuvar and Kañoilitumunnurravar. (T. A. S. Vol. VII. p. 58)

Puṭugrāmam (*Agastīśvaram*)

No.	Place of inscription.	Dynasty.	King.	Date.	Language and Alphabet.	Remarks.
1	On the south wall of the central shrine of the Aḷakiyamaṇavālaperumal Temple near Puṭugrāmam. (25/1093)	...	...	Ko. 358 Tulām 13	Tamil.	Records gift of land to the temple of Udaiyamārttāṇḍa-Viṇṇakar-Emperumān at Puṭugrāmam *alias* Rājanārāyaṇacaturvēdimangalam in Nāñjināṭu, while the king was staying in his palace at Kōṭṭāru. (T A. S. Vol. VI p. 188)
2	Do. (26/1093)	...	...	Ko. 544, Cingam 14	Do.	Relates to the grant registered in No. 25. The king of this record who is not mentioned by name, but who was staying at Amarāpati, was the younger brother of the person who made the gift. (T. A. S. Vol. VI. p. 188)
3	On the south base of the Kailāsanātha temple at Karuppukkōṭṭai near Puṭugrāmam. (104/1099 and 29/1093)	...	...	Ko. 338, Vṛścika 2, Jupiter in Kanni	Do.	Records gift of land by Sēkharan *alias* Gangaikoṇḍacoḷa Valluvanāṭṭāḷvān of Kariōtturai for daily worship to the God Śrī Kailāsamuṭaiya-Mahādēva in the temple at Karumpaluvu. (T. A. S Vol. VI. p 182).

4	On the slab set up in the compound of the same temple. (105/1099 and 28/1093)	...	...	Saka 1676, Kollam 930, Tai 15, Friday Su. 12. Vaidhṛtiyōgum, Simhakaraṇam Makayiram	Do.	Registers gift of land by Viṛayaperumal Sivatāṇuvan for offerings and worship to the God Kailāsamuṭaiya-Nayinār at Karuppukkōṭṭai. (T. A. S. Vol. VI. p. 184)
			Puravaššeri (Agastīśvaram)			
1	On the north wall of the Viṣṇu temple at Puravaššeri. (2/1093)	...	...	Ko. 663, Tai 28, su. di. 11, Thursday, Mṛga śīrṣa	Tamil.	Records gift of 401 *kaliyugarāman paṇam* for feeding a *Brahman* in the temple of Puravari Viṇṇavar Emperumān. The donor was a certain Vangippurattu Nārāyaṇa bhaṭṭan. (T. A. S. Vol. VII. p. 15.)
2	On the south base of the *garbhagṛha of* the same. (3/1093)	Travancore	Vīra Ravi Varman	Ko. 336 + 1, Iṭavam 6, Saturday, Makayiram	Do.	Records gift of land by agents of the king Vīra Ravi Varman of Vēṇāṭu for worship in the temple of Puravari-Viṇṇakar-Āḻvār. (T. A. S. Vol. VII. p. 81 & Indian Antiquary Vol. 24. p. 257).

Puravaśśēri (*contd*)

No.	Place of inscription.	Dynasty.	King.	Date.	Language and Alphabet.	Remarks.
3	On the north and west bases of the central shrine of the same. (4/1093).	Pāṇḍya.	Kōnērinmelkoṇḍān Kulaśēkharadēva.	16+1st year 16th year and 465	Tamil.	Records a royal gift of land at Vīrakeralamangalam, a *Brahmadeya* in Vaikuṇṭhavalanāṭu, a subdivision of Nāṭṭāuṟṟppōkku for the expenses of the temple of Puravari-Viṇṇakar Ālvār at Puravari-caturvēdimangalam. (T. A. S. Vol. VII. p. 5.)
4	On the south base of the *ardhamaṇḍapa* of the same. (5/1093 s. a. 60/1100).	Vēṇāṭu.	Vīra Rāma varman.	Ko. 372 Vṛścikam 21	Do.	End to be traced. Records gift of land as *kiṭaivirutti* for two teachers who had to teach *Rig* and *Yajur* vēdas. There are also 4 pieces with beginning lost. (T. A. S. Vol. VII. p. 14.)
5	On the north base of the central shrine of the same. (6/1093).	Pāṇḍya.	Māravarman *alias* Tribhuvana cakravartin Śrī Vallabhadēva.	16 + 4 and 96th day	Do.	Records that at the instance of Siṅgan Raṅgan of Paśungulam the king while he was staying in his palace Tirunelveli in Kīlvēmpanāṭu

						made a gift of land at Virakeralamangalam in Nāṭṭāṟṟuppōkku to the temple of Puravarivinnakar Ālvār. Mentions the seat called மூனீட தலைமயன். (T. A. S. Vol. VII. p. 3.)
6	On the north and west-bases of the central shrine of the same. (7/1093)	Pāṇḍya.	Do.	16 + 1 years	Tamil.	Records an agreement tendered by the Sabha of Virakeralamangalam promising to supply 7 kalam of paddy as tax and 2 *Kiramam* as antarāyam.
7	On the south base of the garbhagṛha of the same. (8/1093)	...	...	...	Do.	Fragmentary.
8	On the south base of the *maṇḍapa* in front of the same. (9/1093)	...	...	...	...	Fragment. Seems to register gifts of money for offerings, lamps, etc.
9	On the north and west bases of the central shrine of the same. (12/1093)	...	...	...	...	Fragmentary.

Puravaśśēri—(*contd.*)

No.	Place of inscription.	Dynasty.	King.	Date.	Language and Alphabet.	Remarks.
10	On the north base of the central shrine of the same. (12/1093)	...	...	...	Do.	Pieces wanting. Seems to register a gift of land for meeting the daily expenses of the temple. Mentions a certain Vīrapāṇḍiya-Āṇkuṭivēlan. (T. A. S. Vol. VII. p. 12.)
11	On the north base of the *maṇḍapa* in front of the central shrine of the same. (14/1093)	...	...	...	Do.	Fragment. Seems to provide money for lamps. (T. A. S. Vol. VII. p. 10.)
12	On the east base of the same. (16/1093)	...	...	...	Do.	Fragmentary. Seems to register a gift of money. Mentions Kurakkēṇi-Kollam. Signed by Paṭṭāḷi Gōvindan and Siṅṅan-Vikkiraman.

13	On the north wall of the same. (55/1100 and 10/1093.)	Travancore	...	Ko. 33 (6,). Iṭavam 5 (expired), Saturday, Makayiram.	o.	Continuation lost. States that Singan-Rangan of Pasungulam in Tennāṭu colonised the village of Puravaricaturvēdimangalam with eighteen families of *Bramans*, apparently by free grants of land to them. (T. A. S. Vol. VII. p. 2.)
14	On the base of the east wall of the same temple. (56/1100)	Travancore.	Vīra Ravivarman (governing Vēṇāṭu.)	..... Iṭavam 5, (expired), Saturday, Makayiram.	Do.	Some stones missing. This is the original, of which the record published in I. A., XXIV, p. 251, is a counter-agreement. It registers the gift of 10 *mamundirikai* of land by the residents of Tāḻaikkuṭi for providing some offerings and for burning a perpetual lamp in the temple of Āḻvār at Puravaricaturvēdimangalam. (T. A. S. Vol. VII. p. 9)
15	On the base of the north wall of the *maṇḍapa* in the same temple. (57/1100 and 15/1093)	...	...	Ko. 335 1, Iṭavam	Do	Registers the gift of 1 *ma* of land by Tirumarumaruvan of Kuruṅguṭi for providing offerings to Puravarivinnakar-Āḻvār. Nanatisvaram-uṭaiyār is also mentioned. (T. A. S. Vol. VII. p. 6.)

Puravaśśēri—(*contd.*)

No.	Place of inscription.	Dynasty.	King.	Date.	Language and Alphabet.	Remarks.
16	On the base of the same *maṇḍapa*. (58/1100 and 13/1093)	...	...	Ko. 335 + 1, Iṭavam 6, Sunday, Tiruvātirai	Do.	Registers gift of land by Dāmōdaran-Kaṇṭan *alias* Vikramacōḻa-Ankuṭivēlan for providing offerings of 2 *nāḻi* of rice every day to the God Puravari-viṇṇakar-Āḻvār. (T. A. S. Vol. VIII. p. 11.)
17	On the same wall. (59/1100)	...	...	Ko. 335 + 1.	Do.	Registers the document of the Tennan Villattur-velan who took over the land for the above-mentioned donation of Vikramacola-Ankuṭivēlan and Vīra Pāṇḍya-Ankuṭivēlan in Turakkōṭu in Kundurkavu, agreed to measure out the daily rations of rice to the temple.
18	On the base of the south wall of the mahāmaṇḍapa in the same temple. (61/1100)	Pāṇḍya	Kulaśēkharadēva	4th year	Do.	Built in. Only the King's name is visible.

19	On the same wall (59/1100)	...	...	...	Do.	Refers to the *sadāsēvai* of Kēralan-Eduttāyidamuṭai-yān (who has figured in the Ericcikulam record of Kollam 804.
20	On the base of the wall of the same temple. (63/1100)	Pāṇḍya	...	Ko.* 10.	Tamil.	Refers to the agreement given by three garisons called Arikulakesari-termidavillikal and Satyasraya-kulakala-terindavillikal for some offerings to the God at Puravaśśeri. (T. A. S. Vol. VII. p. 13,)
21	On the same wall. (64/1100)	....	...	Ko. 340, Cingam, 6	Do.	Continuation of lines is missing. Registers the gift of some lands for providing 4 *nāḻi* of offering to the God and for feeding two *Brāhmans* with it. (T. A. S. Vol. VII. p. 13.)
22	On the base of the north wall of the maṇḍapa in the same temple. (65/1100)	...	...	...	Do.	Fragmentary. Registers gift of land by three individuals for the recitation o *Tiruvāymōḻi* in the temple. (T. A. S. Vol. VII. p. 10.)

Puttēri (Tōvāḷa)

No.	Place of inscription.	Dynasty.	King.	Date.	Language and Alphabet	Remarks.
1	On a stone standing on the roadside near Puttēri. (53/1100).	...	...	Śaka 1547, Ko. 801, Āvaṇi (10), Wednesday, ba. [illegible], Dhṛtiyōga, Vṛṣabha-karaṇa, Uttiraṭṭāti.	Do.	Registers a gift of land for a wayside choultry by Govindan of Kurakkēṇi-Kollam.

Quilon.

No.	Place of inscription.	Dynasty.	King.	Date.	Language and Alphabet	Remarks.
1	On the west base of the Gaṇapati temple at the bazar street, Quilon. (51/1084.)	...	...	Ko. 671	Sanskrit in Malayalam	Records that Nityaprajñā-muni, author of क्रमदीपिका-व्याख्या consecrated (?) Govinda in Nētrapura. Mentions Keralavarman *alias* Jayasimha. (T. A. S. Vol. II. p. 26.)

2	On a stone set up on the north-east corner of a small building known as the office of Col. Munro at Quilon. (52/1084)	Travancore.	...	Ko. 652	Tamil.	The King is said to have been residing in Tinnevelly; he ordered that the Tarakukōṇam in Kurakkēṇikkollam (Quilon) occupied by the 18 classes of people, be named *Cempakarāman-teruvu* and *Añcinān* pukaliṭam. (T. A. S. Vol. VII. p. 98.)
3	On the south base of the central shrine of the same. (54/1084)	...	...	Ko. 513	Tamil.	Gift of land. (T. A. S. Vol. V. p. 46)
4	On a slab set up in the south side of the Rāmēśvara temple at Quilon. (54/1095 same as No. 53/1084)	Vēṇāṭu ?	Rāmar-Tiruvaṭi	(1102 A. D.) Ko. 278, Jupiter in Kanni, Simha 9; 2 14th year.	Tamil in Vaṭṭeḻuttu.	Damaged. In order to expiate the sin arising from an enmity with the Ārayas, it was decided, in the presence of the king's officer Kulaśēkhara-cakravartin who was then in the palace in Panaiṅnāvu in Kurakkēṇi-Kollam that a festival should be conducted in the temple of Rāmēśvaram. Mentions Kumāran Udaiyavarman of Vēṇāṭu, Kaṇṇan Devan of Melkkāṭu and Satti Piraman. (T. A. S. Vol. V. p. 40.)

Quilon—(*contd.*)

No.	Place of inscription.	Dynasty.	King.	Date.	Language and Alphabet.	Remarks.
5	On another slab set up on the north side of the same temple. (55/1095.)	...	...	...	Tamil.	Mutilated and damaged. Seems to register a gift of land for offerings and lamps. (T. A. S. Vol. VII. p. 102)
6	On two slabs and on four sides of the man-ḍapa in front of the Bhagavati temple at the same village. (56/1095.)	...	...	A. D. 1828, May 12.	Do.	Records that the temple of Bhagavati was constructed in this year. Mentions several Officers of the Army, Col. Hood Woosh, Wiry Schmidt etc. (T. A. S. Vol. VII. p. 103.)
7	On a stone slab embedded in the Mudakkara church at Quilon. (1/1099.)	...	...	A. D. 1771, January 31.	Latin.	States that Clemens Joseph S. J. of Cochin, was interred at Quilon on the day mentioned.
8	On a marble niche *mihrab* kept in the Kollampaḷḷi, Quilon. (2/1099.)	...	...	Ramzan Hijra 726, (A. D. 1326.)	Arabic.	Records that the *mihrab* was the gift of Amir Ahmed, son of Abul Fath of Gazrun (Persia).

9	On a stone set up in the west wall of the Syrian Church at Quilon. (8/1100 same as 95/1092)	...	...	Ko. 826, Iṭavam 15, Tuesday.	Malayalam in Vāṭṭeḻuttu.	Records that (Ko)si Cheriyan died on that date.
10	On the same stone. (9/1100)	...	...	Ko. 812, Mithunam 20.	Malayalam in Vaṭṭeḻuttu.	States that a copy was made from a copper-plate document.
11	On the south base of the Rāmēśvara temple at Quilon. (1/1098)	...	...	Ko. 513.	Tamil.	Records the Sattan Marudapillai redeemed certain temple lands and that Offerings and lamps to the temple at Rāmēśvaram were provided from the income. (T. A. S. Vol. V. p. 46.)
12	On the lintel of the eastern gateway in front of the same. (2/1098)	...	...	Ko. 516, Cittirai.	do.	States that Tiruvottajamamalagiyar of Navalur constructed the gateway in stone. (T. A. S. Vol. V. p. 47)

Sāmbūr Vaṭakarai. (near Cenkōṭṭa)

No.	Place of inscription.	Dynasty.	King.	Date.	Language and Alphabet.	Remarks.
1	On the south base of the *mahāmaṇḍapa* of the Śiva temple at Sāmbūr Vaṭakarai. (19/1086)	*Pāṇḍya.*	Śivala ma ran Vara-gunarāman Pāṇḍya Kulaśēkhara Sōmaśiyār.	S. 153 (8)* 3rd year	Tamil.	Gift of land. (T. A. S. Vol. I. p. 148)
2	On the south base of the same. (20/1086)	Do.	Jatil. Kula-śēkharadēva *alias* Tiru-nelvēlip perumāl son of Abhirāma Parākrama Pāṇḍyadēva	S. 1474, 2nd Paritāpi	Do.	Records the appointment of certain persons as temple servants. (T. A. S. Vol. I. p. 272)

3	Do. (20/1086)	Do	Jatil. Tribh. Parākrama Pāṇḍyadēva born in the MṛgasIrṣa nakṣatra.	31st + 4th	Do.	Records additional grants made to the *Brahmanas* of the Parākrama Pāṇḍyacaturvēdimangalam, as the previous grant was found insufficient to sustain their livelihood. (T. A. S. Vol. I.p. 255)
4	On the south wall of the same. (22/1086)	Do.	Māra. Tribh. Arikēsaridēva.	2nd + 32nd	Do.	Further grants made by the king in addition to those already made by Aṇṇālvi Parākrama Pāṇḍyadēva and his brother ŚrIvallabhadēva. The day of the grant was Uttara nakṣatra, the natal star of SrIvallabha. (T. A. S. Vol. I. p. 252)
5	On the south wall of the same. (23/1086)	Do.	Perumāl Parākrama Pāṇḍyadēva. (Arikēsari)	30th + 2nd	Do.	On the MṛgasIrṣa nakṣatra of the given month etc., certain pieces of land were granted to two *Brāhmanas*. (T. A. S. Vol. I. p. 255)

Sāmbūr Vaṭakarai (contd.)

No.	Place of inscription.	Dynasty.	King.	Date.	Language and Alphabet.	Remarks.
6	On the north wall of the same. (24/1086)	Pāṇḍya.	Jatil. Tribh, Ponnin Perumāl Parākrama Pāṇḍyadēva *alias* Vīra Pāṇḍya-dēva, born in Aviṭṭa nakṣatra.	2nd + 5th	Tamil.	Mentions the previous grants of uncle (mamadi) of Parākrama Pāṇḍyadēva and then of uncle (mamadi) of the ruling king, Srīvallabha and records further grants by the king. (T. A. S. Vol. I. p. 259)
7	On the north wall (facing west) of the same. (25/1086)	Do.	Jatil. Tribh. Ponnin Perumāl Parākrama Pāṇḍyadēva *alias* Vīra Pāṇḍyadēva (born in Aviṭṭa nakṣatra).	2nd + 5th	Do.	Do. (T A. S. Vol. I. p. 257)

8	On the north wall of the central shrine of the same. (26/1086)	...	...	...	Tamil.	Gift of land for celebrating the Pradōṣa festival. (T. A. S. Vol. I p. 194)
9	On the north base of the *mahāmaṇḍapa* of the Siva temple, Śāmbūr Vaṭakarai. (27/1086)	Pāṇḍya.	Jaṭāvarman Tribh. Parākrama Pāṇḍyadēva (Arikēsarivarman).	2nd + 23rd	Do.	Grant of land for the *pūja* of the God Tiru-Mūlasthānam Uṭaiyār of Vindanūr, on the Mṛgasīrṣa nakṣatra, the natal star of the king. (T. A. S. Vol. I. p. 254)
10	On the north wall of the *mahāmaṇḍapa* of the same. (28/1086)	Do.	Alakanperumāl. Ativīrarāma *alias* Śrīvallabhadēva son of Tirunelvēliperumāl *alias* Kulaśēkharadēva.	S. 1494, Angirasa, 10th year	Do	Records the grant of land and house as *pattukkāniyātci*. (T. A. S. Vol I. p. 279)
11	On the north wall of the *mahāmaṇḍapa* of the same. (29/1036)	Do.	Alakanperumāl son of Jatil. Tribh. Tirunelvēliperumāl Kulaśēkhara-perumāl.	S. 1492, Pramoduta 8th year	Do	Grant of land and house to one Tirumēniyalakiyān Brahmādarāyan *alias* Tandaikkal Brahmādarāyan as *arccanabhogam.* (T. A. S. Vol. I. p. 277)

Sāmbūr Vaṭakarai (contd.)

No.	Place of inscription.	Dynasty.	King.	Date.	Language and Alphabet.	Remarks.
12	On the east wall (proper left) of the entrance of the *mahāmaṇḍapa* of the same. (30/1086)	Pāṇḍya.	Tirunelvēlipperumāl son of Abhirāma Parākrama Pāṇḍyadēva born in the Aśvati nakṣatra.	S. 1471, Saumya	Tamil.	Grant of land to God Abhimuktīśvara of the Parākrama Pāṇḍya Caturvēdimangalam *alias* Perumāl-akaram. (T.A. S. Vol. i. p. 263)
13	On the east wall (proper right of entrance) of the *mahāmaṇḍapa* of the same. (31/1086)	Do.	Alakanperumāl Ativīrarāma *alias* Srivallabhadēva son of Kulaśēkharadēva.	S. 1487, Krōdhana, 3rd year	Do.	Appointment of Rakkada perumāl Kallapirān, *alias* Sivala-Kalingarāyan, as the *Śrībhandārakkaṇakku*. (T.A. S. Vol. I. p. 274)

14	On the north, west and south bases of the central shrine of the same. (32/1086)	Do.	Caṭaiya Tribh. Parākrama Pāṇḍyadēva.	2nd × 20th	Do.	Built in several places.
15	On the south wall (the stones facing west) of the *mahāmaṇḍapa* of the same. (33/1086)	Do.	Jatil. Tribh. Śrīvallabhadēva, born in the Tiruvātirai nakṣatra.	2nd + 30t	Do.	Grant of land to a *Brāhmaṇa*. Refers to the grant made before by Mamadi Parakrama Pāṇḍyadēva. (T. A. S. Vol. I. p. 264)
16	On the east wall, (proper left of the entrance) of the *mahāmaṇḍapa* in front of the Amman shrine of the same. (34/1086)	Nāyaka.	Muttu Vīrappa Nāyaka.	S. 1527	Do.	Appears to record a gift for *abhiṣēka* of the God Mūlasthānamuṭaiyār in the temple at Vindanūr. (T. A. S. Vol. V. p. 193)
17	Do. (35/1086)	Do.	Muttu Vīrappanāyaka.	S. 152 (6) Sobhakrit Citrai 27	Do.	Grant of land. (T. A. S. Vol. V. p. 192)
18	On the east wall (proper right of the entrance) (36/1086)	Do.	Do.	Do.		Do. Do.

Sāstamaṅgalam (Trivandrum).

No.	Place of inscription.	Dynasty.	King.	Date.	Language and Alphabet.	Remarks.
1	On a boulder in the garden belonging to the Kūvakkaraipōtti at Śāstamaṅgalam. (18/1084)	...	...	....	Tamil in Vaṭṭeḻuttu.	Fragment, mentions Tirucāttamaṅgalam (T.A.S. Vol. VII. p. 134)
	Śāstānkōṭṭai (Kunnattūr)					
1	On the south side of the back entrance of the Śāsta temple at Śāstānkōṭṭa. (36/1090)	Travancore.	Jayasimhanāṭṭu Svarūpam Uṇṇikērala.	*Vṛścika 5	Malayalam.	Mentions the name of the king.
	Sattakulam (Kunnattunaṭu.)					
1	On the east base of the *maṇḍapa* in front of the Siva temple of Sattakulam. (129/1096)	...	...	1078 Makaram, 24	Malayalam.	This is the work of Vettungal Tambi Pillai (T. A. S. Vol. VII. p. 98)

Śucīndram (Agastiśvaram).

1	On the rock inside the compound of the Srī-kailāsam shrine in the Sthāṇunāthasvāmin temple at Sucīndram. (58/1086)	Cōḷa.	Parakēsari-Varman.	34th.	Tamil in Vaṭṭeḻuttu.	Gift of sheep for a lamp. (T. A. S. Vol. I. p. 237)
2	On the rock outside the compound of the same. (59/1086)	Do.	Rājarājakēsarivarman.	10th.	Do.	Do. (Ep. Ind. Vol. V. p.44 & T. A. S. Vol. I. p. 238)
3	On a rock inside the same. (63/1086 & 23/1090)		(*Cōlan-ralai koṇḍa*) Kō-Vīra Pāṇḍya *alias* Vīra Nārāyaṇa.	4 + 3	Do	Built in, gift of land for offerings, lamp and a flower garden by Araiyan Vīranārāyaṇan *alias*......Anukkappallavaraiyan. (T. A. S. Vol. III. p. 60)
4	On a rock inside the same. (64/1086)	Do.	Vīranārāyaṇa *alias* Vīra Pāṇḍya, who took the head of Cōḷa.	Lost.	Do.	One half built in ; records the gift of land for a flower garden and a perpetual lamp and offerings by......Araiyan Vīranārāyaṇan *alias* ... . Anukkappallavaraiyan.

Śucīndram (*contd.*)

No.	Place of inscription.	Dynasty.	King.	Date.	Language and Alphabet.	Remarks.
5	On the south base of the central shrine of the Nambi Śāstān temple, at Śucīndram. (65/1086 and 12/1107)	...	...	Ko. 404.	Tamil.	Gift of land to the God (Viṣṇu), Dvārakai-Emperumān. Mentions Gōvindaprajña Bhiṭāra Tiruvaṭi.
6	On the south base of *ardha-maṇḍapa* of the same. (66/1086)	...	...	Ko. 404.	Do.	Gift of land. Mentions Gōvindaprajñā Bhaṭāra Tiruvaṭi.
7	On the west and south base of the central shrine of the same. (67/1086)	...	...	Ko. 399	Do.	Gift of land for a perpetual lamp and a flower garden to the temple of Dvārakai-Emperumān. Mentions Gōvindaprajña Bhaṭāra Tiruvaṭi.
8	On the west base of the central shrine of the same. (68/1086)	...	....	Ko. 40 (4).	Do.	Gift of land. Damaged. Gōvindaprajña Bhaṭāra Tiruvati is mentioned.
9	On the north base of the central shrine of the same. (69/1086)	...	...	Ko. 402.	Do.	Gift of land for offerings. Gōvindaprajñā Bhaṭāra Tiruvaṭi is mentioned.

10	Do. (70/1086)	...	...	Ko. 406.	Tamil.	Deals with the appointment of the Śāntikkārs. Mentions in addition to the person already referred to, a Periya Tiruvaṭi who looked after the affairs of the temple at Tiruvanantapuram.
11	On the north base of *ardhamaṇḍapa* of the same. (71/1086)	...	...	...	Do.	Sale of land. Mentions Tiruvikkiramapurattālvār.
12	On the north base of the *mahāmaṇḍapa* of the same. (72/1086)	...	...	Ko. 400.	Do.	Gift of gold for burning a lamp in the temple of *Dvārakai Emperumān*, the donees receiving which arranged to burn the lamp, and the gold was utilised for a *paṭṭam* to be worn by the image of Śucīndramuṭaiyār.
13	On the west base of the ruined *Cuṟṟumaṇḍa a* of the same. (73/1086)	...	...	Ko. 362, Iṭavam.	Do.	Fragmentary.

Śucīndram (*contd.*)

No.	Place of inscription.	Dynasty.	King.	Date.	Language and Alphabet.	Remarks.
14	On a natural rock in the north west corner of the *prākāra* of the same. (74/1056)	...	...	Lost	Tamil.	Gift of land.
15	On the south-eastern wall of the *maṇḍapa* in front of the Sthāṇunātha temple at Sucīndram. (92/1087)	Pāṇḍya.	Jatil. Tribh. Parākrama Pāṇḍya.	20th year Mēṭam 20, su. 3, Mṛgaśīrṣa.	...	Registers a gift of land for conducting certain services in the temple. (T. A. S. Vol. I. p. 281)
16	On the rock near the Kailāsa shrine in the Śiva temple at Sucīndram. (21/1090)	Pāṇḍya.	Caṭaiyamāran.	8 Simha.	Tamil in Vaṭṭeḻuttu.	Fragment. Seems to register gift of sheep for a lamp to the temple at Sucīndram.
17	On the same. (22/1090)	....	...	...	Do.	Fragment.
18	Do. (24/090)	Pāṇḍya.	Caṭaiyamāran.	2nd + 10th, Makaram 20	Do.	Gift of 50 sheep for a lamp to the temple at Śucīndram by Kannipalanci in this. (T. A. S. Vol. IV. p. 123)
19	Do. (25/1090)	Do.	Tennapirān *Vīrakēraḷan.*	10th.	Do.	Gift of 25 cows for a lamp to the same temple.

20	On the rock near the Kailāsa shrine in the Śiva temple at Sucīndram. (26/1090)	Cōḷa.	Rājarāja-Rājakēsari.	10th.	Tamil in Vaṭṭeḻuttu.	(Ep. Ind.)
21	Do. (27/1090)	Pāṇḍya.	Vīra-Pāṇḍya who took the head of Cōḷa.	4 + 6th.	Do.	Gift of 50 sheep for a perpetual lamp. (T. A. S. Vol. III. p. 74.)
22	Do. (28/1090)	...	...	...	Do.	Damaged. Mentions Śivindirattu Mādēva.
23	Do. (29/1090)	Pāṇḍya.	Vīra-Pāṇḍya who took the head of Cōḷa.	4 + 4th	Do.	Damaged. Mentions O-. Dēvakar of Tennāṭu. (T. A. S Vol. III. p. 73)
24	On the same. (30/1090)	Do.	Do.	12 + 1	Do.	Registers a gift of 30 *Īḻakkāśu* by Cērāntakapallavaraiyan *alias* Maran accan for a perpetual lamp. (T. A. S. Vol. III. p. 72.)

Śucīndram (*contd.*)

No.	Place of inscription.	Dynasty.	King.	Date.	Language and Alphabet.	Remarks.
25	On the wall near the rock adjoining the Kailāsa shrine of the same. (31/1090)	Pāṇḍya.	Vīra Pāṇḍya who took the head of Cōḷa.	15 ; 4th	Tamil.	Refers to a transaction and the findings of the assembly of Śucīndram. (T. A. S. Vol. III. p. 71.)
26	On the wall of the 2nd prākāra of the Sthāṇumāthasvāmin temple at Sūcindram. (32/1090 & 30/1093)	...	...	Kollam 420, Mithunam 28.	Do.	Records a gift of 10 accu of gold by the Parasiva Dēvan Śucīndravāsi to the temple of Śucīndiramuṭaiya-Nayanār for a lamp.
27	On the pillar in the maṇḍapa opposite to the same temple at Śucīndram. (52/1092)	...	...	...	Do.	This is the *Sadāsēvai* of a certain lady named Śivakāmi the daughter of Maṇimālai, to the temple of Śucīndram.
28	Do. (53/1092)	...	...	...	Do.	This is the *Sadāsēvas* of Āṇḍicci the daughter Valladevan.
29	Do. (54/1092)	...	...	...	Do.	This is the Sadāsēvai of Deyvaputtira Māṭan Kuṭṭi-Iraiyumaikuṭṭi.

30	On the north wall west side of the door of gōpura gate of the same temple. (55/1092)	...	...	Ko. 796, Mārkaḻi 4.	Tamil.	Damaged. Registers a gift of a lamp by a private individual.
31	On the wall of Cempakarāman *maṇḍapa* near the right side of *dvajastambha* of the same. (56/1092)	Travancore	Rāmavarma.	Kollam 654. Expressed by the chronogram '[illegible]'	Sanskrit in Grantha.	Records the construction of the maṇḍapa by King Rāmavarma. (T. A. S. Vol. VIII. p. 23)
32	On the south wall at the west side of the *gōpura* of the same. (57/1092 and 103/1096)	...	...	Sādhāraṇa Āvaṇi 6.	Tamil.	This is the Sadāsēvai of Vasuvana-Nāyakar son of Tippayya-Nāyaka, Periya Rāmappa Nāyaka and Ciru Rāmappa-Nāyaka sons Vasuvana-Nāyaka for the prosperity and continuance and freedom from sin of the family.
33	On the east wall of *dvajastambha maṇḍapa* near the left of *Dvajastambha* in the same. (58/1092)	...	...	Ko. 757, Arpaśi 28, Saturday, Anuṣa, su. 2	Tamil.	Registers gift of a gold *tāli* and pot (kuṭam) to the temple at Śucīndram by Īccammaikuṭṭi Ammai living on the eastern side of the *gōpura* at Tiruvaṭṭāru.

Sucīndram (*contd.*)

No.	Place of inscription.	Dynasty.	King.	Date.	Language and alphabet.	Remarks.
34	On the left side post of the threshold at the west side of the door of the gōpura gate of the same. (59/1092)	...	...	Ko. 766, Mārkaḻi 13.	Do.	Registers gift of 40 *paṇam* for a lamp to be burnt near the image of Nandīccurar-Tampirān on the right side of the *gōpura* of the Sucīndra-muṭaiya-Nayinār.
35	On a pillar at the north side of *Nāṭaka-śālai-mukappu* of the same. (61/1092)	...	...	...	Do.	The pillar is the gift of Jātavēdan Dēvaki-Ammai of Puttillam at Śucīndram.
36	On a pillar at the right side of Garuḍa installed in front of *dvajastambha* of the same. (62/1092)	...	...	...	Tamil.	Damaged. Mentions a certain Kēśavan Kēśavan.
37	On a pillar on the north side of the Kutira-vāsal *maṇḍapa* of the same. (63/1092)	...	...	...	Do.	Mentions Nācciyār, daughter of Umaiyammai, who probably presented the pillar.

39	On a pillar on the right side of the big *Vṛṣabha* of the same. (64/1092)	...	...	...	Do.	This is the *saddāsāvai* of Karumpan.
40	On the north wall on the west side of the door of the *gōpura* gate of the same. (65/1092 and 7/1111)	Travancore.	Śankaranārāyaṇa Muṭivēḷaikkāran Venṟuman Koṇṭa vīra Bhūtala Rāmavarman of Jayatunganāṭu.	(7) 22 Tulām śu. di. 2 Tuesday, Anuḷam	Do.	Registers provisions made for the offerings *sri bali* etc., to the shrine of the Teṉ-Tiruvēngaṭa Viṇṇavar-Emberuman. The King was encamped at Talaikkulam in Malaimaṇḍalam while ordering the gift.
41	On the right side post of the threshold on the west side of the door of gōpura gate of the same. (66/1092)	...	...	Ko. 805, Arpasi 10.	Tamil.	Registers a gift of 100 *paṇam* by Irāman Tiruvaṭi Ammai of Mullai-illam from the interest on which lamps had to be maintained in the shrine of Śankarānārayaṇa in the inner enclosure of Sucīndiramuṭaiya-Nayinār.

Sucīndram ··(contd.)

No.	Place of inscription.	Dynasty.	King.	Date.	Language and Alphabet.	Remarks.
42	On the south wall of *dvajastambha maṇḍapa* on the west side of the central gate of the same. (67/1092)	Travancore.	Adityavarman *alias* Jayatunganāṭṭu-Mutta-Tiruvaṭi	Kali 4584, Ko. 659, Māsi 14, su, 13, Monday, Pusam.	Tamil.	A piece missing or built in. Rāmavarman Ciravāymuttavar was the younger brother of the king. Records an order for the removal from the registers the demands of revenue, on certain lands granted to the temple of Sucīndrum by the king and his younger brothe:. The order was made while the king was staying in Cempakarāmacaturvēdimangalam in Tirukkurunkuṭi Patinettunāṭu is stated to lie to the east of Panrivāykkal to the south of Vaippāru to the north of stone and to the west of the sea. The lands were situated in Tapporunaikkarai, Nattarrankarai Paocaraiyarai, Tenkaraināṭu, Amindakanavalanāṭu Manaveravalanadu Papakudi Purattānāṭu Karingulanāṭu and Nānjināṭu.

43	On the east wall of *dvajastambha maṇḍapa* on the right side of *dvajastambha* of the same. (68/1092)	...	...	Ko. 724, Māsi 14, su., 12, Saturday, Puṣya.	Do.	Relates to the appointment of an accountant by the *Srīkāryamceyvār* and the assembly.
44	On the right side post of the threshold in the central gate of the south wall of *dvajastambha* of the same. (69/1092)	...	...	Ko. 745, Ṛṣabha 28, Thursday Aviṭṭam, ba. di. 6.	Do.	Relates to the appointment of Ādiccan Adiccan of Tiruvaṭṭāru as the accountant in place of his brother Tikkellām Pukaḻum Perumāl.
45	On the left side of the same. (70/1092)	Travancore.	Sakalakalai Mārttāṇḍa Varmar *alias* Ciraivāy Mutta Tiruvaṭi	Kollam 716 Āni 9 su, di. 13, Monday.	Tamil	Records that on a representation made by the temple authorities of Sucīndira muṭaiya-Ṅayinār to the king regarding to their disabilities in cultivation a royal order was issued removing the disability. Mentions the ānaivāl Tikkellāmpukaḻum perumāl.
46	On the north wall of Vināyaka shrine on the left side of gōpura of the same. (71/1092)	...	...	...	Do.	Provides for offerings to the shrine of Piḷḷaiyār set up to the north of the *maṇḍapa* in the inner side of the *gōpura*.

Sucīndram. (*contd*)

No.	Place of inscription.	Dynasty.	King.	Date.	Language and Alphabet.	Remarks.
47	On a stone on the right side of the sculpture of a, king facing east in the 2nd *prākāra* of the same. (72/1092)	...	...	...	Tamil.	Fragment. Contains the names of a few signatories of a record.
48	On the top of the wall of the right side of the sculpture of a king facing east in the end *prākāra* of the same. (73/1092)	Travancore.	Mārttāṇḍavarman.	Kollam 586, Saka 1332, Jupiter in Simha, Tula month Punarvasuday	Sanskrit in Grantha.	States that Mārttāṇḍavarman built a maṇḍapa for God Śiva. (T. A. S. Vol. VIII, p. 28)
49	On the wall of Munnūṟṟunaṅkai Amman temple on the north bank of the Padmatīrtha tank at Sucīndram. (74/1092 and 33/1093)	...	...	Ko. 817 Āṭi 5	Tamil.	Provides for conducting a festival on the asterism Pūram in the month of Āṭi and for procession to the Goddess Munnūṟṟunaṅkai by Mādammai-Kuṭṭi a dancing girl of the temple.

50	On the rock inside the enclosure of the Kailāsa shrine in the same. (29/1093)	Pāṇḍya.	Māranca-ṭaiyan.	23rd year	Tamil in Vaṭṭeḻuttu.	Gift of buffaloes for a lamp to the temple of Tiruccivindirattu-Emperumān by Sēnāvarayan *alias* Tattan-Andari of Tiruvellur in Tiruvaḻutivaḷanāṭu.
51	On a pillar in the *maṇḍapa* on the south of the Pañca linga shrine in the same. (30/1093 and 7/1107).	Travancore.	Mārttāṇḍavarman.	Kollam 586, Śaka 1332, *rāgālōkēśakābdē*, Sun in Tula, Sunday.	Sanskrit in Grantha.	Damaged. Records the construction of the *sabhāmaṇḍapa* in the temple of Śambhu at Sucīndram. (see 73/1093).
52	On the north wall of the first prākāra of the same. (78/1096).	Vēṇāṭu.	Kōtai Kēraḷavarman.	Ko. 320, Mīnam.	Do.	Registers gift of land in Tenvaḷanallūr which was included in *Dēvadāna* village of Nirupaśēkaranallūr for daily offerings in the shrines of Sucīndiramuṭaiya-Mahādēva and Tiruvēnkaṭanilai-Ālvār. The gift was made in accordance with a royal order. (T. A. S. Vol. IV. p. 19).

Sucīndram. (contd)

No.	Place of inscription.	Dynasty.	King.	Date.	Language and Alphabet.	Remarks.
53	On the same wall. (79/1096).	Vēṇāṭu	Kōtai Kēraḷavarman.	Kollam 320.	Do.	Records an order, appointing a private individual to prepare the offerings mentioned in No. 78 above and to have a share of the offered food for his wages. (T. A. S. Vol. IV. p. 20.)
54	Do. (80/1096).	Pāṇḍya.	Māravarman *alias* Tribhuvana Cakravartin Śrīvallabhadēva.	8th year and 407th day.	Do.	Records that the king, while he was seated on the throne called Paḷḷipīṭam-Munaiyadaraiyan in the hall of Palliyaraikkuḍam within the palace at Rājarājacaturvēdimangalam in Muḷḷināṭu, ordered the grant of certain lands in Pullamangalam in Puraṭṭāya-nāṭu, to the temple of Śucīndiramuṭaiya-Mahādēva at Sucīndram *alias* Sundara-Pāṇḍya-Caturvēdimangalam in Nāñji-nāṭu, in.

						order to meet the daily expenses in the shrines of the God Kuttāṭuntēvar and his consort. Mentions Andapillai Bhatta-Atiratrayaji and the temple of Tumburu-Nārada-Īśvaramuṭaiyār at Irukkandurai in Purattāyanāṭu. (T. A. S. Vol. IV. p. 125).
55	Do. 81/1096) and (32/1093).	...	...	Ko. 309. Jupiter in Ṛṣabha, Mithunam.	Tamil.	Incomplete. Registers a gift of land for offerings, to the image of Umākānta-sahitan-tirumēni, set up in the temple of Sucīndira-muṭaiya-Mahādēva, by Arangan Tiruvikkiraman of Śrī-vallabhamangalam.
56	Do. (82/1096)	Vēṇāṭṭu.	Kōtai Kēra-ḷavarman.	Ko. 325	Do.	Registers a provision made for the shrine of Vaṭa-Tiru-vēngaṭattālvār at Sucīndram.

Śucīndram (contd)

No.	Place of inscription.	Dynasty.	King.	Date.	Language & Alphabet.	Remarks.
57	Do. (83/1096)	Do.	Do.	Ko. 325 + 1, Jupiter in Kanni, Vṛści-kam.	Do.	Registers gift of land by the offices of the king, for offerings to Vaṭa-Tiruvēngaṭattālvār. The land was situated in Karkāṭu *alias* Nirupaśēkharanallūr a village in Nānji-nāṭu. (T. A. S. Vol. IV. p. 21).
58	Do. (84/1096)	...	...	Ko. 384, Mīnam.	Do.	Records that the Assembly of Sucīndram *alias* Sundara-cola-caturvēdimangalam conferred on Sankaranārāyaṇan, a vāriyan of Raṇasinkanāṭu, the duty of obtaining paddy and supplying the required quantity of rice, to the temple of Srīmad-Dvarakai-Ālvār, at the rate of four to ten. (T. A. S. Vol. IV. p. 105.)

59	At the left of the entrance Cempakarāman-maṇḍapa in the north wall of the same temple. (85/1096.)	Travancore.	Venṟu-maṇkoṇḍa Bhūtalavira Virakēraḷa varman of Jayatunga-nāṭu.	Kollam 720. Karttikai 27, Aśvati, Monday, śu. di. 11.	Do.	Records that the king conferred the appointment of treasury accountant in the temple of Sucīndramuṭaiyār at Sucīndram, on a certain Uṭaiyān Kuṭṭi called also Dikkellām-pukaḻum Perumāl a native of Vijayankuṭi in Kurunguṭi-nāṭu. (T. A. S. Vol. IV. p. 105).
60	On the north wall of the *Cempakarāman-maṇḍapa* in the same temple. (86/1096)	Travancore	Vīrarāma Rāmavarman, Tiruppāppūr-Mūttavar of Kīlappērūr house Jayasimha-nāṭṭu illam.	Kaliyuga 4572, Ko. 646, Cittirai 12, saturn in Ṛṣabha and Jupiter in Kanya.	Tamil.	Records that, while the king was staying in the *Cenpakarāman-maṇḍapa* of the Tāṇu temple, he made grants of lands, money etc. to a resident of Sivindiram in Tenkōṭu and one *poduval* for conducting the morning worship in the temple, for feeding and for the expenses to be met on the natal star of the king *i. e.* Rēvati & for lamps. (T. A. S. Vol. IV. p. 94.)
61	On the rock near the Kailāsa shrine in the same temple. (87/1096)	Do.	Venṟumaṇkoṇḍa Bhūtalavīra	Ko. 712, Cittirai 19, sudi 6, Sunday.	Do.	Records that, while the king was encamped at Paṇakuṭi in Murattā-nāṭu, he

Sucīndram.—(*contd.*)

No.	Place of Inscription.	Dynasty.	King	Date.	Language and Alphabet.	Remarks.
			Ravivarman	Purnavasu.		ordered the grant of lands in Pullamangalam, Veppangulam included in Irukkandurai in the same nāṭu, as a dēvadāna, to the temple of Sivindiramuṭaiya-Nayinār, in order to meet the expenses of the service called Udaiyam-ārttāṇḍan-sandi, instituted in that temple. Signed by Ayyan Tendiccuramuṭaiyān the architect. (T. A. S. Vol. IV. p. 102.)
2	On the same rock. (88/1096)	Cōḻa-Pāṇḍya.	Jaṭavarman *alias* Sundara Cōla Pāṇḍyadēva.	9th year.	Do.	Registers a gift of cows for lamps made by Śaṅkarappadiyan Kaḻani Venni *alias* Madhurāntakappēraraiyan a resident of Kōṭṭāru *alias* Mummuṭicōḻanallūr to the shrine of Ten-Tiruvēṅgaṭattāḻvār at Sucīndram *alias*

						Sundaracola-Caturvedimangalam which was a *Brahmadeya* of Nañjinātu in Uttama cōla-vaḷanātu, a district of Rājarāja Pāṇḍinātu. (T.A.S. Vol. IV. p. 134).
63	Do. (89/1096)	Travancore.	Sānkaranārāyaṇa Venrumaṇkoṇḍa Bhūtalavīra Udaiyamārtāṇḍavarman Tiruppāpur Mūttavar of Jayasimhanāṭu.	Ko. 710, Māsi 23, ba. di. 13. Sunday, Uttirāṭam.	Tamil.	Records that while the king was encamped at Vaṭaśēri, he ordered the grant of certain lands, in Tāḷaikkuṭi as a *dēvadāna* of the temple of Sucīndramuṭaiya-Nayinār. Signed by Rāman Rāman and Ayyan the architect and Tendiccuramuṭaiyan, the engraver of the inscription. (T. A. S. Vol. IV. p. 2).
64	Do. (90/1096 and 61/1086.)	Pāṇḍya.	Caṭaiyamāran.	2+14th year.	Tamil in Vaṭṭeḻuttu.	Registers gift of sheep for a lamp to the temple of Tiruccucīndirattu-Mahādēva, by Kunran Sūlapāṇi a resident of Ten-Kuṇavāy. (T. A. S. Vol. IV. p. 120.)

Sucīndram (contd.)

o.	Place of inscription.	Dynasty.	King.	Date.	Language and Alphabet.	Remarks.
65	Do. Do. (91/1096 and 62/1086)	Do.	Mārancaṭaiyan.	2+1st year, Karkaṭakam.	Do.	Gift of sheep for a lamp to the temple of Tiruccivindirattu-Emperumān by Iyakki Cellan *alias* Tennavan Uttara mandiri a resident of Kaniyarpalli in Malaināṭu. (T. A. S. Vol. IV. p. 117).
66	Do. Do. (92/1096).	...	...	Ko. 665, Avaṇi 21.	Tamil.	Records a gift of land by a dancing girl for worship and offerings in the temple of Sivindiramuṭaiya-Nayinār. Mentions Segaraneri and Vira keralan-kulam. (T. A. S. Vol. IV. p. 131.)
67	Do. Do. (93/1096)	Cōḷa Pāṇḍya.	Jaṭāvarman alias Uṭaiyār Srī-Cōḷa-Pāṇḍya-dēva.	25th year.	Do.	Records gift of land by purchase from the assembly of Sundaracōla-Caturvēdi-mangalam, a *Brahmadēya* in Nāñjināṭu a sub-division of Uttamacōla-vaḷanāṭu which was a district of Rājarāja-Pāṇḍināṭu, to the temple

							of Sucīndiramuṭaiya-Paramasvāmin by Vēnkadan Sānkaran *alias* Sēnāpati Malaiyappiccōlan of Uttamacōlanallūr in Nalarrur-nāṭu, a sub-division of Rājādhirāja-Vaḷanāṭu which was a district of Cōḷamaṇḍalam, for offerings etc. Mentions a flower garden called after Unnataraman. (T. A. S. Vol. IV. p. 131).
63	Do. (94/1096)	Do.	Do.	Do.	24th year, Mithunam 29.	Do.	Records that the assembly of Sundaracōla-casurvēdimangalam a *brahmadeya* in Nanji-nāṭu met together in the *maniambalam* and sold a piece of land to Velar-Tennavan-Devar-Gandan *alias* Abhimānacōla-Viḷupparaiyan of Madhurāntaka-Catur-vēdimangalam in Karukkaināṭu, a sub-division of Vatakarai Rajendrasinga-valanāṭu, which was a district of Cōlamaṇḍalam for being granted to the temple for sacred lamp. (T. A. S. Vol. IV, p. 138).

Sucīndram. (contd.)

No.	Place of inscription.	Dynasty.	King.	Date.	Language and Alphabet.	Remarks.
69	On the same rock. (95/1096).	Cōḷa-Paṇḍya.	Jaṭavarman *alias* Uṭaiyār Śri-Cōḷa-Pāṇḍyadēva.	25th year.	Tamil.	Registers a gift of sheep for a lamp to the temple of Śucīndiramuṭaiya-Paramasvāmin at Sucīndiram *alias* Sundara-Cōḷa-caturvēdimangalam by the *Daṇḍanāyaka* Velan Cōḷa-keralan *alias* Karikālacōola Vaidumbarāyan Marudattūr in Tiruvalināṭu, a sub-division of Valanāṭu in Cōḷa-maṇḍalam. (T. A. S. Vol. IV. p. 136).
70	Do. (96/1096).	Cōḷa.	Rājarājakēsari varman.	14th year.	Tamil in Vaṭṭeḻuttu.	The conquests of the king extended over Kāntaḷūrśālai, Gangapādi Nulambapādi, Tadiyaivaḻi and Vengai-nāṭu. Records that at the instance of Periyan-Mūvēndavēlār the tax in paddy on certain tax-paying lands were raised. (T. A. S. Vol. IV. p. 129).

71	Do. (97/1096).	Pāṇḍya.	Māran Caṭaiyan.	2+23rd „	Do.	Registers gift of land by purchase and some gold to the temple of Śucīndiram-aṭaiya-Emperumān by Tennavan Tongappallavaraiyan of Kilkundaru in Koluvūrkūṟṟam. (T. A. S. Vol. IV p. 118)
72	On the same rock (outside the prākāra of the Kailāsa shrine) (98/1096 s. a 60/1086).	Do.	Caṭaiya-māran.	2 10th „ year Makaram 20	Do.	Registers a gift of sheep for a lamp to the temple of Tiruccivindirattu-Emperumān by Kanni-Palanji, an *arugai vanigan* of Ilakkandura in Purattāyanāṭu. (T. A. S. Vol. IV. p. 123)
73	Do. (99/1096)	Cola.	Abhaiyaṅ	32nd year.	Tamil (verse).	Records that Puvanavan Kari of Seyalurman set up the immage of the Goddess in the temple of Śucīndram. (T. A. S. Vol. IV. p. 130)
74	On the east *Gōpura* of the same temple, right side. (100/1096 and 5 of 1111)	Vijaya nagara.	...	Kollam 720, Āvaṇi, Kṛṣṇa Jayanti.	Sanskrit in Grantha.	Records that Viṭṭhalēśa and his younger brother constructed the gōpura of the Śucīndram temple on the Kṛṣṇa Jayanti day of Kollam 720 Āvaṇi.

Śucīndram (contd).

No.	Place of inscription.	Dynasty.	King.	Date.	Language and Alphabet.	Remarks.
75	Do. (101/1096)	Vijaya-nagara.	Abhaiya.	Kollam 796, Mārkaḷi 4.	Sanskrit in Grantha.	Registers a gift of money by Nāgammai, daughter of Nāgamaṇi of Terūr, for making a lamp borne by an image and for keeping it burning.
76	On the same *gōpura* left of entrance (108/1096 and 60/1092).	...	...	Ko. 795, Kārttikai 8.	Do.	Registers a gift made by the temple managers (*Srīkāriyamceyvār*) for conducting the Kārttikai festival in the month or Karttikai and for burning a bonfire.
77	On the south base of the *ardhamaṇḍapa* Nambi Sasta temple, Śucīndram (80/1099).	...	...	Ko. 404 Tulām 1.	Tamil.	Records gift of a tank by Govindapra jnābhiṭāra to the temple of Śrīmad Dvārakai-Emperumān of Śucīndrum.

78	On the west base of the *curumandapa* (81/1099).	...	...	Ko. 362 Thulam 1.	Tamil.	Fragmentary: relates to the gift of land.
79	On a small boulder in the *prākāra* (82/1091)	...	...	Probably Ko. 404, Mithunam 2.	Do.	Built in at the beginning. Seems to record gift of land to the temple. Mentions Śrisālāgrama-Bhagavan and Gōvindaprajña-Bhaṭāra Tiruvaṭi.
80	On the west base of the Perumāl Shrine Sthāṇunāthasvāmin temple, Śucīndrum 1/1103).	...	...	?	Do.	Damaged. Seems to record the gift of land for lamp to be lighted in the temple.
81	On the left post of the threshold in the right entrance of the Cempakarāman maṇḍapam of the same temple. (1/1103).	...	...	Ko. 720 Mārkaḻi 14 Friday Anusam Ba. 13	Do.	States that the Assembly etc. of Śucīndrum temple executed, a deed in favour of Kaṇakku Uṭayānkuṭṭi, Tikkellāmpukaḻumperumāl who were to write the accounts as usual and enjoy aṭukkuvatu, Uṭamai and other privileges.

Śucīndram (contd).

No.	Place of inscription.	Dynasty.	King.	Date.	Language and Alphabet.	Remarks.
82	On a pillar in the Konraiyaṭinātha shrine in the same. (3/1103).	Cōḷa.	Rājēndra Cōḷa.	...	Tamil.	Records that the Tiruppaṇi was executed by Kāli Nallaśivan.
83	On another pillar (4/1103).	...	...	...	Do.	Records the Sēdasēvai of Āṇḍār Mārāyakuṭṭi and the work contributed by him.
84	On a stone set up in a house at Kākkumūr 1 Sucīndrum (5/1103).	...	...	S. 1675 Ko. 932 Kārttikai 20 Wednesday Śu. 10 Rēvati.	Do.	Much damaged. Seems to refer some endowment of land.
85	On the eastern wall (north) of the Cempakarāman maṇḍapam of the Sthāṇunāthasvāmi temple, Śucīndrum. (1/105.)	Travancore.	Rāma Varma.	Ko. 654	Sanskrit in Grantha.	Records that king Rāmavarma constructed the Maṇḍapam in front of God Sthāṇunāthasvāmi at Śucīndrum.

86	On the eastern face of Western wall of the Udaiya-Mārttāṇḍa Maṇḍapam to the west of *Cempakarāman-Maṇḍapa* in the same temple. (2/105)	...	...	Ko. 403 Kanni.	Tamil in Tamil & Grantha.	Registers that the Brahmasvam properties be possessed and enjoyed by members of the assembly, and those who give them in mortgage or in sale to any foreigners outside the village be punished by gold of 12 Kaḻanju and five kāṇams, and the temple and village affairs be looked after by the elders of the assembly.
87	On a standing stone near the Piḷḷaiyār Sannidhi Street, Sucīndrum. (3/1105)	...	...	Ko. 781 Āṭi 17.	Tamil.	Registers that Cendan Sivindravādi of Puttillam constructed the temple and left provisions for offerings, lights etc.
88	On the basement of the steps to the same temple. (4/1105)	...	...	... 57	Do.	Refers to the Sadāsevai of Nanampi.

Śucīndram (*contd.*)

No.	Place of inscription.	Dynasty.	King.	Date.	Language and Alphabet.	Remarks.
89	On the northern outer wall of the first *Prākāra* just south of the Jayantīśvaramahādēva shrine in the Sthāṇunāthasvāmin temple at Śucīndrum. (4/1107)	...	...	Ko. 301 Jupiter Vṛṣabha Mithunam.	Do.	Damaged at the end. Registers the gift of land for offering to God Umāskanda Sahita Tiramēni set up by Arangan Tiruvikraman of Śīvalamangalam.
90	On the central *Uttara* stone in *Jayantīśvara-maṇḍapa* below the new opening of the same. (5/1107)	...	....	Kuli expressed by "वन्यौषधिस्य सूर्ये" Makara saptami Rōhiṇi, Jupiter in Dhanu, Monday Kōlamba, expressed in the Chronogram Jātasamjñe (769).	Tamil. Grantha & Sanskrit.	States that the Brahmin of Navabhavanam (Puttillam) residing at Śucīndram consecrated the God Śambhu with Goddess Gouri.

91	On the south base of the Subrahmaṇya temple in the same. (6/1107.)	...	...	Ko. 413 Mēṭam 1.	Tamil.	The Major part of this inscription under this ground mentions Sivintiram Uṭaiya Nayanār.
92	On the eastern wall of the first *Prākāra* of the same (in front of the Vaṭakkeṭam) (8 1107)	Travancore.	...	Ko. 318 Mithunam 1 Thursday Tiruvātirai.	Do.	States that Kēraḷan Vikramacōḷadēvanēn made a gift of 71 *accu* to Sucīndramuṭaiya Nayanār for offering Tiruamutu while chanting Mantras.
93	On the western *prākāra* north of the *Vāhanappura* of the same. (9/1107)	Pāṇḍya.	Vīra-Pāṇḍya.	Ko. 432 Dhanu 19 Thursday Ēkādaśi.	Do.	This is a *Jayakaṭa Ōlai* written by the assembly and *Śrī Kāriyam* of the Sucīndrum temple and records that Cokkattāṇḍāḷ *alias* Ulakamuḷutuṭaiyāḷ, the Nambirāṭṭiyār of Vīrapāṇḍyadēva made a gift of 200 *Puṭupon*-Accu for daily *tiruamutu* of Sucīndramuṭaiya Nayanār and for feeding 3 *Brahmins* during the time of the *Pujas*.
94	On the western *Prākāra* facing the Pancalinga shrine of the same (10/1107)	...	...	Ko. 328 Iṭavam 8.	Tamil.	Damaged.
95	Do. (11/1107)	...	...	Kō. 340.	Do.	Do.

Sucīndram (*contd.*)

No.	Place of inscription.	Dynasty.	King.	Date.	Language and Alphabet.	Remarks.
96	On the north base of the Ardhamaṇḍapa of the Dvārakai Emperumān temple near Sucīndrum Satram. (3/1107)	...	...	Ko. 400	Do.	Registers gift of 10 *accu* for burning a perpetual lamp in the same temple. Mentions Palikkal Nāyar.
97	On the western *prākāra* inside of the *vāhanappura* of the Sthāṇunāthasvāmin temple at Sucīndram (39/1108).	....	...	Jupiter in Makaram	Do.	Damaged. Seems to register a gift of land.
98	On the western base of the *Garbhagṛha* of Dvārakai Emperumān temple Do. (40/1108)	...	...	Ko. 301 Kanni 30 Friday Puraṭṭāsi.	Tamil.	Registers a gift of land for lighting a perpetual lamp in the Dvārakai Emperumān temple and for maintaining a flower garden by the assembly of Śucīndram who met in Sucīndramuṭaiyanayinār temple when Gōvinda Prajñābhiṭārar-tiruvaṭi of Cerumukkil was present.

99	On the western base of the *Garbhagṛha* of the same. (41/1108)	...	...	Ko. 404 Karkaṭakam Tuesday Pūram Ko. 404 Dhanu.	Do.	Registers a gift of land for offering to Dvārakai Emperumān by Kaṇṇan.
100	Do. Do. 42/1108)	...	...	Ko. 404 Dhanu.	Do.	Refers to a gift of land by Kēśavan Āraṅgan of Putumāṭam to the said God
101	On the four sides of a standing stone west of the eastern *gōpura* in the same. (6/1111)	Travancore.		Ko. 880 Māśi 26 Su 10 Thursday.	Tamil.	Registers a settlement of accounts in connection with puja *Viśēṣapūja*, *Sāntiuṭamai*, etc. between *Svarūpam* and temple assembly.
102	On the western wall of the *Cempakarāman-maṇḍapa* in the same (Sucīndram)(12/1112)	Do.	Do.	Ko. 722 Āṭi 14.	Do.	Registers a gift of land for conducting the service of Cempakarāman-*sandhi* in the same temple.

Tāḷakkuṭi. (Tovāḷa)

No.	Place of inscription.	Dynasty.	King.	Date.	Language and Alphabet.	Remarks.
1	On the south wall of the entrance of the *gopura* of the Śiva temple at Tāḷakkuṭi. (17/1093)	...	...	...	Tamil.	This is the Sadāsēvai of Tirunāvukkaraśu-Pillai Ārumukapperumāḷ. (T.A.S. Vol. VI. p. 103)
2	On the south base of the *ardhamaṇḍapa* of the same. (18/1093)	...	...	...	Do.	Fragment. Mentions the service called after Cempakarāman. (T. A. S. Vol. VI. p. 103)
3	On the south base of the *mahāmaṇḍapa* of the same. (19/1093)	...	...	...	Do.	Mentions a certain Nāgammai. (T. A. S. Vol. VI. p. 103)
4	Do. (20/1093)	...	...	...	Do.	Mentions first rate land under the first kaṇṇāru in Puravu. (T. A. S. Vol. VI. p. 103).

5	Do. (21/1093)	....	...	Ko. 782 Āvaṇi 30.	Do.	**Fragement. Seems to provide for lamp and offerings. Mentions Tāḻaikkuṭi in Nāñjināṭu. (T. A. S. Vol. VI. p. 103)**
6	On the east base of the *mahāmaṇḍapa* (proper left of entrance) of the same. (22/1093)	...	...	Ko. 744, Puraṭṭāśi 15.	Do.	Registers gift of land for a flower garden to the temple of Sēndan̄ccuramuṭaiya-Tampirāṇār at Tāḻaikkuṭi. (T. A. S. Vol. VI. p. 103)
7	On the east wall of the *mahāmaṇḍapa* (proper left of entrance) of the same. (23/1093)	...	...	Ko. 735, Pankuni 25.	Do.	Records gift of land irrigated by Vīrakēraḷappērēri for a flower garden to the temple of Sēndan̄ccura-muṭaiya Nayinār at Tāḻaikkuṭi in Nāñjināṭu. (T.A.S. Vol. VI. p. 102)
8	On the wall of the Kīḻaimaṭham at Tāḻakkuṭi. (90/1099)	...	...	Śaka 1559, Ko. 853, Pingala, Kārttikai 19, su. 5, Monday, Tiruvōṇam.	Do.	Records some gift of land by Nallanayinān Pariyērum-perumāḷ, the accountant of Sucīndrum for offering worship to the image of Piḷḷaiyār in the stone-maṭham built by him at Tāḻakkuṭi. (T. A. S Vol. VI. p. 104)

Tāḷakkuṭi (contd)

No.	Place of inscription.	Dynasty.	King.	Date.	Language and Alphabet.	Remarks.
9	On the south wall of the central shrine of the Jayanteśvara temple in the same village. (91/1099)	Travancore.	Jayatunganāṭṭu Śaṅkaranārāyaṇa Venṛumankoṇḍa Bhūtalavīra Vīra Udaiya mārttāṇḍavarman Tiruppāppūr-Mūttaṭu.	Ko. 708, Karttikai 12, su. 13, Sunday, Aśvati.	Tamil.	Registers that while the king was staying in the new palace at Vīramārttāṇḍa caturvēdimaṅgalam in Kaḷakkāṭu *alias* Coḷakulavalli-puram, he appointed Ariyan Cokkan Periyaperumāḷ *alias* Mārttāṇḍa Brahmādarāyan of Śucīndrum as the accountant of the temple of Jayantīśvaram-uṭaiya-Nayinār at Tāḷakkuṭi. (T. A. S. Vol. VI. p. 131)
10	On the western wall of the same temple. (92/1099)	...	...	...	Do.	Fragment. Refers to a tax on each oil-mill for offerings to the temple. (T. A. S. Vol. VI. p. 103)

			Talaikkuḷam (Kalkuḷam)			
1	On the base of the south wall of the Viṣṇu-temple at Talaikkuḷam. (53/1095)	...	...	...	Tamil.	Records that Kaṇḍan Perumāḷ *alias* Vīrakēraḷa-Pallavadaraiyar of Iraṇaśiṅgappādividu in Paṭaippānāṭṭillam repaired the temple of Aḷagapperumāḷ-Nayinār and re-consecrated the gold in it. The repairs were commenced in *Kollam* 660, *Tai* 26, *Aśvati* and completed in *Kollam* 662, *Vaikāśi* 7, Friday, su. di. 12. (T. A. S. Vol. VII. p. 35)
			Tirukkaṭavūr. (Quilon)			
1	On the north and west bases of the Śiva temple at Tirukkaṭavūr. (33/1090)	...	...	...	Malayāḷam.	Damaged. Records a gift of land to the temple.
2	On the east *gōpura* of the Śiva temple at Tirukkaṭavūr. (34/1090)	...	...	...	Do.	"This is the service instituted by Iṭṭiyādiccan Valiyattān"
3	On the west *gōpura* of the same. (35/1090)	...	—	Ko. 964, Vṛścika 20.	Do.	States that another service was instituted on this day.

Tirukkaṭittānam. (Caṅṅānācēri)

	...ce of inscription.	Dynasty.	King.	Date.	Language and Alphabet.	Remarks.
1	On the north base of the central shrine of the Viṣṇu temple at Tirukkaṭittānam. (88/1086)	...	...	...	Tamil in Vaṭṭeḻuttu.	Records that one Kaṇḍankumāran *alias* Māluvakkōn of Kilumalai gave some lands for the maintenance of a lamp which was entrusted to some private persons in the presence of 300 of Nanruḻanāṭu. (T. A. S. Vol. V. p. 181)
2	On the north and west bases of the central shrine of the same. (89/1086)	Cēra.	Kō-Pākkaran Iravivarma Tiruvaṭi.	6th + 7th.	Do.	An order that the *ūrālars* and *paruṭaiyar* shall not interfere with the arrangements made for the Tiruvamirtu, nandāviḷakku, tiruvakkiram and Mābāratam and certain rules regarding the management of and appointment of temple servants is engraved. (T. A. S. Vol. II. p. 36)

3	On the west, south and east bases of the same. (90/1086 and 19/1097)	Do.	Kō-Iravi Irāman.	2nd + 1st.	Do.	Records the arrangements made by the Officer Iyakkan Sirīkaṇḍan of Maṇalmanṟam ruling over the Nanrulaināṭu regarding......... (T. A. S. Vol. V. p. 174)
4	On the south base of the central shrine of the same. (91 1086)	Do.	(Bhāskara Ravi-varman.)	2nd and 24th.	Do.	Orders that the people of the two quarters of the town of Nārāṇamangalam should, before the specified time, give the temple the quantity of oil they have engaged themselves to supply. (T. A. S. Vol. II. p. 41)
	On the south base of the same. (92/1086)	Cera.	...	...	Do.	Gift of land for offerings. (T. A. S. Vol. V. p. 180)
6	Do. (93/1086)		Bhāskara Ravivarma Tiruvaṭi.	2nd + 24th.	Do.	Records certain rules regarding temple servants. Mentions Vēṇāṭuṭaiya Gōvarddhana............and Iravi Rāman. (T. A. S. Vol. II. p. 40)
7	On the north and west bases of the same. (95/1086)	Do.	Do.	(1 + 14th.)	Do.	Gift of something for feeding 12 *Brāhmanas*. Incomplete and damaged. (T. A. S. Vol. II. p. 45)

Tirukkaṭittānam. (contd)

No.	Place of inscription.	Dynasty.	King.	Date.	Language and Alphabet.	Remarks.
8	On the west south bases of the shrine of the same. (69/1086)	Cēra.	Do.	...	Tamil in Vaṭṭeluttu.	Records the gift for offerings.
9	On the north wall of the central shrine in the Viṣṇu temple at Tirukkaṭittānam. (17/1097)	...	Bhāskara Ravivarman.	Jupiter in Ṛṣabha Kumbha, Monday Tiruvōṇam.	Do.	Records gift of Nelvāvil *alias* Cērikkal by Kaṇḍan Kumāran *alias* Māluvakkōn of Kelumalai to the temple of the Bhaṭṭāraka at Tirukkaṭittānam for lamps. (T. A. S. Vol. V. p. 182)
10	On the west and south bases of the same temple. (18/1097)	...	Do.	2 + 12th year.	Do.	Records gift of paddy by the chief of Nanrulaināṭu appointed by Gōvarddhanamārttāṇḍavarman of Vēṇāṭu for sacred offerings. (T. A. S. Vol. V. p. 177)

11	On the south base of the central shrine in the Adbhutanārāyaṇa temple at Tirukkaṭittānam. (48/1099	...	...	2nd + 24th year.	Do.	Contains some restrictions relating to the mortgage of the lands belonging to the temple servants. Gōvardhana-Mārttāṇḍan, the governor of Vēṇāṭu is mentioned. (T. A. S. Vol. V. p. 179)
12	On the same base. (49/1099)	...	...	...	Do.	Registers certain gifts of land by Dēvan-Irāman of Muttūru for the expenses of providing day-offerings to the God at Tirukkaṭittānam. (T. A. S. Vol. V. p. 180)
13	On the base of the central shrine of the same. (6/1100)	...	...	2nd year.	Do.	Incomplete and one stone missing in the middle. Registers the arrangements made for the *Uttiram*-festival instituted by the Vēṇāṭu ruler Srivallabhankōtai when ...... Marttāṇḍavarman was ruling Nanrulai-nāṭu. (T. A. S. Vol. V. p. 189)

Tirukkākkarai. (Kunnattunāṭu.)

No.	Place of inscription.	Dynasty.	King.	Date.	Language and Alphabet.	Remarks.
1	On the east base of the central shrine of the Viṣṇu temple at Tirukkākkarai (proper right of the entrance) (95/1084)	Cēra.	Kō-(Pār) karan Iravivarman.	2nd 26th.	Tamil in Vaṭṭeḻuttu.	Gift of gold; damaged.
2	Do. Do. (86/1094.)	...	...	...	Do.	Damaged. Mentions Kunṟappōḷan and Kōtaikēraḷan. (T. A. S. Vol. III. p. 175)
3	On the proper left of the entrance into the first prākāra of the same. (97/1084)	...	...	...	Do.	Records the scale of expenditure under the various items of the temple service. (T. A. S. Vol. III. p. 186)
4	On the outside east base of the *Cuṟṟu-maṇḍapa* proper left of the entrance into the first *prākāra* of the same. (98/1084)	...	...	...	Do.	Gift of gold ornaments by Kōtai-Puraiyan.

5	Do. (99/1084)	...	Pōḻan-Iravi.	Jupiter in Tulām Kanni.	Do.	Gift of ornament by Kōtai-Puraiyan and Kōtai Śrī Kaṇḍan (T. A. S. Vol. III. p. 185).
6	On the outside south base of the same proper right of the entrance. (100/1084)	...	...	Jupiter in Mīnam.	Do	Gift of land by a dancing girl. (T. A. S. Vol. III. p. 188).
7	On the outside south base of the same. (101/1084).	...	...	3705* (of what era is not mentioned.)	Do.	Damaged. Mentions one Cāttan Cinnan, Ruler of Tirukkākkarainādu. (T. A. S. Vol. III. p. 184).
8	Do. east base, proper left. (102/1084)	...	Kō-Pārkaran Iravivarman.	2nd + 21st.	Do.	Gift of land for offerings. (T. A. S. Vol. II. p. 39).
9	Do. Do. proper right. (103/1084)	Cēra.	Kō-Ind Kōtai.	11th + 5th	Do.	Records the gift of money for feeding by several people including Kaṇṇan Puraiyan the officer in charge of the Tirukkākkarai-nāḍu. (T. A. S. Vol. III. P. 166)

Tirukkākkara. (*contd.*)

No.	Place of inscription.	Dynasty.	King.	Date.	Language and Alphabet.	Remarks.
10	On the outside east base, proper right. (104/1084)	Cēra.	Pārkkaran Iravivarman.	2nd + 4th, Jupiter in Ṛṣabha, Karkaṭaka.	Tamil in Vaṭṭeḻuttu.	Registers a gift of money by Kōtai Kēraḷan of Cirumaṟṟapuḷai to the temple of Tirukkākkarai for feeding Brahmins. (T. A. S. Vol. III. p. 180)
11	On the outside base of the *Cuṟṟumaṇḍapa*, south and east base, proper right in the same place. (105/1084).	...	Kō Indu Kōtai Tiruvaṭi.	Jupiter in Dhanu.	Do.	Beginning and large portions of the middle are built in. (T. A. S. Vol. III. p. 172)
12	Do. (106/1084)	...	...	Jupiter in Kanni, Simha.	Do.	Damaged. Registers a gift of money made by Kaṇṇankumaran to purchase certain lands. (T. A. S. Vol. III. p. 176)
13	Do. (107/1084)	...	...	Jupiter in Simha, Kumbha.	Do.	Do. Gift made when Yakkan Kunra Pōḻan of Panritturutti, was the ruler. (T. A. S. Vol. III. p. 174)

14	On the outside base of the (*Cuṟṟumaṇḍapa*, south and east bases, proper right, in the same place. (107 A/1084)	...	...	...	Do.	Gift by Kunran Puraiyan of Tirukkākkarainātu.
15	Do. (108/1084)	Cēra.	Ko-Pākkaran Iravivarman.	4th + 5th.	Do.	Damaged in the beginning; Gift of offerings and feeding Brāhmaṇas and Śrīvaiṣṇavas. (T. A. S. Vol. II. p. 47)
16	Do. (109/1084)	...	Do.	Do.	Do.	Damaged. Records gift of gold for a perpetual lamp. (T. A. S. Vol. II. p. 41 and T. A. S. Vol. III. p. 182)
17	On the east base (on the outside) of the *Cuṟṟumaṇḍapa* of the same. (110/1084)	...	...	Jupiter in Mithunam.	Do.	Records an arrangement for the management of the temple routine. (T. A. S. III. p. 178)
18	On the east base of Valiyambalam of the Viṣṇu temple, Tirukkākkarai. (9/1091)	Cēra.	Bhāskaran Iravi.	58th year.	Do.	Seems to register a gift of a perpetual lamp. (T. A. S. Vol. II. p. 48)

Tirukkāriyūr. (Mūvāṟṟupuḻa)

No.	Place of inscription.	Dynasty.	King.	Date.	Language and Alphabet.	Remarks.
1	On a stone built into the flight of the tank in front of the Śiva temple at Tirukkāriyūr. (105/1085).	...	...	...	Tamil in Vaṭṭeḻuttu.	Fragmentary.
2	On the four sides of the base of the flagstaff in the same. (106/1085).	Travancore.	Ramavarman	Ko 1073	Sanskrit in Malayalam.	Records the rebuilding of the temple.

Tirukkunnapuḻai. (Kārttikappaḷḷi)

No.	Place of inscription.	Dynasty.	King.	Date.	Language and Alphabet.	Remarks.
1	On the west and south bases of the *maṇḍapa* in front of the Perumāḷ shrine in the Śāsta temple at Tirukkunnappuḻai. (5/1088)	...	...	Ko. 931, Makaram 27.	Malayalam.	States that the God Perumāḷ, which was brought from the seaside, was set up here by Manayattāṟṟu Nārāyaṇan-Nambūtiri. (T. A. S. Vol. VII. p. 63).

Tirukkunnappuḻai. (*contd*)

2	On the east base of the Perumāḷ ambalam in the same. (6/1088)	...	...	...	Malayalam in Vaṭṭeḻuttu.	Refers to the consecration of the God by Nilakara-Iśvaran under the orders of Senior ruler (Valiya-Tamburan) of Elannallur. (T. A. S. Vol. VII. p. 63.)
3	On the east base of the central shrine of the Śāsta temple at Tirukkunnappuḻai. (7/1088)	...	...	...	Do.	Damaged. Seems to give the name of the persons who built the temple. (T. A. S. Vol. VII. p. 63)

Tirumaṇivēnkaṭapuram. (Vaikam)

1	On the base of the *Balikkal* in the Viṣṇu temple at Tirumaṇivēnkaṭapuram. (5/1099)	...	...	Jupiter in Kumbham, Karkaṭakam	Tamil in Vaṭṭeḻuttu.	Registers a resolution to the effect that without the consent of certain temple officials, the *paṭṭāyam* (wooden chest) shall not be kept in the *cuṟṟu maṇḍapa* of the temple. (T. A. S. Vol. VII. p. 139)

Tirunandikkarai (Kalkuḷam)

No.	Place of inscription.	Dynasty.	King.	Date.	Language and Alphabet.	Remarks.
1	On the east wall of the rockcut shrine at Tirunandikkarai. (26/1084)	Cōḷa	Rājakēsari-varman (Rājarāja-dēva I).	18th	Tamil in Vaṭṭeḷuttu.	Grant of the village of Muṭṭam under the name of Mummuṭicōḷanallūr for the celebration of a festival in the month of *Aippaśi* and for a perpetual lamp; damaged. (T. A. S. Vol. I. p. 292)
2	On a pillar on the left side of the rock-cut cave at Tirunandikkarai. (44/1096 and 27/1084)	...	...	...	o.	Registers gift of land by Nārāyaṇan Suvākaran, a native of Mangalaccēri, to the shrine of Tiruvallaval-Bhaṭāra and to the temple of Tirunandikkarai-Bhaṭāra, for worship, lamps etc. (T. A. S. Vol. III. p. 204)
3	On another pillar in the same cave. (45/1096 and 28/1084)		...	The year of destruction of the ships at Talaikkuḷam.	do.	Registers a gift of land by the assembly of Tirunandikkarai to Nambi-Gaṇapati, for offerings to the temple.

Tirunandikkarai. (contd.)

						The gift-land was constituted into a village under the name Nandimangalam- (T. A. S. Vol. III. p. 202)
4	At the entrance into the same cave. (46/1096 and 25/1084)	...	...	The year of destruction of the ships at Karaikandiśvaram.	Tamil in Vaṭṭeluttu.	Registers gift of lamp to the temple of Tirunandikkarai-Bhaṭāra by Sittakkutti Ambi *alias* Annuṟruva-Muttaraiyan of Veyngomalai in Nānji-nāṭu. (T. A. S. Vol. III. p. 206)
5	At the base of the path leading to the kitchen in the Śiva temple of the same village. (47/1096)	...	...	...	Do.	Registers gift of gold for a lamp, to the temple of Tirunandikkarai-Bhaṭāra by Kilanaṭikaḷ, the queen of Vijaiyarāgadēva and the daughter of Kulaśēkharadēva. (T. A. S. Vol. IV. p. 144)
6 to 11	On rafter shoes from Tirunandikkara. (3 to 8/1113)	...	...	...	Do.	Mentions the names of private individuals who probably contributed to the construction of the temple.

Tirupporaiyāru (Kunnattunāṭu)

No.	Place of inscription.	Dynasty.	King.	Date.	Language and Alphabet.	Remarks.
1	On a slab in the court yard of the Śiva temple at Tirupporaiyāru (135/1096)	...	...	...	Tamil in Vaṭṭeḻuttu.	Fragment in archaic characters. (T. A. S. Vol. VII. p. 101)
	Tiruppatisāram (Tōvāḷa)					
1	On the east wall (right of entrance) into the first *prākāra* of the Viṣṇu temple at Tiruppatisāram. (63/1084)	...	..	Kollam 789.	Tamil.	Gift of money for offerings. (T. A. S. Vol. V. p. 160)
2	On a slab of stone built into the floor next to the entrance into the first *prākāra* of the same. (64/1084)	...	...	Kollam 961.	Do.	Records the building of the orraikkal *maṇḍapa* and having the front *maṇḍapa* with stone by a person of Kalkuḷam Piḷḷaiyārkōyil. (T. A. S. Vol. V. p. 160)

			Tiruppatisāram. (*contd*)			
3	On the west base of the second *prākāra* of the same. (65/1084)	...	...	Kollam 304.	Tamil.	Mentions that Nāṭancetti of Viḷiñam *alias* Rājēndracōḷapaṭṭaṇam made some gift (?) to the God of Tiruppatisāram ; incomplete. (T. A. S. Vol. IV. p. 198.)
			Tirupparappu (Kalkuḷam)			
1	On the north wall (outside) of the Śrīkōyil of the Mahādēva temple at Tirupparappu. (73/1085)	...	...	Kollam 407.	Tamil in Vaṭṭeḻuttu.	Gift of a lamp to a private person. (T. A. S. Vol. VI. p. 75)
2	On a pillar in the south east of the *namaskāramaṇḍapa* in front of the *Śrīkōyil* in the same. (74/1085)	...	...	Kollam 664.	Tamil in Kōleḻuttu.	States that Maṟṟattil Nārāyaṇan Nārāyaṇan provided for the burning of a lamp. (T. A. S. Vol. VI. p. 75.)
3	On a stone in the middle of the first *prākāra* of the same. (75/1085)	...	...	...	Tamil in Vaṭṭeḻuttu.	Refers to the sale of lands, the names of some of which are similar to those found in the Huzur Office plates. (T. A. S. Vol. VI. p. 78)

No.	Place of inscription.	Dynasty.	King.	Date.	Language and Alphabet.	Remarks.
4	In the *maṇḍapa* on the river, situated to the south of the same. (76/1085)	Travancore.	Rāmavarma	Kollam 1054 "Dhīmanayam."	Sanskrit in Malayalam.	Records the construction of the *maṇḍapa*. (T. A. S. Vol. VI. p. 77.)
5	On a rock in the bed of Kōtayāru in front of the same. (77/1085)	Do.	Do.	Do.	Sanskrit in Nāgarı.	Records the construction of the *maṇḍapa* and expresses the wish that the God of Tirupparappu may use it long. (T. A. S. Vol. VI. p. 78)
6	Do. (78/1085)	Do.	Do.	Do.	Do.	Do. Do. (T. A. S. Vol. VI. p. 78.)
		Tirupparamalà (Viḷavankōṭu)				
1	On the *balikkal* in front of the Viṣṇu temple at Tirupparamala. (44/1098)	...	...	Jupiter in Vṛścika Tula.	Tamil in Vaṭṭeḻuttu.	Records the gift of eight buffalloes to Vikkiraman Accan and his brothers who had to measure out 14 *nāḻi* of ghee for maintaining two perpetual lamps in the temple of Karumāṇikkattāḻvār at Tirupparamala.

2	On the south base of the same temple. (45/1098)	...	...	...	Do.	Much damaged. Three fragmentary inscriptions. Seems to refer to the maintenance of a perpetual lamp and the feeding of *Brahmins*.
3	On another stone in the same temple. (46/1098)	...	..	...	Do.	Damaged. Mentions one Kṛṣṇan-Subrahmaṇyan of Cembaramangalam, who was a lessee of the temple lands and who had to provide some offerings to the God.
			Tiruppalaṅgāṭu	(Viḷavankōṭu)		
1	On the south wall of the central shrine in the Śiva temple at Tiruppalaṅgāṭu. (34/1096)	...	...	Jupiter in Kumbha, Ṛṣabha.	Tamil in Vaṭṭeḻuttu.	Damaged and portions lost. Records a mortgage deed, made in favour of the *devarkanmis* of the Mahādēva at Pullalankōṭu. (T. A. S. Vol. VII. p. 130)
2	On the same wall. (35/1096)	...	...	Jupiter in Kumbha, Iṭavam.	Do.	Damaged. Seems to register a gift of land to the same temple. (T. A. S. Vol. VII. p. 130)

Tirunayinārkuricci. (Kalkuḷam.)

No.	Place of inscription.	Dynasty.	King.	Date.	Language and Alphabet.	Remarks.
1	On the south base of the central shrine of the Karaikkaṇḍeśvara temple at Tirunayinārkuricci. (67/1093)	...	...	Ko. 395, Kumbham.	Tamil.	Records gifts of money for offerings, lamps and flower garden to the temple of Karaikkandēśvaramuṭaiya-Mahādēva at Kaṭikaippaṭṭiṇam in Kurunāṭu a sub-division of Tennāṭu. The donor was Ādiccan Kōtai of Ayirappuḷai. (T. A. S. Vol. IV. p. 82).
2	On the west base of the same. (68/1093)	...	...	Ko. 403, Makaram 15, Thursday Ōṇam.	Do.	Records gift of land for *Sri-bali* in the same temple and by the same donor as in No. 68 the engraver of the record was Suriyan Porkodi *alias* Ravivarma-Acari, (T. A. S. Vol. IV. p. 84)

3	On the south wall of the *mahāmaṇḍapa* of the same. (69/1093)	...	...	Ko. 339, Māṣa 24, Thursday, Mūlam.	Tamil.	Records gift of money for conducting *cittirai-tirunāl* in the same temple by Sivanukkiniyār of Perumbaṟṟappuliyūr. It is also stated that a drama should be staged on that occasion. (T. A. S. Vol. VII. p. 30)
4	On the east base of the *mahāmaṇḍapa* of the same. (70/1093)	...	...	...	do.	Records that Kēraḷan Kunran built the *bali piṭha*. (T. A. S. Vol. VII. p. 35)
5	do. (71/1093)	...	...	Ko. 608, Cittirai 26, Rōhiṇi.	do.	Records that on this day the temple was renewed and reconsecrated by a certain Kēraḷappallavaraiyan. (T. A. S. Vol. VII. p. 31)
6	On the two beams of the *mahamaṇḍapa* of the same. (72/1093)	...	...	Śaka 1629, Ko. 882, Avaṇi 13, Wednesday, Uttiraṭṭāti, ba. di. 2.	do.	Pieces are not fully numbered. Refers to the construction of a *maṇḍapa* in the temple of Kuraikkaṇḍesvaramuṭaiya-Nayinār of Kaṭilaippaṭṭinam in Kurunāṭu a subdivision of Rājarāja tennāṭu. Mentions Sivanukkiniyār. (T. A. S. Vol. VII. p. 33)

Tirunayinārkuricci (*contd*).

No.	Place of inscription.	Dynasty.	King.	Date	Language and Alphabet.	Remarks.
7	On a rock near the sluice of the Periya-kuḷam near Tirunayinār-kuricci. (73/1093)	Cōḷa,	Rājarāja,	27th year.	Tamil in Vaṭṭeḻuttu.	Damaged. Begins with திருமகள்போல and seems to register a gift of land. (T. A. S. Vol. VI. p. 1[illegible]5)
8	On a rock near the Periyakuḷam near Tiru-nayinārkuricci. (74/1093)	Travan-core.	Ravivarman Kulaśēkhara Perumāḷ.	Ko. 77 2or3) Cittirai 14	Tamil.	Damaged. Registers gift of land for worship to the God consecrated in *Ravi-varman Tirumaṭham*. (T. A. S. Vol. VII. p. 33)
9	Do. (75/1093)	...	...	Ko. 440, Tulām 30, Monday, Ut-tirāṭam.	Do.	Damaged. Mentions Dē-varaṭiyān Peṟṟān Kunran *alias* Ādiccavarma Paṇṇai-ceyvān of Karaikkaṇḍe-śvaram, the assembly of Cēra-mangalam and the *Urār* of Kaṭikaippaṭṭinam. (T. A. S. Vol. VII. p. 31)

11	On the South base of the Viṣṇu temple at Cēramangalam near Tirunayiṇarkuricci. (76/1093 S.a. 66/1098)	Cōḷa Pāṇḍya.	Jaṭāvarman Sundara Cōḷa Pāṇḍya	19th.	Tamil in Vaṭṭeḻuttu.	Pieces not fully numbered. Records gift of lamp to the temple of Tentiruvarangam uṭaiyār at Cēramangalam by Tiru-Orraiccēvakamayilatti of Mukkarai alias Mummuṭi Cōḷapuram, Arumolidēva-Vaḷanāṭa in the Cōḷa-maṇḍalam. (T. A. S. Vol. V. p. 29)
12	On the south base of the Viṣṇu temple at Cēramangalam near Tirunayinārkuricci. (77/1093 and 65/1098)	..	Jaṭāvarman Sundara Cōḷa Pāṇḍya	19th year.	Do.	Registers the agreement given by Ayiravan Dēvan to stand as surety to another tenant of the temple. (T. A. S. Vol. V. p. 30)
13	Do. (78/1093 S.a. 67/1098)	...	...	...	Do.	Fragment. Mentions Iraṇasinga (nallūr) in Cēramangalam. (T. A. S. Vol. V. p. 31)
14	On a pillar in the *maṇḍapa* in front of the *mahāmaṇḍapa* of the Viṣṇu temple at the same. (79/1093)	...	...	...	Tamil.	Contains the words. Ten Tiruvarangattu-Āḻvār. (T. A. S. Vol. V. p. 31)

Tirunayinārkuricci (*contd*)

No.	Place of inscription.	Dynasty.	King.	Date.	Language and Alphabet.	Remarks.
15	On a detached stone lying in the yard of the Viṣṇu temple at Cēramangalam near Tirunayinārkuricci. (80/1093)	...	...	Jupiter in Ṛṣabha.	Tamil. Vaṭṭeḻuttu.	Mentions Adiyanūr *alias* Alakiyapan .... and Cēramangalam. (T. A. S. Vol. V. p. 31)
16	On the base of the balikkal of the same temple. (68/1098)	...	...	...	Do.	Incomplete. States that Cēramangalam was a *Brahmadeya in* Rājārajattennāṭu. (T. A. S. Vol. V. p. 31)

Tiruvalla.

No.	Place of inscription.	Dynasty.	King.	Date.	Language and Alphabet.	Remarks.
1	On the base of the pial (proper left of the entrance) of the gate leading into the first *prākāra* of the Viṣṇu temple at Tiruvalla. (10/1087)	...	...	...	Tamil in Vaṭṭeḻuttu.	Mentions Venmai Kovan Narayanan.

2	On the north base of the *maṇḍapa* in front of the central shrine of the Śiva temple at Tiruvāṟṟuvāy in Tiruvalla. (2/1091)	...	...	Jupiter in Mitunam Kumbham.	Do.	Registers a gift of money for bathing the God of Tiruvāṟṟuvāi with ghee and for feeding offering etc. (T. A. S. Vol. III. pp. 196-197)
3	On two pillars of the *Vātil māṭam* of the Śiva temple at Tiruvāṟṟuvāy in Tiruvalla. (2/1091)	...	...	...	Malayalam.	States that the pillar was erected by Kilvare Menon.
4	Do. (3/1091)	...	...	Do.	Do.	States that the pillar was set up by Palakkil nambi.
5	On the east base of the central shrine of the Viṣṇu temple at Perungara in Tiruvalla. (4/1091)	...	...	Jupiter in Mīnam Makaram.	Tamil in Vaṭṭeḻuttu.	States that Nārā (ya) ṇan Senan of Perungaraceri bathed (the God) in butter.
6	On a slab set up in the *Samūhamaṭham* Kṛṣṇankōyil at Tiruvalla. (19/1098)	...	...	...	Malayalam Later Vaṭṭeḻuttu.	States that for 120 parai of land belonging to Vaṭakkēpurattu-pōtti or Mepparadēśam 400 *paṇam* was paid and given for expenses of worship to God Kṛṣṇa.

Tiruvalla (*contd'*)

No.	Place of inscription.	Dynasty.	King.	Date.	Language and Alphabet.	Remarks.
7	On the same slab. (23/1098)	...	...	...	Malayalam.	Is a detailed Malayalam copy of the above lease deed.
8	On the brim of a well in the Śiva temple at Neṭumpuram near Tiruvalla. (21/1098)	...	...	Kollam. ... Makaram 26	...	States that Koccu-Śakti of Vaikkattu-illam constructed the well.
9	On the lampstand in front of the Śāsta temple at Tiruvalla. (22/1098)	...	...	Kollam 1059 Vrischika 29	...	States that the lamp was set up by the residents of Kāvungal.
10	On a pillar in the Vātilmāṭam of the Śāsta temple at Tiruvalla (23/1098)	...	...	Kollam 910 Dhanus 20	Malayalam.	States that the pillar was the gift of Ayyappan-Kumaran of Vaikkanpalli.
11	On another pillar. (24/1098)	...	...		Do.	States that the pillar was the gift of Ayyappan Padmanabhan.

12	On another pillar (25/1098)	...	...	...	Do.	States that the pillar was the gift of Rāman Kṛṣṇan of th● East coast (keḻakkētti).
13	On three sides of a stone standing behind the central shrine of the Śrī Kṛṣṇa temple. Kāvumbhagām, Tiruvalla. (12/1105)	...	...		Tamil in Grandha, Tamil and Vaṭṭeḻuttu.	Damaged Seems to refer to some gift of land by Ramapaṭṭar for conducting *pūja of* God Kṛṣṇa. Mentions Mēpradēṣa

Tiruvallam (Neyyāṟṟinkara)

1	On the north base of the Brahma shrine in the Paraśurāmēśvara temple at Tiruvallam. (28/1095 and 48/1084)	Vēṇāṭu.	Vīra Kēraḷa varman.	Ko. 399, Jupiter in Vṛścikam Makaram	Tamil in Vaṭṭeḻuttu	Registers gift of the *Jīvita* rights on Nigamam in Tenganāṭu for offerings to the Gods Mahādēva, Tirukkaṇṇappar and Gaṇapati. (T. A. S. Vol. III. pp. 4) 40
2	On the east base of the same shrine. (29/1095 & 50/1084)	...		Ko. 482 Jupiter in Dhanu Makara 10 expired, Sunday Rēvati	Do.	Provides for feeding, worship and offerings in the shrines of Mādēvan-Tiruvaṭi and Tirukkaṇṇappan. (T. A. S. Vol. III. p. 39 and T. A. S. Vol. I. p. 297)

Tiruvallam (*contd*)

No.	Place of inscription.	Dynasty.	King.	Date.	Language and Alphabet.	Remarks.
3	On the west base of the maṇḍapa in front of the same shrine (30/1095 and 49/1084)	...	...	Kollam 411 Jupiter in Vṛścikam Makaram 5, Pūram	Do.	Registers a gift made by Vijayan Iravi of Tekkinkāvu and mentions Mukundōttama Paḷārar-Tiruvaṭi. (T. A. S. Vol. III. p. 43)
	Tiruvālūr. (Parūr.)					
1	On a stone built into the floor of the passage leading into the Siva temple at Tiruvālūr (near Asamanūr.) (8/1090)	Vēṇāṭu.	Vīra Kēraḷa varman.	...	Tamil in Vaṭṭeḻuttu.	Damaged.
2	On a slab built into the eastern entrance of the Śiva temple at Tiruvālūr. (128/1096)	Cēra.	Kulaśēkhara Perumāḷ.	2nd and 1st year.	Do.	Records the *kiḻśānti* appointed in the temple of Aralūr should perform duties of both the *mēlśānti* and *kiḻśānti* up to *Viṣu* and receive certain remuneration. Mentions Nārāyaṇan Ravi of Kaṭaiṃnōtu. (T. A. S. Vol. IV. p. 145)

Tiruvāṭṭāru. (Kalkuḷam.)

No.	Place	State	King	Date	Language	Remarks
1	On the north and east bases of the central shrine of the Ādikeśavapperumāl temple at Tiruvāṭṭāru. (22/1084)	Travancore.	Śrī Vīra Ravi Ravivarman Kulaśekharapperumāl of Kiḷappērūr Illam and Tiruppāppūr Svarūpam.	Ko. 780, Ko. 4704. Ko. 779, Āni 26, Saturday, Hasta, su. 7.	Tamil.	Records the additions and repairs made to the temple by the king, his two younger brothers, Ādityavarman and Rāmavarman, their consorts Iraiyumakuṭṭiyammai, Nācciyārammai and a lady referred to as Nambirāṭṭiyār. (T. A. S. Vol. I. p. 177)
2	On a pillar of the *Currumaṇḍapa* of the same. (23/1084)	...	...	...	Do.	Records that that portion was built by two private persons. (T. A. S. Vol. VII. p. 122)
3	On a second pillar of the same. (24/1084)	...	...	...	Do.	Mentions that the row of pillars was set up by Deyvaputtiran Iravi. (T. A. S. Vol. VII. p. 122.)
4	On the south wall (outside) of the *Śrikōyil* of the Ādikēśavapperumāl temple at Tiruvāṭṭāru. (65/1085)	Travancore.	Vīra Udaya mārttāṇḍavarma Tiruvati.	Ko. 3 (4) 8.	Tamil in Vaṭṭeḷuttu.	Gift of land for services in the temple of Ādikeśava. Mentions Kōtainallūr Kilacceri (Vēṇāṭṭu-ilaṅgūru at that time). (T. A. S. Vol. I. p. 296)

Tiruvāṭṭāru. (*contd*)

No.	Place of inscription.	Dynasty.	King.	Date.	Language and Alphabet.	Remarks.
5	Do. (66/1385)	...	...	...	Do.	Damaged. Fragmentary.
6	On the south wall (bottom) of the western side of the same. (67/1085)	...	...	...	Do.	Damaged. Stones out of order.
7	On the north wall (bottom) of the western side of the 1st *prākāra* of the same. (68/1085)	...	...	...	Do.	Records repairs and additions effected to the temple and grants of land for lamps. The stones are all misplaced. Damaged.
8	On the western side of the temple of the same. (69/1085)	...	...	...	Do.	Records arrangements made for temple services.
9	On the south side of No. 65 above. (70/1085)	...	...	...	...	Damaged. Fragmentary.

10	On the north and west bases of the *Oṟṟaikkal maṇḍapa* of the same. (71/1085)	Travancore.	Vīra Ravi Ravivarman *alias* Kulaśēkharapperumāl, born in the Kēṭṭai nakṣatra to Umai Ammai, who was born in the Rōhiṇi nakṣatra.	Kali 4704, Vṛścika, Ko. 778, Citrai 7, Monday, Rōhiṇi.	Tamil.	Records that the *Oṟṟaikkal maṇḍapa* was constructed by the King. King was born in Kēṭṭai nakṣatra. His brothers and his queen are also mentioned. (T. A. S. Vol. I. p. 178)
11	On a pillar on the south side of the west wing of the same. (72/1085)	...	...	...	Do.	Mentions the name of an accountant of Vilavūrdēśam.
12	On the balikkal in the same. (129/1099)	...	...	Ko. 757, Jupiter in Dhanus, Vṛścika 12, Saturday, Rōhiṇi, ba. pratipada.	Do.	Records that the metal casing of the stone balikkal in the temple of Ādikēśavaperumāl who is pleased to be in Tiruvāṭṭāru was put up by Kuttatti-Īccammakuṭṭi. (T. A. S. Vol. VII. p. 120)

Tiruvāṭṭāru (*Contd*)

No.	Place of inscription.	Dynasty.	King.	Date.	Language and Alphabet.	Remarks.
13	On the base of the wall to the south of the *Udayamārttāṇḍan-maṇḍapa* in the same. (29/1100)	Cōḷa.	...	...	Tamil in Vaṭṭeḻuttu.	Contains a portion of the historical introduction of the Cōḷa king Rājēndracōḷadēva I (A. D. 1013-45). Mentions Tiruvāṭṭāru, Cōḷakulavallipuram and Gangaikoṇḍacōḷa-Nulambar. (T. A. S. Vol. VI. p. 146)
14	On the base of the wall to the north of the same maṇḍapa. (30/1100)	....	...	Ko. 442 + 1st year, Kanni 12, Thursday, Ōṇam.	Do.	Damaged at the end. Appears to record some gift of lands made by Araśu-Keśavan of Dēvancēri in Iraṇasinganallūr for offerings to the God Perumāl of Tiruvāṭṭāru. (T. A. S. Vol. VII. p. 120)
15	On the south base of the *maṇḍapa* in the first prākāra. (31/1100)	Travancore.	Vīra Udaiyamārttāṇḍavarman.	...	Do.	Fragmentary. Only the name of the king is mentioned together with the names of some fields. (T. A. S. Vol. VII. p. 118)

16	On the same base. (32/1100)	Travancore.	Vīra Kōtai-Mārttāṇḍavarman.	Jupiter in...... Rēvati, śu. 13.	Tamil in Vaṭṭeḻuttu.	Some portions are lost. Appears to record that some repairs were made to the temple by the agents of Vīra Kōtai-Mārttāṇḍavarma when he was the heir-apparent of Travancore, that the old inscriptions of the temple were re-engraved on the walls, and that certain revisions were made in the establishment. (T. A. S. Vol. VII. p. 118)
17	On the north base of the same *maṇḍapa*. (33/1100)	Do.	Ravivarman *alias* Kulaśēkhara-perumāl.	Kollam 780, Vaikāśi 16.	Tamil.	States that Ayyappan-Ayyappan built a portion of the *maṇḍapa* during the time of Ādityavarman the king's younger brother. (T. A. S. Vol. VII.p. 121)
18	On the base of the *maṇḍapa* in the north-east corner of the inner *prākāra*. (34/1100)	Do.	Do.	...	Do.	Built in. States that the *maṇḍapa* was built by an individual of the Tekkineṭattu-illam in Tiruvāṭṭāru-dēśam. (T.A.S. Vol. VII. p. 122)

Tiruvāṭṭāṟu (*contd.*)

No.	Place of inscription.	Dynasty.	King.	Date.	Language and Alphabet.	Remarks.
19	On the same base. (35/1100)	Do.	Kulaśēkhara Kēraḷādhīśvara.	...	Sanskrit in Nāgari.	Damaged. Appears to be a Sanskrit version of the same inscription. (T. A. S. Vol. VII. p. 122)
20	On several detached stones in the base of the eastern *maṇḍapa*. (36/1100)	...	...	...	Tamil in Vaṭṭeluttu.	The writing belongs to the end of the 12th century; but the inscription is fragmentary and contains the names of fields etc. (T. A. S. Vol. VII. p. 119)
21	On the base of the southern verandah. (37/1100)	...	...	...	Tamil.	States that one paṭṭi was contributed by Kiṭṭipan-Kiṭṭipan. (T. A. S. Vol. VII. p. 123)

22	On a stone partly under ground in street called Taḷiyal at Tiruvaṭṭār. (6/1105)	...	...	...	Tamil Vaṭṭeḻuttu.	Records that Dattan Kaṇḍan of Māmballi gave Tāmaraitturutti purayiṭam for a perpetual lamp to be lighted in the temple of Ādikēśavaperumāl of Tiruvaṭṭār and in the temple of Mahādēvar of Taḷiyal.
			Tiruviṭaikkōṭu (*Kalkulam*)			
1	On a rock in the south side, of the second *prākāra* of the Śiva temple at Tiruviṭaikkōṭu. (5/1084)	Travancore.	Iravi Iravivarman of the Kiḻapperur ruling over Vēṇāṭu.	Ko. 548	Grantha or early Malayālam.	Gift of land; mentions Srīvallabhacaturvedimaṅgalam in the Kil-kaḷa-kuṟṟam. (T. A. S. Vol. V. p. 142)
2	Do. (6/1084)	Vṛṣṇi or Yādavakula.	Ko-kkaruṇandaḍakkar.	2+12 year	Tamil. in Vaṭṭeḻuttu.	Gift of a perpetual lamp. (T. A. S. Vol. I. p. 14)
3	Do. (7/1084)	Do.	Do.	2+(2)0	Do.	Do. (T. A. S. Vol. I. p. 15)
4	On the rock on the south side of the second *prākāra* of the same. (8/1084)	...	...	Jupiter in Vṛścikam	Do.	Records the gift of land for, a perpetual lamp and offerings; mentions that Tiruviṭaikkōṭu belonged to Marudattur. (T.A.S. Vol. III. p. 198)

Tiruviṭaikkoṭu (*contd.*)

No.	Place of inscription.	Dynasty.	King.	Date.	Language and Alphabet.	Remarks.
5	On the rock on the south side of the second prākāra of the same. (9/1084)	...	...	Jupiter in Tulām, Mēṣa.	Tamil.	Records gift of land by two individuals of Marudattūr for feeding 7 *Brāhmans* on *Dvādaśi* days in the temple of Tiruviṭaikkōṭu. (T. A. S. Vol. V. p. 145)
6	On the rock Do. (10/1884)	...	...	...	Do.	Gift of land. Fragmentary. (T. A. S. Vol. III. p. 200)
7	Do. (11 1084)	...	...	...	Do.	Records that provision made by a private individual for feeding 12 *Brahmans* on the new-moon days. Damaged. (T. A. S. Vol. V. p. 144)

8	On the four faces of a pillar set up on the east side of the 2nd prākāra of the same. (12/1084)	...	...	Ko. 835.	Do.	Records the gift of land for the maintenance of a way-side charitable institution (*ambalam*) (T. A. S. Vol. V. p. 147)
9	On another pillar set up on the south east corner of the second prākāra of the same. (13/1084)	...	...	S. 1649 , Ko. 902, Plavanga	Do.	Gift of land for feeding *Brahmans* on Dvādaśis by a native of Maṇavāḷakkuricci belonging to Kaṭikaippaṭṭiṇam in the Kurunāṭu, a sub-division of Rājarāja-Tennāṭu. (T. A. S. Vol. V. p. 149)
10	On a stone set up in the second prākāra of the Śiva temple at Tiru-viṭaikkōṭu. (13 a/1084)	...	...	...	Tamil in Vaṭṭeḻuttu.	Damaged.
11	Ōn the Rock in the south *prākāra* of the same. (47/1098)	Vēṇāṭu.	Iravi-Iravi-varman of Kiḻappērūr.	Kollam 548, Kanni 10.	Grantha or early Malayalam.	Same as No. 5/1084 which was recopied for a better impression. Records gift of land for conducting the *Viśākha* festival. (T. A. S. Vol. V. p. 142)

Tiruviṭaikkōṭu. *(contd)*

No.	Place of inscription.	Dynasty.	King.	Date.	Language and Alphabet.	Remarks.
12	On the same rock. (48/1098)	...	...	...	Early Tamil.	Damaged. Relates to the gift of money by Karpaka Śeṭṭi of Āḷūr *alias* Vikramacōḷapāṇḍiyapuram for the feeding of 12 *Brāhmans* on new moon days. (T. A. S. Vol. V. p. 144.)
13	On the same rock. (49/1098)	...	...	Jupiter in Tulām, Mēṭam.	Tamil.	Records gift of land by Uṭayān Ponnāṇṭi and Udayamangala-nangai of Marudattūr in Kurunāṭu for feeding *Brahmans* during every Dvādaśi of the first fortnight in the temple of Tiruviṭaikkōṭu. (T. A. S. Vol. V. p. 144)

14	On a pillar in the *Cuṟ-ṟumaṇḍapa* of the same. (50/1098)	...	...	...	Do.	States that Nāgan-Ādiccan gave 120 *paṇam* for the erection of a *patti* (row of pillars). (T. A. S. Vol. V. p. 152)
15	On another pillar. (51/1098.)	...	...	...	Do.	States that Munbayyan-Kaṇṇan erected the *patti*. (T. A. S. Vol. V. p. 152.)
16	On a third pillar. (52/1098)	...	...	...	Do.	States that Rāman-Dēvan of Kaḷaikkūṭṭam gave money for the *patti* of pillars. (T. A. S. Vol. V. p. 152)
17	On a fourth pillar. (53/1098)	...	...	...	Do.	States that the *patti* was erected by the Oṟṟuviḷākavīṭṭil house in Pārthivaśēkharamangalam. (T. A. S. Vol. V. p. 152)
18	On a fifth pillar. (54/1098)	...	...	...	Do.	States that the *patti* was erected by Dharman-Kiṭṭiṇan of Perumanai in Kuttamangalam-dēśam. (T. A. S. Vol. V p. 152).

Tiruviṭaikkōṭu (*contd*)

No.	Place of inscription.	Dynasty.	King.	Date.	Language and Alphabet.	Remarks.
19	On a sixth pillar. (55/1098)	...	...	...	Do.	States that Īśvaran-Ayyappan of Marudattūr-dēśam gave money for a *patti*. (T. A. S. Vol. V. p. 152)
20	On a seventh pillar. (56/1098).	...	...	...	Do.	States that the pillar was set up by Caṭaiyan-Saṅkaran of Putuvūr. (T. A. S. Vol. V. p. 152)
21	On an eighth pillar. (57/1098).	...	...	...	Do.	States that one *patti* was made by Cātan-Araṅgan of Kulikkāṭu. (T. A. S. Vol. V. 152)
22	On a ninth pillar. (58/1098)	...	...	...	Do.	States that Murugan-Nangan of Pallam made one *patti*. (T. A. S. Vol. V. p. 152)

23	On a tenth pillar. (59/1098)	...	...	...	Tamil.	States that Nallattan-Perumāl contributed one *patti*. (T. A. S. Vol. V. p. 152.)
24	On an eleventh pillar. (60/1098)	...	...	Kollam 769 Arpasi 12	Do.	Records gift of 120 *paṇam* by Periyatiruvaṭi–Anantāḷvān of Mudavampuram in Māccikkōṭu for a *patti* of pillars. (T. A. S. Vol. V. p. 152.)
25	On a twelfth pillar. (61/1098)	...	...	...	Do.	States that the southern entrance and a portion of the *maṇḍapa* was erected. The name is damaged. (T. A. S. Vol. V. p. 152.)
26	On an oblong stone-slab in the same temple. (62/1098)	...	...	...	Do.	States that Dēvan-Śaṅkaran made the slab for tying flower garlands. (T. A. S. Vol. V. p. 153)
27	On another stone. (63/1098)	...	...	...	Do.	States that Caṭayappar contributed 140 *paṇam* for a stone *podigai*. (T. A. S. Vol. V. p. 153)

Tiruvikkramamangalam (Trivandrum)

No.	Place of inscription.	Dynasty.	King.	Date.	Language and Alphabet.	Remarks.
1	On the south wall of the *mukhamaṇḍapa* in the Trivikrama-Perumāl temple at Tiruvikkramamangalam. (14/1095)	...	...	...	Tamil in Vaṭṭeḻuttu.	Built in the middle. Registers gift of land in Iṭaikkōṭṭūr for a lamp to the temple of Tiruvikkramamangalattu-Perumāl. (T. A. S. Vol. VI. p. 61)
2	On the same wall. (15/1095)	...	...	...	Do.	Gift of land for feeding and Vṛścika-lamps to the same temple, by Cattankunran of Pullanūr in Era-nāṭu. (T. A. S. Vol. VI. p. 61)
3	On the north base of the *namaskāra maṇḍapa* in the same temple. (16/1095)	...	...	...	Do.	Contains the name Vikkiraman Kumaran. (T. A. S. Vol. VI. p. 62)

4	On the south base of the same maṇḍapa. (17/1095)	...	...	...	Do.	Unfinished. Mentions Tiruvikkiramangalam. (T. A. S. Vol. VI. p. 62)
5	On the same base. 18/1095)	...	...	Jupiter in Dhanus, Vṛścika 16, Wednesday, Rēvati.	Do.	Provides for offerings and feedings on the day of *Pāṭam* of each month, in the temple of Tiruvikkiramangalattu-Perumāl. (T. A. S. Vol. VI. p. 61.)
6	Do. (19/1095)	...	...	...	Do.	Records that the *maṇḍapa* was built by the merchants Puttan Tiruvikkiraman *alias* Virasetti and Vikkiraman Kattiran of Viḻiñam. (T. A. S. Vol. VI. p. 62)
7	On the north base of the *prākāra* of the same temple (inside). (20/1095)	...	...	Jupiter in Mēṭam.	Do.	Provides for offerings to the same temple by the assembly of Tiruvikkiramangalam. (T. A. S. Vol. VI. p. 60)
8	On the base of the balipīṭha in the same temple. (21/1095)	...	...	...	Do.	Records that Kaṇḍan *alias* Parakesarippallavaraiyar constructed the *balipīṭha*. (T. A. S. Vol. VI. p. 62)

Tiruvitāṅkoṭu (Kalkuḷam)

No.	Place of inscription.	Dynasty.	King.	Date.	Language and Alphabet.	Remarks.
1	On the west base of the Central shrine of the Siva temple at Tiruvitāṅkōṭu. (48/1093)	...	...	...	Tamil in Vāṭṭeḻuttu.	Registers a gift of five buffaloes for a perpetual lamp by Arangan Tiruvaypaṭi of Vēmbanūr.
2	On the east base of the same. (49/1033)	...	...	...	Tamil in Vaṭṭeḻuttu.	Records the gift of land for lamp. (T. A. S. Vol. III. p. 79)
3	On a rock situated on the south of the Central shrine of the same. (52/1093)	Cōḷa Pāṇḍya.	Jaṭāvarman *alias* Sri Sundara Cōḷa Pāṇḍya	20th year	Do.	Records gift of gold *Kāśu* for a lamp to the temple by a native of Tirukkaṇankōṭu (T. A. S. Vol IV. p. 140)
4	On the south wall of the Central shrine in the same. (65/1096)	...	...	Kaliyugam 1451 191 days.	Tamil in Vaṭṭeḻuttu (Archaic)	Records that Singan Kunrapōḷan, the headman of Omayanāṭu gave six *kalam* of paddy into the hands of the Assembly for making offerings to the temple of the Mahādēva, twice a day.

5	On the north wall of the *Maṇḍapa* in front of the same. (50/1093 & 66/1096)	Travancore.	**Ravivarman.**	Ko. 814 (dvipade) Mithunam 4 **Anarādhā** Su. di 13 Monday.	Sanskrit verse in Malayalam.	Records that at the instance of the king, his prime-minister Vasudeva repaired the temple of Vatakotara Nayaka in 3 *Paksas* and provided for feeding *Brahmaṇas* in it. A certain Balarama composed the verse. (T. A. S. Vol. VI. p. 78.)
6	On a stone set up near the Girls' school in the same village. (67/1096)	...	...	Ko. 628 Citirai.	Tamil in Vaṭṭeḻuttu.	Records that as the Vellanāṭar had been offending against the Veḷḷāḷas, this inscription prohibiting their right was caused to be engraved on the lines of two previous records on the subject. (T. A. S. Vol. V. p. 90)
7	On a stone set up near the mosque in the bazaar street in the same village. (68/1096)	Travancore.	**Vīrakēraḷa varman Ciravāy Mūttavar.**	Ko. 871 Tai 25.	Tamil.	Records an order of the king, issued when he was encamped at Kalkuḷam, regarding certain disabilities of Caste-Hindu ladies in connection with *Pulappēṭi* and *Maṇṇāppeṭi*. (T. A. S. Vol. VII. p. 26)

Tiruvitāṅkoṭu (contd)

No.	Place of inscription.	Dynasty.	King.	Date.	Language and Alphabet.	Remarks.
8	On a slab set up at Purūr near the same village. (69 1069)	...	...	Ko. 894.	Do.	Records that certain residents of Putuvūr and Paḷḷiccal built an *ambalam* at Putuvūr and presented lands for its upkeep. (T. A. S. Vol. V p. 89)
9	On a pillar in the Maṇḍapam in the same hamlet. (70/1096)	...	...	Ko. 836.	Tamil.	Records that Iccuvaran Iccuvaran of Paḷḷiccal built the *ambalam* and that others gave lands to it.
10	On a slab set up near the Śāstā temple at Mayilōṭu near the same village. (71/1096)	...	...	Jupiter in Simha Ko. 942 Arpaśi 6 Wednesday, Makayiram ba. di 5.	Do.	Registers a gift of land under the tank called Āmarāvatikuḷam in Tiruvitāṅkōṭu to the *Ambalam* built in Palakkōṭu, one of the hamlets of that village for supplying water, butter, milk, chunam etc.

11	On a tomstone within the R. C. Church at Tiruvitāṅkōṭu. (47/1100)	...	...	A. D. 1860	Do.	Records that Fr. Adrinus who was born at Madrid in 1818 and had been ordained in A. D. 1850 died at Tirukkanankōṭu in A. D. 1860 and was buried in the Tiruvitāṅkōṭu church. (T. A. S. Vol. VII. p. 61)
12	On the step of the tank near the Muhammadan mosque at the same place. (48/1100)	...	...	Ko. 17 Vaikasi 4.	Do.	Illegible. The writing is modern. Mentions the name of some Rāvuttars who were apparently responsible for the stone steps of the tank.
				Toṭupuḷai.		
1	On the base of the pial in the *balikkalpurai* of the Bhagavati temple at Kārikkōṭu near Toṭupuḷai. (89/1087)	...	...	...	Tamil (Modern.)	The prostration of the temple servant Iramavanmarayar to the Malaininrar Puttinagari-Paramēśvari.
2	On the base of the *Cuṟṟu maṇḍapa* of the Śiva temple at Kānjiramaṟṟam near Toṭupuḷai. (90/1087)	...	...	...	Do.	The same individual (as in No. 89) adorns the Śiva at Kānjiramaṟṟam.

Toṭuveṭṭi **(Viḷavankōṭu)**

No.	Place of inscription.	Dynasty.	King.	Date.	Language and Alphabet.	Remarks.
3	On a stone built into the floor behind the central shrine of the Viṣṇu temple at Toṭupuḷai. (91/1087)	...	...	...	Modern Malayalam.	The same individual as in Nos. 89 and 90 figures in this also.
1	On a slab set up in the market at Toṭuveṭṭi. (29/1096 and 43/1108.)	Travancore.	Ravivarman ciravāymūttavar.	Ko. 819, Āvaṇi 20.	Tamil.	Records that this order, issued by the King in respect of certain offenders was engraved and set up in the *Koṭṭali-ambalam*. (T. A. S. Vol. VIII. p. 58.)

Tōnnal **(Trivandrum)**

No.	Place of inscription.	Dynasty.	King.	Date.	Language and Alphabet.	Remarks.
1	On the south base of the *maṇḍapa* in front of the Bhagavati temple at Tōnnal. (24/1095.)	...	...	Ko. 654, Mithunam 29, Saturday, Hastam, Saptami.	Tamil in Vaṭṭeḻuttu.	Records that Nārāyaṇan Suvaran of Cirrur commenced repairs in Kollam 650, Mīnam 12 and completed them and consecrated the Goddess in Kollam 654, Mithunam 29. (T. A. S. Vol. VI. p. 35.)

	***Toṭṭappaḷḷi* (Ambalappuḻa)**					
	On a slab in the pavement of the Bhagavati temple at Tōṭṭappaḷḷi. (100/1100)	...	...	Ko. 840.	Malayalam.	A fragment containing the date.
	Tōvāḷa.					
1	On the south base of the central shrine of the Kṛṣṇasvāmin temple at Tōvāḷai. (11/1087)	Vēṇāṭu.	Venru maṇkoṇḍa Bhūtalavīra Udayamarttāṇḍavarman.	Ko. 700.	Tamil.	Incomplete. Grant to the Kṛṣṇasvāmin temple at Tōvāḷai. (T. A. S. Vol. IV. p. 101.)
2	On a rock near the Piḷḷaiyārkōyil near the Government Satram at Tōvāḷai. (12/1087 and 89/1099)	Do.	Do.	Do.	Do.	Relates to the appointment of a *Brahmin* named Arian Cokkan Periya Perumāḷ Mārttāṇḍa Brahmādhirājan as temple accountant. (T. A. S. Vol. IV. p. 100.)
3	On the rock in front of the Vināyaka temple at Tōvāḷa. (88/1099 and 13/1087)	...	...	Kollam 670, Kumbham 2.	Do.	States that the king, while he was camping at his new palace Vīrakēraḷēśvaram near Muttalaikkuruċċi made a gift of the taxes on certain lands for the conduct of worship and feeding in the temple of (Adittaviṇṇakar-Emperumān at Tōvāḷai, a village in Nāñjināṭu. (T. A. S. Vol. VI. p. 174.)

Trivandrum

No.	Place of inscription.	Dynasty.	King.	Date.	Language and Alphabet.	Remarks.
1	On a stone set up at the entrance of the Napier Museum, Trivandrum. (15/1084.)	Pāṇḍya.	Kō-Māran-caṭaiyan.	27th year.	Tamil in Vaṭṭeḻuttu.	Records that Raṇakīrtti, a faithful servant of the king, fell in the siege of Karaikkōṭṭai. (T. A. S. Vol. I p. 458.)
2	On the base of the *maṇḍapa* in front of the central shrine of the Padmanābhasvāmin temple at Trivandrum. (29/1084.)	ravan-core.	Vīra Rāma kēraḷavarman ruling over vēṇāṭu.	Ko. 384 (385.)	Tamil in Vaṭṭeḻuttu.	End built in, grant of land for feeding Brahmanas, flower gardens, &c., mentions....... Tongappallavaraiyan, Tiruvanandapuram and Mitrānandapuram. (Published by Mr. Sundaram Pillai in Ind. Ant. Vol. V. p. 305 and T. A. S. Vol. VI. 66.)
3	On the south and east sides of the huge slab forming the floor of the *oṟṟaikkal maṇḍapa* in the same. (30/1084.)	Do.	Bālamārttāṇḍavarman.	Ko. 906 Cinnidhi.)	Sanskrit in Malayalam.	Records that the stone for the oṟṟaikkal maṇḍapam reached the Trivandrum Fort. (T. A. S. Vol. I. p. 41.)

4	On the south side of the front maṇḍapa close to the oṟṟaikkal *maṇḍapa* (31/1084.)	Do.	Do.		Do.	The image of Padmanābha was set up with the help of Bālāraṇyakṣōṇidēva and his disciples. Compare No. 32 below. (T. A. S. Vol. I. 41.)
5	Do. (32/1084.)	Do.	Do.	Ko. 904, Bhūnala, Ko. 908 Janadhi.	Do.	Balamārttāṇḍavarman, the nephew of Rāmavarman and the new ruler of the Vañcibhūmi began reconstructing the temple of Padmanābha. (T. A. S. Vol. I. p. 40.)
6	On a pillar of the Namaskāra maṇḍapa of the same. (33/1084.)	...	...	908.	Tamil.	Mentions a private individual.
7	On the Tulābhārakkal in the same. (34/1084.)	Travancore.	Vīra Ravi Ravi Varma Kulaśēkhara-pperumāl of the Kiḻappērūr illam and Tiru-ppāpūr Svurupam.	Ko. 776 Ka. 4702.	Sanskrit in Malayalam.	Records the building of the Tulāpuruṣamaṇḍapa by the King's consort Iraiyumakkuṭṭiyammal. (T. A. S. Vol. II. p. 29.)

Trivandrum (contd)

No.	Place of inscription.	Dynasty.	King.	Date.	Language and Alphabet.	Remarks.
8	On the ***balikkal*** in the Kṛṣṇa shrine of the temple. (35/1084)	Travancore.	....	.....	Tamil in Vaṭṭeḻuttu.	Damaged. Mentions Sarvāṅganāthan Tiruppāḷpūr Mūtta Tiruvaṭi (Sri Vira Iravivarman).
9	On the *maṇḍapa* in front of the Kṛṣṇa shrine in the same. (36/1084)	Do.	Ādityavarman.	...	Sanskrit in Grantha.	Built the temple of Kṛṣṇa, the maṇḍapa in front of it and the *gōśala*. (T. A. S. Vol. I. p. 172)
31	On the northern wall of the central shrine of the Kṛṣṇa shrine in the same. (37/1084)	Do.	Gōdamārttāṇḍa, lord of Kōlamba.	Ko. 359 or 371.	Sanskrit in Malayalam.	Presented to the God of Gosṭhālaya, a silver drum. (T. A. S. Vol. III. p. 46.)
11	Do. (38/1084)	Do.	....	...	Tamil in Vaṭṭeḻuttu.	Mentions some Bhaṭāratiruvaṭi. Records the gift of drum, and money for offerings. (T. A. S. Vol. III. p. 46.)

12	Do. (39/1084.)	Travancore.	Sarvāṅganātha.	Cōḷapriye (1296.S)	Sanskrit in Malayalam.	Records the construction of the Kṛṣṇa shrine, its front *maṇḍapa* and the gōśāla; compare No. 36 above. (T. A. S. Vol. I. p. 171.)
13	On the south wall of the Kṛṣṇa shrine in the same. (40/1084.)	.....	...	Jupiter in Mīnam.	Tamil in Vaṭṭeḻuttu.	Gift of two lamps. Mentions Prajñādhyakṣa Puḻārati. (T. A. S. Vol. III. pp. 44—46.)
14	On the same. (41/1084.)	...	...	Jupiter in Karkaṭakam.	Do.	Gift of land for a lamp by Kāman Kunṛappōḷan. (T. A. S. Vol. III. pp. 44—46.)
15	On the east wall of the same. (42/1084.)	...	...	Jupiter in Mēṣam.	Do.	Gift of land for bathing in oil the God of Tiruvāyambāṭi. (T. A. S. Vol. VII. p. 132.)
16	Do. (43/1084.)	...	.	Jupiter in Vṛścikam.	Tamil in Vaṭṭeḻuttu.	Damaged.
17	On the south base of the Śāstāmkōyil at Taikkāṭu in Trivandrum. (78/1084.)	...	...	Ko 775, Pankuni.	Kōleḻuttu & Malayalam.	Damaged. Mentions Vikkiraman Kēyavan (T. A. S Vol. VII. p. 134)

Trivandrum (contd)

No.	Place of inscription.	Dynasty.	King.	Date.	Language and Alphabet.	Remarks.
18	On a stone built into the floor of the first *prākāra* of the Mahādeva temple at Cālai, Trivandrum. (79/1085)	Cōḷa.	(Rājēndra-Cōḷadeva.)	...	Sanskrit in Grantha & Tamil.	Contains the first half of the historical introduction of the Cōḷa king Rājēndracōḷadeva I. (T. A. S. Vol. VI. p. 149.)
19	On a stone lying to the west of the lamp-post in the 1st *prākāra* of the same. (80/1085)	Vēṇāṭu.	Tribhuvana-cakravartti-Kulaśēkhara-dēva Sangrāma-dhīra	...	Tamil in Vaṭṭeḻuttu.	Incomplete. The introduction is similar to that on pp. 145—152 of Ep. Ind. Vol. IV. (T. A. S. Vol. II. pp. 58/59.)
20	On a stone set up in front of the same. (81/1085)	...	...	...	Tamil in Vaṭṭeḻuttu.	Very much damaged.
21	On the front four faces of a stone set up in front of the Śrīvarāha temple at Trivandrum. (42 1086)	Travancore.	Vīra Iravi-varman.	...	Do.	Records gift for the supply of flower garlands.

22	On the south base of the central shrine of the same. (43/1086)	...	...	Ko. 660.	Malayalam.	Records that the temple was repaired in the time of Srī Yādavēndrānubbūti Bhaṭārar.
23	On the north eastern corner of Nālukeṭṭu of the house of Paramēśvaran Mūttatu, Superintendent of Vaidyaśāla, Mitrānandapuram, Fort, Trivandrum. (43/1090)	...	...	Ko. 1030 Iṭavam 5.	Do. (modern.)	One big inscription about the defalcation made in the Muncirai maṭham. (T. A. S. Vol. VII. p. 23.)
24	On the west wall of the Brahma shrine at Mitrānandapuram. Trivandrum. (22/1095/ & 47/1084).	...	...	Jupiter in Makaram, Vṛścika.	Tamil.	Unfinished. Registers gift made in the presence of Rāmajña—Bhaṭāra Tiruvaṭi, by Pūrṇakīrti Rāma varman of Pulamaṇ in Vēṇāṭṭu—Iḷaṅkuru, incomes in paddy and gold, to the shrine of Dakṣiṇasvarṇamukai—Bhaṭāra, at Mitrānandapuram. (T. A. S. Vol. III. p. 25)
25	On the south wall of the same shrine. (23/1035)	...	...	Jupiter in Makaram, Makaram.	Do.	Registers gift of *rakṣābhōga* by Dēvan Cakrāyudhan of Śaṅkaramaṅgalam, for offerings to the same temple. Mentions Rāmajña—Bhaṭārar. (T. A. S. Vol. III. p. 26.)

Trivandrum (contd)

No.	Place of inscription.	Dynasty.	King.	Date.	Language and Alphabet.	Remarks.
26	At the left base of the entrance into the Viṣṇu temple in the same place. (24/1095 and 45/1084)	...	...	Kollam 600. Jupiter in Vṛścikam and Mīnam.	Do.	Records that in Kollam 660 repairs were executed to the temple, the image of the God set up and the pinnacle covered with copper. Mentions Yādavendrānubhūti-Paḷarar—Tiruvaṭi. (T. A. S. Vol. III. p. 27.)
27	On the yāḷi stone at the left of entrance into the same shrine. (25/109 same as No. 44 of 1084.)	Vēṇāṭu.	Maṇikaṇṭha Rāmavarman.	Jupiter in Karkaṭakam, Kumbham 1.	Tamil Vaṭṭeḻuttu.	Records gift of lands in Marudattūr and Cempaḻanti Nenmalimagalam for offerings to the temple of Mitrānandapurattu-Bhaṭārar. Mentions Kaṇḍan Udayanan of Kaitaivay, Govindan Kumaran of Paṭṭāḷi and Vikkiraman Parannavan of Punalūr. (T. A. S. Vol. III. p. 28)

27	In the same place. (26/1095)	...	...	...	Do.	Registers gift of land in Iṭaimālai for offering to the temple of Mitrānandapurattu —Perumāḷ by Pugali Selvan *alias* Tiruvālavāyil Danma-seṭṭi, a merchant of Tirukkōlūr. (T. A. S. Vol. III. p. 30.)
28	On a slab set up in the verandah of the Napier Museum, Trivandrum. (1/1096)	...	...	Kollam 229 (A. D. 1054) Simha.	Tamil in Vaṭṭeḻuttu.	Registers a transaction made by the people of 18 cities, 32 *vellam* 64 *kadikait-tavalam*, the *settis* living in them as well as the 1500 of Kurakkēṇi–Kollam. Mentions Kēraḷakēsari Ayyan and Aiyappolipura-Paramesvari.
29	On another slab in the same place. (2/1096 same as No.17 of 1084.)	...	...	Jupiter in Dhanus, Kollam 257, Āṭi 10 expired, Monday, Mūla sudi. 13.	Tamil.	Records that Picca Piḷḷai–Kaṇṭan Pillai of Manjaviḷā-kaṇivīṭu in Kulutturai-dēsam constructed a shed to the east of the market, sunk a well, fitted with a water-cistern in stone; and provided for supplying drinking matter, pickles, *Chunam*, *suttu* (flambeau consisting of

Trivandrum (*contd.*)

No.	Place of inscription.	Dynasty.	King.	Date.	Language and Alphabet.	Remarks.
					Tamil.	palm-leaves etc, for the convenience of travellers. Mention is made of Pākōṭu and Aṇṭukōṭu. (T. A. S. Vol. V. p. 134.)
30	On a third slab in same place. (3/1096 same as No. 16 of 1084)	...	...	Jupiter in Dhanus, Kollam 839 Cittirai 3, expired, Thursday, su. di. 15.	Tamil.	Registers a gift of land in Neyyāṟṟinkarai—dēśam by Iccammatikuttiyamma and Ayyappan—Mārttāṇḍan of Ceruvallivīṭu in Cirayinkil for maintaining a flower garden etc., attached to a shed. The gift—land was originally assigned to the donees by the king (Mutta—Tambiran). Mentions Kāndaḷūrśālai—mādēva. (T. A. S. Vol. V. p. 129).

			Turavūr (Cārttala)			
1	On the base of the *dvajastamba* in the Vaṭakkinnakokam temple at Turavūr. (20/1100)	...	...	Kali *sōsaudēvah* (4877, 951,) Mēṣa 22, Mithuna-lagna.	Latin.	States that the flagstaff was erected in the Nṛsimha temple at Turavūr (svarpuri) by king Rāmavarman of Travancore (Vanci).
2	On a brass plate fixed on a door in the same temple. (21/1100)	...	...	Kollam 922, Mithunam Kollam 924, Mēṭam.	...	States that Śrīkōyil was built in Kollam 922, Mithunam and was consecrated in Mēṭam of Kollam 924.
	On a stone in the flooring of the same temple. (22/1100)	...	...	..	...	Contains the name Pallattil Itti-Ādiccan.
4	On the base of the ruined *dvajastambha* of the Tekkinnakam temple in the same village. (23/1100)	...	...	...	...	Mentions Devan-Kumaran of Turuttikkāṭu.
			Udayagiri (Kalkuḷam)			
1	On a tombstone within the ruined chapel on the Udayagiri hill, Puliyūrkuricci. (59/1099)	...	...	A. D. 1765, September 14, Saturday.	...	States that John Eustace Benedict Le Lannoy, who was born in 1745 and who was wounded at the storming of the Fort of Kaḷakkāṭu, died the day mentioned. (T. A.S. Vol. VI. p. 51.)

Udayagiri (*contd.*)

No.	Place of inscription.	Dynasty.	King.	Date.	Language and Alphabet.	Remarks.
2	On the same tomb stone. (59/1099)	...	...	Kollam 941, Puraṭṭāśi 9.	Tamil.	Contains the same particulars as the above and mentions in addition that John Eustace de Lannoy was the son of the Valiya Kappittān. (T. A. S. Vol. VI. p. 52.)
3	On a second tomb stone in the same place. (60/1099)	...	...	A. D. 1777, June 1.	Latin.	Records that Eustace Benedict de Lannoy, the General in-chief of the troops of Travancore, having subjected all the kingdoms from Kāyamkuḷam to Cochin during his service of nearly 37 years died at the age of 62 years, 5 months. (T. A. S. Vol. VI. p. 53)

4	On a same tombstone. (61/1099)	...	..	Kollam 952 Vaikāśi 22, Sunday night.	Tamil.	Contains the same particulars as the above in incorrect Tamil. (T. A. S. Vol. VI. p. 55.)
5	On a third tombstone in the same place. (62/1099)	...	...	11th Septr. 1782.	Latin.	States that Margaret de Lannoy, who was called the 'Mother of the poor' on account of her charitable disposition, died on the day mentioned. (T. A. S. Vol. VI. p. 55.)
6	On the same tomb stone. (63/1099)	...	...	Kollam 953, Āvaṇi 29.	Tamil.	Contains the same particulars as the above. (T. A. S. Vol. VI. p. 55.)
7	On a fourth tomb stone in the same. (64/1099)	...	...	16th March 1750	Latin.	States that Peter Plory, a lieutenant of the Travancore army, died at the age of 55, after having served the king for 36 years. (T. A. S. Vol. VI. p. 57.)
8	On the same tomb stone. (65/1099)	...	...	Kollam 955, Panguni 6, Wednesday.	Tamil.	Contains the same particulars as the above. (T. A. S. Vol. VI. p. 57.)

Udayagiri (*contd.*)

No.	Place of inscription.	Dynasty.	King.	Date.	Language and Alphabet	Remarks.
9	On a fifth tombstone in the same place. (66/1099)	...	...	Kollam 978, Puraṭṭāsi 11.	English Tamil.	Damaged. Relates to the death of Major Charles Everard of the Travancore military Service. (T. A. S. Vol. VI. p. 56.)

Udiyanpērūr (Vaikam.)

No.	Place of inscription.	Dynasty.	King.	Date.	Language and Alphabet	Remarks.
1	On the base of the maṇḍapa in front of the Peruntirukkōyil at Udyaupērūr. (6/1099)	Travancore.	Kīḻappērūr Sri Vīra Kōtai-Raviva rman, Vēṇāṭṭaṭikaḷ.	...	Granthain Malayalam.	States that the Maṇḍapa was constructed by Nārāyaṇan at the instance of the king. (T. A.S. Vol. VI. p. 65)
2	On slab let into the flooring of the prākāra of the same temple. (7/1099)	...	...	...	Vaṭṭeḻuttu. (12th century).	Very much damaged. Seems to record some donations made to the temple for offerings and burning a perpetual lamp. (T.A.S.Vol. VI. p. 65)
3	On a tombstone kept in the R. C. Church at Udiyanpērūr. (9/1099)	...	...	...	Malayalam Vaṭṭeḻuttu.	Records the death of Matten Kora of Kadaparam. (T. A. S. Vol. VI. p. 66)

4	On another tombstone. (10/1099)	...	..	Kollam 897, Mīnam 28.	Do.	Do. of a certain Thoma. (T. A. S. Vol. VI. p. 67.)
5	On a third tombstone. (11/1099)	...	...	Kollam 846, Dhanu 13.	Do.	Records the death of Vaṭakkeṭattu Mattu (Mathew) Kattanar of Udiyanpērūr. (T. A. S. Vol. VI. p. 67)
6	On a fourth tombstone. (12/1099)	...	...	Kollam 734, Mēṭam 22.	Do.	Registers the death of Matten Ka da ta Panikker. (T A. S. Vol. VI. p. 66.)
7	On a fifth tombstone. (13/1099)	...	...	Kollam 836, Makaram 25.	Do.	Do. of Aruvara Varkki. (T. A. S. Vol. VI. p. 67.)
8	On a sixth tombstone. (14/1099)	...	...	Kollam 827, Mithunam 3	Do.	Do. of Panikker. (T. A. S. Vol, VI p. 67)
9	On a seventh tombstone. (15/1099)	...	...	Kollam 865, Mēṭam 5.	Do.	Do. of Mariya ....
10	On an eighth tombstone. (16/1099)	...	...	A. D. 1701 (Month 2), (day) 9.	Do.	Registers the alleged death of VillārvaṭṭamThommarājāvu, who was living in Cēnōnnalam. (T.A.S. Vol. VI. p.68)
11	On a ninth tombstone. (17/1099)	...	...	....	Do	Contains a few syllables.

Kuḷitturai. (Viḷavankōṭu)

No.	Place of inscription.	Dynasty.	King.	Date.	Language and Alphabet.	Remarks.
			Uḷiyannūr (Parūr).			
1	On the south base of the central shrine in the Śiva temple at Uḷiyannūr (130/1096 & 107/1085)	Travan-core.	Kīḻappērūr Sri Vīra Kōtai Ravivarman Vēṇāṭṭaṭikaḷ.	...	Tamil in Vaṭṭeḻuttu.	Records that a certain Kaṇṭan Kaṇṭan constructed the temple. (T. A. S. Vol. VII. p. 99).
2	On a slab in the Namaskara maṇḍapa in front of the same. (131/1096 &108/1085).	...	...	...	Do.	Provides for offerings and lamps to the (same) temple. (T. A. S. Vol. VII. p. 98.)
			Vaṭivīśvaram (Agastīśvaram)			
1	On the east wall of the second *prākāra* of the Śiva temple at Vaṭivīśvaram (near Nāgarkōyil.) (34/1087)	...	...	Kollam 694.	Tamil.	Gift of land. (T. A. S. Vol. VI. p. 133.)

2	Do. (35/1087)	Vēṇāṭu.	Bhūtalavīra Venrumaṇkoṇḍa Ravivarman.	Kollam 712.	Do.	Gift of land. (T. A. S. Vol. VI. p. 134.)
3	Do. (36/1087)	...	...	Kollam 786.	Do.	Refers to a document executed by the residents of Kōtaccapillai akaram. (T. A. S. Vol. VI. p. 134.)
				Vaikam.		
1	On the base of the *maṇḍapa* in front of the central shrine in the Peruntṛkōyilappan temple at Vaikam. (24/1100)	...	...	...	Tamil in Vaṭṭeḻuttu.	Damaged. Mentions the name Vaikkattu-Bhaṭārakar.
2	On two pillars of the *Curṟumaṇḍapa* in the same temple. (25/1100)		...	...	Malayalam.	The names of Ariyappaḷḷi-Paṇikkar of Tekkumkūru and Śankaran are mentioned.
3	On a pillar in the Tekke-ambalam in the same place. (26/1100)	...	...	...	Do.	States that the pillar was set up on behalf of the Kāryakār of Kaniyampadikkal.
4	On another pillar. (27/1100)	...	...	...	Do.	Mentions the name of Paramēśvara of Pallippuram.
5	On a pillar in the western *Curṟu-maṇḍapa*. (28/1100)	...	...	...	Do.	Gives the names of the men who carved the pillar.

Vāḻappaḷḷi (*Caṅganācēri*)

No.	Place of inscription.	Dynasty.	King.	Date.	Language and Alphabet.	Remarks.
1	On the north base of the central shrine in the Śiva temple at *Vāḻappaḷḷi*, Caṅganācēri taluk. (29/1098)	...	...	Kollam 840, Iṭavam 1.	Tamil in Vaṭṭeḻuttu.	States that the repairs were completed and that consecration was celebrated. (T. A. S. Vol. VII. p. 136.)
2	On a pillar in the *namaskāramaṇḍapa* in front of the same shrine. (30/1098)	...	...	...	Malayalam.	States that a certain Dēvan set up the pillar. (T. A. S. Vol. VII. p. 136.)
3	Do. (31/1098)	...	...	...	Do.	States that Tuppan-Tuppan of Acceri set up the pillar. (T. A. S. Vol. VII. p. 136.)
4	Do. (32/1098)	...	...	...	Do.	States that Mādhavan-Śrīkumāran set up the pillar. (T. A.S. Vol. VII. p. 136.)
5	Do. (33/1098)	...	...	...	Do.	States that Tuppan-Tuppan of Pilakkuṭi set up the pillar. (T. A. S. Vol. VII. p. 136.)

6	On the pedestal of the copper bull in the Siva temple at Vāḻappaḷḷi. (7/1100)	...	...	Kollam 810, Mīnam.	Tamil in Vaṭṭeḻuttu.	States that the bull was cast at the instance of or by Kocci (nai; ... —of Kunrampelli in the northern corner of Vāḻappaḷḷi. (T. A. S. Vol. VI, p. 135)
			Vālviccakōṭṭam (*Kalkuḷam*)			
1	On the south wall of the central shrine in the Bhagavati shrine at Vālviccakōṭṭam. (72/1096)	...	...	Kollam 410, Mēṣa.	Tamil in Vaṭṭeḻuttu.	Records that the temple of Bhagavati, intended to protect the Vēṇāṭṭaṭikaḷ and his kingdom, was constructed by Nārāyaṇan Araṅṅan of Melamarudūr. (T. A. S. Vol. VI p. 171)
2	At the right of entrance into the same temple. (73/1096)	...	...	Kollam 798 Panguni 25, Kārttikai su. do. 3.	Tamil verse.	Records that a certain Dāmōdaran of Mullamangalam executed the repairs of the temple and obtained *paralōkam*. (T. A. S. Vol. VI, p. 172)
3	At the left of the same entrance. (74/1096)	Travancore.	Ravivarman.	Kollam 798, Arpaśi, Daśami, Aviṭṭam Friday.	Do.	Records that a certain Tiruvikkiraman of Mullamangalam constructed the *Mukhamaṇḍapa* of the Bhagavati temple at Vālvaittakōṭṭam. (T. A. S. Vol, VI. p. 171)

Vālviccakōṭṭam—(*contd.*)

No.	Place of inscription.	Dynasty.	King.	Date.	Language & Alphabet.	Remarks.
4	Above one of the images in a pillar of the *maṇḍapa* in front of the same temple. (75/1096)	...	...	...	Malayalam.	Contains the name K (ā) li Sankaran who was the *Sri-paṇḍārakkaṇakku-Vāriyan.* (T. A. S. Vol. VI. p. 171)
5	On the *balikkal* in front of the Tiruppannikōṭu temple near the same village. (76/1096)	...	...	...	Tamil in Vaṭṭeḻuttu. (Archaic)	Records that a certain native of Kuḻikkōṭu constructed the *bali-pīṭha*. (T. A. S. Vol. VI. p. 171).
6	On the east wall of the *Cuṟṟu-maṇḍapa* of the same temple. (77/1096)	...	...	Ko. (4) 51, Ṛṣabha	Tamil ?	Registers gift of land for lamp, offering, etc., to the temple of Tiruppannikōṭu.
	Vāriyūr (Agastīśvaram.)					
1	On a slab of stone set up in Veyyilu koṇḍa-amman shrine situated in the centre of the vāriyūr salt pans, near Vāriyūr. (48 1086)	Cōḻa.	Cakravartin-Kulōttunga cōḻadēva (i)	38th	Tamil.	Gift of salt pans to the God of Agastīśvaram for the merit of king. (T.A. S. Vol. I. p. 243)

2	On the three faces of a stone lying in the cocoanut garden north of the salt factory near Vāriyūr. (49/1086)	Do.	Cakravartin Kulōttunga cōḷadēva.	4 (9)	Do.	Gift of 2 salt pans at Vāriyūr for a lamp to the God of Sucīndram, for the merit of the king, by Ponpaṟṟi-uṭaiyaṉ Avaiyan Mūvāyirattoruvan *alias* Kurukularāyan of Amarapurimangalam in the Uttamacōla-Vaḷanāṭu of Rājarājappāṇḍināṭu; Vāriyūr is otherwise known as Parākkirama-Cōlappēraḷam. (T. A. S. Vol. I. p. 248)
			Varkala (Cirayinkīḻ)			
1	On the south base of the central shrine in the Janārdana temple at Varkalai. (109/1096 same as No. 2 of 1084)	Vēṇāṭu.	Vīra Pattanābhamārttāṇḍavarma Tiruvaṭi.	Kollam 427 Ṛṣabha 21, Wednesday, su. do. 5, Karkaṭaka Rāśi.	Tamil in Vaṭṭeḻuttu.	Records that the king built of stone the central shrine (from the *adhiṣṭhāna* to the *uttiram*) of the temple of the Bhaṭṭāraka at Varkalai-Udaiyamārttāṇḍapuram, had the *śrīvimāna* covered with copper-sheets, renewed the mukha *mandapa* and consecrated the God. (T. A. S. Vol. IV. p. 151)

Varkala—(*contd.*)

No.	Place of inscription.	Dynasty.	King.	Date.	Language and Alphabet.	Remarks.
2	On the north base of the maṇḍapa in front of the same shrine. (110/1096 same as 3/1084)	Do.	Mārttāṇḍa.	Kollam 655, expired by the chronogram (*mameta*) Ṛṣabha 15, Thursday, Mārgaśīrṣa, Vidhi tithi, Thursday	Malayalam.	Published by Prof. Kielhorn in Ep. Ind. Vol. IV. pp. 203f. In the published text the syllables svasti sri' are omitted at the beginning and 'gate' has been misread as 'ite.'
3	On the east prākāra wall of the same temple. (111/1096)	Travancore.	Ravi Kulaśēkhara Perumāḷ of Āṟṟingal Svarūpam, who had his *hiraṇya garbha* and *tulābhāra* ceremonies performed at Tiruvanandapuram.	Kollam 70 Ṛṣabha 16.	Malayalam.	Fragmentary and damaged. Seems to relate to the repairs executed in the temple.

4	On the east and north bases of *dvajastambha* in the same temple. (1112/1096 same as No. 4/1084.)	Do.	Rāmavarman.	Kollam 1071 expressed by the chronogram Pārtha nandye), Sun in Mṛgaśīrṣa, Makara 4, Thursday.	Do.	Records that by the command of the king the flag-staff was set up.
5	On the bell in the same. (41/1100).	...	...	A. D. 1757.	English.	Contains the name of Michael Everard.
			Vellalūr. (Cirayinkil)			
1	On the north base of the Siva temple at Vellalūr. (114/1096)	Vēṇāṭu.	Vīra-Rāman-Kerala Tiruvaṭi of Kiḷappērūr.	Jupiter in Makaram. Thulam.	Tamil in Vaṭṭeḻuttu.	Registers a gift made by the king, for offerings to the shrine, built on the north side of the temple at Tiruvellalūr. (T. A. S. Vol. IV. p. 71.)
			Vellanāṭu (Neṭumangāṭu)			
1	On the *bali-pitha* in Subrahmaṇya temple at Vellanāṭu. (44/1095)	...	...	...	Tamil in Vaṭṭeḻuttu.	Records that Kaṇṇan Accan built the *bali-pīṭha* and provided lands for offerings. (T. A. S. Vol. VII. p. 37).

Veḷḷāṇi (Neyyāṟṟinkara)

No.	Place of inscription.	Dynasty.	King.	Date.	Language and Alphabet.	Remarks.
1	On the south base of the *maṇḍapa* in front of the Viṣṇu temple at Veḷḷāṇi. (27/1095).	Vēṇāṭu.	Vīra-Ravi varman.	Ko. 371 Mēṣa 24, Jupiter in Karkaṭakam.	Tamil in Vaṭṭeḻuttu.	Registers gift made by the officers of the king for offerings and lamps to the temple of Tirukkuṇakarai *alias* Yādavanārāyaṇa Viṇṇakar-Āḻvār at Senkottāru-cerikkal. Mentions Kaṇḍan Kaṇḍan of Kokkopparappu, Keralan Suvaran Danamankōtu, Vikkiraman of Parannavan of Punalur and Govindan Kumaran of Paṭṭāḻi. (T. A. S. Vol. III. p. 35).

Velunnannūr (Koṭṭarakkāra)

No.	Place of inscription.	Dynasty.	King.	Date.	Language and Alphabet.	Remarks.
1	On two pillars of the nālambala near the entrance of the Srī-Rāmasvāmin temple, Velunnannūr. (3 & 4/1104)	...	...	...	Malayalam.	Mentions Keralan Ādiccan of Nellittanam and Kavunkal Ayyappilla.

Vindanūr (Cenkōṭṭa)

1	On the east wall of the *maṇḍapa* in front of the central shrine proper right of the entrance of the Sundararājapperumāḷ temple Vindanūr, near Sambūrvaṭakarai. (37/1086)	Pāṇḍya.	Tirunelvēlipperumāḷ son of	Lost.	Tamil.	Damaged and fragmentary.
2	On the south wall of the maṇḍapa of the same. (38/1086)	Do.	Kulaśēkharadēva *alias* Parākrama Pāṇḍyadēva son of Jatil. Tribh. Abhirāma Parākrama Pāṇḍyadēva, born in the Aśvati nakṣatra.	S. 1472, Sādhāraṇa, 7th year.	Do.	Appointment of an accountant to the temple. (T. A. S. Vol. I. p. 272)
3	On the east wall of the maṇḍapa of the same. (39/1086)	Do.	Tirunelvēlipperumāḷ Kulaśēkharadēva, son of Jatil. Tribh. Abhirāma Pāṇdyadēva.	S. 1474, Paritāpi, 2nd 1st.	Do.	Records the appointment of a man in the temple service. (T. A. S. Vol. I. p. 273)

Vindanūr (contd)

No.	Place of inscription.	Dynasty.	King.	Date.	Language and Alphabet.	Remarks.
4	On the north base of the central shrine of the same. (41/1086)	Pāṇḍya.	A̲ḻakamperumāḷ Parākrama Pāṇḍyadēva born in Tiruvātirai nakṣatra and who is called Annāḻvi.	2nd + 9th	Tamil.	Grant of land to the Srī vaiṣṇavas for making midday offerings to the God A̲ḻakiya Maṇavāḷapperumāḷ. Mentions A̲ḻakiyamaṇavāḷappērēri. (T. A. S. Vol. I. p. 262)
5	On the south base of the central shrine of the same. (41/1086)	Do.	Jatil. Trib. Srīvallabhadēva.	2nd + 10th	Do.	Grant of land to the God A̲ḻakiya Maṇavāḷapperumāḷ.

Vīranārāyaṇaśēri (Kalkuḷam)

No.	Place of inscription.	Dynasty.	King.	Date.	Language and Alphabet.	Remarks.
1	On a stone standing on the road side at Vīranārāyaṇaśēri. (7/1112)	...	...	Ko. (2?) 31? A. D. 1756	Tamil.	Records that a private individual made a gift of land for a wayside charitable institution. Damaged.

Copper—plates.

1	Aṟṟūr plates.	Travancore.	Vīraravi Udaya Mārttāṇḍa Varman Ciravāy Mūttavar of Kiḻappērūr.	Sa. 1173 Ko. 426 Mēṣa 19 Mūla, ba. di 5.	Malayalam.	Records that the king conferred on a resident of Kaṇṇanūr in Malaimaṇḍalam the right of Kōyinma Urāṇma and sthāna in the temple of Mahādēva at Muttalakkuricci alias Vīrakēraḷapuram.
2	Do.	Do.	Ravivarman Cirāvaymūttavar of Kiḻappērūr.	Ko. 821 Mīnam 22 expired Friday, Uttiram, Paurṇami.	Tamil.	Records gifts of lands to, and privileges conferred on, a resident of Kaṇṇanūr in Malaimaṇḍalam for conducting festivals in the temple of Vīrakēraḷapuram. Reference is made to the grants made by previous kings in the Kollam years 332, 335, 337, 491, 628 and 782.
3	Cēnnamangalam Paliattu Accan.	Cochin Rajas.	....	322nd year of the Putuvaippu era.	Malayalam in Vaṭṭeḻuttu.	Copy of a treaty of alliance entered into between the Rāja of Cochin and the Honourable Dutch East India Company.

Copper—plates (*contd.*)

No.	Place of inscription.	Dynasty.	King.	Date.	Language and Alphabet.	Remarks.
4	Do.	Vṛṣṇi or Yādava.	Varaguṇa.	...	Sanskrit and Tamil in Nāgari.	Records the grant of certain lands to the temple of Tirumūlavātam. Tamil portion is fragmentary.
5	Cittiattu Church Plate.	...	...	Ko. 894.	Malayalam in Vaṭṭeḻuttu.	Registers the gift of some land made by Ravirāma Kaimal to the Carmelite Fr. Mathew to build a Church thereon.
6	Do	...	...	Ko. 936.	Do.	Registers a sale of land by Kumaran Śrīkaṇṭha Tirumulpad of Maṇṇāḍu to Muppan padiri of the carmelite Mission.
7	Do.	...	...	Ko. 956.	Do.	Records that Fr. Franciscos. Muppan Padiri of the Carmelite Mission Purchased some land from Kunnattu Rāman Kumāra Kaimal and his brothers.

8	Dalavāy Agraharam Plates.	Pāṇḍya.	Varatunga-rāma.	Śa. 1504.	Sanskrit in Grantha.	Records that king Varatungarāma granted the village of Muruganeri, to Candraśēkhara, son Cokkappa Paṇḍita, a medical doctor.
9	Do.	Do.	Do.	Śa. 1510.	Do.	Records that king Vīrapāṇḍya granted the village of Silarippatti to Gōvinda Bhaṭṭa, son of Udayam bhaṭṭa.
10	Do.	Do.	Ativīra-rāma.	Sa. 1517.	Do.	Records that Prince Abhirāma alias Ativīra granted the village of Nadikkudi, under the name of Ativīrarāmapura, to a number of Brahmans.
11	Eṭakkāṭṭu Mūttatu near Puliyūr.	Nāyaka.	Tirumala Nāyaka.	Sa. 1574 Nandana, Uttarāyaṇa vasanta, Vaiśākha. Su 11, Sunday Hasta.	Tamil.	Registers the gift of land at Muttūrkūṟṟam to Brahmānubhūtisvami the disciple of Muncirai Kaḷakkāṭṭu Śrīpādangal by Danukkatta Vaniyarttanta vilatta Devar of Kulōttunga Cōḷanallūr

Copper—plates (*contd.*)

No.	Place of inscription.	Dynasty.	King.	Date.	Language and Alphabet.	Remarks.
						in Tukavūrkuṟṟam for the donee's ancestors on paternal and maternal side.
12	Do.	Pāṇḍya.	Parākrama Pāṇḍya.	Sa. 1......31 plus 7.	Do.	Fragmentary. The date of the inscription may be as pointed (31 plus 7) Śaka 1382 and the King Mentioned in this copper plate is Arikēsari Parākrama Pāṇḍya, the builder of Viśvanātha Svāmin temple at Tenkāśi. The introductory stanza shows that the copper plate is the Śāsana of Viśvanātha at Tenkāśi by Parākrama Pāṇḍya and the protection of temple charities by some sanyasins.

13	Kanyākumāri plates.	...	...	Ko. 346 Cittirai 10.	Tamil.	Gives a list of some temple property.
14	Do.	Vēṇāṭ .	Padma-nābha dāsa Bālarāma-varma Kula-śēkhara perumāḷ.	Sa. 1682 Ko. 935 Cittirai 16.	Do.	Gives an account of the receipts and expenses of the temple of Kannimākumari Bhagavati Amman.
15	Kāṭṭātturai plate of cempantōṭṭattu vīṭu.	Do	Vīra Iravi Kēraḷa-varma.	Ko. 329.	Do.	Records that the King was pleased to give certain privileges to Nallā Nācciyār Tangacci, the daughter of Nācciyār.
16	Kiḷimānūr record.	Travancore.	Vīra Udaya Mārttāṇḍa Varman.	Ko. 343 Jupiter in Makaram, Mēṭam 12 Thursday, Uttiram Trayōdaśi Kollam 304 Mēṭam 1 Kollam 341 Mēṭam 1.	Tamil in Vaṭṭeḻuttu. (copied in Tamil).	This is a cumulative list of the gifts of lands made to the temple of Tiruppārkaṭal Bhaṭāraka by Maṇikaṇṭhan Umaiyammaiyāyapillai-tiruvaṭi, Nōtai Āvaṇiyāya Pillaiyar and Devadaran Āvaṇiyāya Pillaiyar-tiruvaṭi. It lays down the scale of expenditure of the temple and remuneration to the servants.

Copper-plates (*contd.*)

No.	Place of inscription.	Dynasty.	King.	Date.	Language and Alphabet.	Remarks.
17	Kōccepiṭāram temple.	Travan-core.	Nayinār Ravivarma alias Kulaśēkhara Perumāḷ.	Sa. 1524 (expired) Ko. 778 Śubhakṛt Kārttikai, 13.	Tamil.	States that Sankaran Kōṭai of Panaiyarai in Malaimaṇḍalam founded an Akaram called Kōṭaiccan akaram alias Udayamārttāṇḍa caturvēdimangalam near Kōṭṭāru Alias Mummuṭi cōḷanallūr in Nānjināṭu built the temple, consecrated the images of Polintuninraruḷiya perumāḷ and his consorts, and provided for offerings and for the conduct of worship to them.
18	Kollūrmaṭham agent.	Vēṇāṭu.	Vīra udaya-mārttāṇḍa Varman.	Ko. 364	Tamil in Vaṭṭeḻuttu.	Registers assignments made for various requirements in the temple of Dēvidēvēccuram built by the mother of King Śrīvallabhankōtai of Vēṇāṭu.

19	Kōṭṭayam Sthāṇuravi Copper plates.	Cēra.	Sthāṇuravi.	5th year of the reign.	Do.	Records that Ayyanaṭikal Tiruvaṭi the Governor of Vēṇāṭu, made a gift of Īḻavers, Īḻakkayyers and Vaṇṇans, to the church of Tarisa remitting all taxes due from them.
20	Kōṭṭayam Sthāṇuravi Copper plates.	Do.	...	...	Do	Records that Ayyanaṭikal Tiruvaṭikal and Rāmatiruvaṭikal have granted some lands to the Tarisāppalli erected by Maruvān Sapir Iso.
21	Kōṭṭayam Sthāṇuravi Copper plates.	Cēra.	Sthāṇuravi.	17th year of the rēign.	Tamil in Vaṭṭeḻuttu.	Records that the Sabha of Tiruvārrūray and the aṭikal made arrangements regarding the feeding on Ōṇam days, for which one Sendan Sankaran of Punseyappadakaram gāve certain lands.
22	Kṛṣṇasamudram copper plates.	Vijaya nagara.	Venkataraya.	Sa. 1508 Vijaya Kartika Uttara-dvadasi.	Sanskrit in Nāgari.	Registers a gift of village named Sri Partikulasēkharanallūr near Kṛṣṇasamudram to a number of Brahmins of different families.

Copper-plates —(*contd.*)

No.	Place of inscription.	Dynasty.	King.	Date.	Language and Alphabet.	Remarks.
23	Malayāṟṟūr R. C. Church.	...	...	Ko. 923 Mēṭam.	Malayalam.	Registers a mortgage deed executed by Nārāyaṇan Tuppan for a loan of 22,023 new paṇam, which he took from the adhikāri of the church at Malayāṟṟūr.
24	Māmbaḷḷi plates.	...	...	...	Tamil in Vaṭṭeḻuttu.	Fragment. Records the incomes of lands granted to the temples of Tiruecceṟ-gunrūr and Siṟṟur, for lamps and other expenses. Mentions Ayurūrmukkāl vaṭṭam.
25	Do.	Vēṇāṭu.	Vīradēva-daran Kēr-aḷavarma Tiruvaṭi (Born	...	Do.	Registers gifts of incomes from lands, granted by the officers of the King, to the temple Vīrakēralapurattu-Bhaṭṭārakar, for daily re-

			in the asterism Āvaṇisravana)			quirements. Mentions Vīra maṇikaṇṭha Rāmavarma Tiruvaṭi and the villages Mēvūrkkal Siṟṟāṟṟankarai, Cirayinkil, Tōnrakkal, Kōṭṭūr, Nirmangalam, Māranallūr, Isariman, Gōvindamangalam Ilavalanātu, Irinnalur, Marudakacceri, Kandalur and Perumbulam.
26	Do.	Do.	Śrī-vallabhan Kōtai	Ko. 159	...	Registers that the temple of Ayurūr and its lands were placed as Kīḻiṟṟu to the temple of Tiruccengunrur by Ādiccan Umayammai of Tirukkalayapuram.
27	Mincirai Maṭham Plate	...	...	Śa. 1692.	Malayalam Vaṭṭeḻuttu.	Records that one Kannur Namburi entered into an agreement with the Svāmi of the Mincirai Maṭham.
28	Do.	...	...	(A. D. 13th Century) Jupiter in Kumbham, Tulām.	Tamil in Vaṭṭeluttu.	Records the gift of money made for feeding on occasions, such as Tiruvōnam, Pūrṇima, Ayana Saṅkrānti.

Copper-plates—(*contd.*)

No.	Place of inscription.	Dynasty.	King.	Date.	Language and Alphabet.	Remarks.
29	Nagercoil District Judge.	...	...	Ko. 826 Virōdhi Puruṭṭāśi 27 Daśami. Monday Tiruvōṇam.	Tamil.	Registers a gift of 10 temples to Śrī Ranga Rāja Pattar Nambiyar of Ālvār-tirunagari under Royal command.
30	Nagercoil Kṛṣṇa-svāmi Temple.	...	...	...	Tamil.	Gift by some private person for offering.
31	Padmanābhapuram Mr. Marudanāyakam Pillai.	Travan-core.	Sakala Kalai Āditya Varma.	Ko. 541, Tai 21	Tamil	This Copper-plate was given to Tampi Aṇṇan Mārttāṇḍa Pillai Mūttaṇṇan by King Āditya Varma while he was staying in the Palace at Vīralakṣmi Viḷākam in the Street called Iravivarma Mahārāja Kulaśēkhara-perumal Perunteruvu and registers that presents and Virudas received for defeating Ayyumenon, the guru of Sāmūri of Neṭiyiruppu

						by Mārtāṇḍa Pillai. Muttaṇṇan and for defeating Tipatīpapulavar, the guru of Vaḷḷiyūr Rājas by Koccu Cēnnan, and the presents Lakṣmīrūpam, Tiru pira, Anumamuttira etc. given by King Āditya Varman himself, be enjoyed as long as sun and moon endure by Tampi Aṇṇan Muttaṇṇan and by his descendants. The descriptions of some social functions also have been stated in the record in detail.
32	Palaiyūr Church.	...	...	Ko. 852 Ṣimha.	Malayalam Vaṭṭeḻuttu.	Registers the sale of the land called Palippparambu in Accalam, a suburb of Palaiyūrdēśam by Kaman Kamar and brothers to the church of Mar Kuriyyako—Sahada at Palaiyūr.
33	Palaiyūr Church.	...	....	Ko. 856 Mthunam.	Do.	Registers a mortgage deed on the land called Kaliyanvittil Parambu, transacted by the Karttanar of the Palaiyūr Church Suri-Itti of Acca Vittil for a loan of 101 Paṇam, with interest payable at 12 % (nērpaliśai)

Copper-plates—(*contd.*)

No.	Place of inscription.	Dynasty.	King.	Date.	Language and Alphabet.	Remarks.
34	Palaiyūr Plates.	....	...	Ko. 918 Mīnam.	Malayalam in Vaṭṭeḻuttu.	Registers the complete purchase, with libation of water, of a free hold property by the Vicar of the Palaiyūr church, from Rāman Paṇṇan and his brothers of Accaḻiyam a hamlet of that Village.
35	Do.	...	...	...	Tamil in Vaṭṭeḻuttu.	Registers a sale of land for interest due on money lent by the Vicar of the church at Palur.
7	Paṭṭāḻi Devaswom.	...	...	Ko. 959.	Malayalam.	Describes certain misunderstandings that had occurred between the Karakkār and Ūrāṇmakkār of the Maṇṇaṭi Bhagavati temple at Paṭṭāḻi and the Kāmpittān the agent of Kandan Kali of Amerkunnam and that these were patched up by the parties at fault swearing in front of the temple that they will no longer infringe on the just authority of the Kāmbittān, in the administration of the temple.

38	Putukkōṭṭai Temple.	Pāṇḍya.	Srī Vallabha and Varatungarāma.	Sa. 1505	Sanskrit in Grantha.	Records that the Village of Putukkōṭṭai was given to a number of Brahmans at the request of one Tirumalairāja, who is described as the right hand of Vīrabhūpati.
38	Shertala Āvalūr Panikker.	...	...	Ko. 972 Makaram.	Malayalam.	Records the gift of land made by Nārāyaṇan Kṛṣṇan of Āvalūr Vīṭu fort he conduct of the Bharaṇi festival at Koṟṟan Kulangara.
39	Do.	...	...	Ko. 1001 Mīnam 4.	Malayalam.	This is an Āḷpaṇaya Kaiccīṭṭu relating to the sale of some Pulaya labourers for 201 Chs.
40	Śrī Villiputtūr plates.	Pāṇḍya.	Abhirāma.	So. 1474.	Sanskrit in Grantha.	Records that King Abhirāma Pāṇḍya made the village of Kṣīrārjuna pura into an agrahāra named Parākramapāṇḍyapura.
41	Śucīndram Vaṭṭappaḷḷi.	..	...	...	Tamil in Vaṭṭeḻuttu.	Fragmentary. Contains the details of certain fields but the temples name is not given. The words 'Devar Kaṇakku' in the margin of the plate seems to show that the God at Śucīndram was the donee.

Copper-plates—(*contd.*)

No.	Place of inscription.	Dynasty.	King.	Date.	Language and Alphabet.	Remarks.
42	Sucīndram Yōgīśvara Śivatāṇu.	...	...	Ko. 621 Arpaśi 25.	Tamil.	Registers that certain yōgi pparadēśis of Sucīndram were appointed as Ānavāḷ of the temple of Sucīndra muṭaya Nayinār for conducting certain temple festivals.
43	Tāḻamana Illam Plate.	Cēra.	Rājaśēkhara dēva.	(9th Century A. D.) 12th year of the reign.	Tamil in Vatteḻuttu.	Records that an arrangement was made by the people of the eighteen nāṭus belonging to Tiruvāṟṟuvāy and the Townsmen of Vāḻaippaḷḷi who assembled under the Presidency of the King Rājaśēkharadēva.
44	Tirukuṟṟālam Plates.	Pāṇḍya.	Śīvalavaraguṇarāma alias Kulaśēkharadēva Dīkṣitar.	Ko. 935.	Tamil.	Records that a sāyarakṣai kaṭṭaḷai is established by the Pillaimars and the Mutalimars in the Kuttālanāthasvāmin temple.

45	Tirukuṟṟālam Plates.	Pāṇḍya	Śrīvala varaguṇarāma alias Kulaśēkharadēva Dīkṣitar.	S. 1675 Ko : 930.	Tamil.	Records that the army of Pāṇḍya King Kulaśēkharadēva Dīkṣitar established a Kaṭṭaḷai to be daily performed in the evenings in the temple of Kuttālanāthasvāmi.
46	Tirunelli Plates.	Cēra.	Bhaskararavi Varman	A. D. 10th Century.	Tamil in Vaṭṭeḻuttu.	Belongs to the Tirunelli temple in Vayanāṭu Taluk in British Malabar.
47	Do.	Do.	Do.	The year opposite 38th year opposite 6th year.	Tamil in Vaṭṭeḻuttu.	Refers to the Śrī Kāryam of Tirunelli temple. Mention also made in the same of Kuññikuṭṭan.
48	Do.	...	...	Jupiter in Makaram.	Tamil in Vaṭṭeḻuttu.	Records that a gift of land was made for a lamp. Mentions Tirunelli and Muḻikkaḷakaccam.
49	Do.	...	...	...	Do.	Refers to certain transactions made in Tirunelli Āḻvār.
50	Do.	...	...	...	Do.	Mentions the agreement made by the Urvāryam, and Śrī Vaiṣṇavas of Tirunelli.

No.	Place of inscription.	Dynasty.	King.	Date.	Language & Alphabet.	Remarks.
51	Tirunelli plates.	...	...	Jupiter in Karkaṭakam.	Tamil Vaṭṭeḻuttu.	Records that Kotai Raman of Valluvanaṭu granted 35 Kalannu of Ponnu (gold) for lamps in the temple of Tirunelli.
52	Do.	...	...	Jupiter in Dhanu, Mēṭam.	Tamil. Vaṭṭeḻuttu.	Illegible.
53	Tirupparappu Siva Temple.	Vṛṣṇi-kula (Yādava-kula.)	Kokarunan-dadakkan.	Lost.	Sanskrit and Tamil in Grantha and Tamil.	The first and the last places alone are found in the set. At the end, it is stated that the engraving was executed by the armour maker to Ko-Karunandadakkar.
54	Trivandrum Cellam vakai.	...	...	Kollam 925.	Malayalam.	Relates to the sale of land to Davida Ikkelparadesi of Kocci.

55	Trivandrum Cellam vakai.	Setupati and Travancore.	Mutturāmalinga Sētupati and Bālarāmavarma Kulaśēkhara perumal.	Sa. 1691 Ko. 945 Virodhi, Arpasi 23 Sunday Uttirāṭam Su. 7.	Tamil in Tamil and Telugu.	Registers the sale deed of the village of Kakkur to the king of Travancore for 4000 varahan for the expenses of conducting worship and providing offerings to the God Rāmanāthasvāmin at Rāmēśvaram.
56.	Trivandrum Husur Office.	Vṛṣṇikula or yādavakula.	Ko-karunandadakkan.	1449087th day of the Kali era.	Tamil.	Records the building of a temple for Viṣṇu and naming the place where this temple stood as Parthivaśēkharapuram and founding a Śālai (feeding house or boarding school) for 95 Vaidik students. Fragmentary.
57	Do.	Do.	Vikramāditya Varaguṇa.	8th regnal year Panguni.	Tamil.	Gift of land for the maintenance of Murukan Sēndi or Āy Kula mādēvi, married by the king. Mentions Pārthivaśēkharapuram.

No.	Place of inscription.	Dynasty.	King.	Date.	Language and Alphabet.	Remarks.
58	Trivandrum Huzur Office.	...	...	...	Malayalam Vaṭṭeḻuttu.	Copy of private documents dealing with transactions such as pāṭṭam, kāṇam, etc.
59	Do. Tiruvella.	...	...	...	Tamil in Vaṭṭeḻuttu.	Records rules laid down by Niraññāpāda paḻāra Tiruvaṭi for the conduct of priests performing worship in temples.
60	Do.	...	...	...	Do.	Gives abstract of contents of earlier grants made to the temple of Tiruvallavāl Appan.
61	Trivandrum Mitrānandapuram Maṭham.	...	...	...	Do.	Registers gift of lands to the temple at Mitrānandapuram.
62	Do	...	...	Jupiter in Vṛścikam Tulām 15.	Do.	Records gift of paddy and money to the same temple by Suvākaran Maṇiyan of Malaiya Manram.

63	Trivandrum Mr. Lakshmana Iyer.	Vijaya nagar.	Venkatapati.	S. 1568 Vyaya Kartikai.	Sanskrit in Nāgari.	Registers gift of the village of Sattupattur to Brahmins of various families, tax-free, at the request of Vīrabhūpa (Vīrappa Nāyaka) son of Kṛṣṇa and grand-son of Viśvanātha.
64	Trivandrum Mr. M. C. Narayana Pillai		Muhammad Mafus khan son of Hazarat Kibila Nawab Sahib Muhammad Anavardi-khan Bahadur.	Sa. 1066 Ko. 920 Krodhana Cittirai, Friday, Su. 7 Punarpūsam.	Tamil in Hindustani.	Records gift of the revenue of 78 rekai-pon liviable from Arripputturai, a village belonging to Aramanaikkarai vasal in Tinnevelly, the southern portion of the Arcot Trichinopoly Samsthānam belonging to the Subha of Hyderabad, which was payable in twelve instalments to Miyan Sheik Ahmad Kabir son of Hazarat Miyan Imam Sahib, and the Guru of Muhammad Mafuz khan.

No.	Place of inscription.	Dynasty.	King.	Date.	Language & Alphabet.	Remarks.
65	Trivandrum Mr. M. C. Narayana Pillai.	Nayaka.	Minakshammagaru.	Sa. 1660 Kalayukti Magha, Su. 12 Friday, Punarvasu.	Telugu.	Registers the gift of two pieces of land to Fakir Imam Sahib by Sri Minakshamma garu, the queen of Vijayaranga cokkanata Nāyaka of the Kasyapa gotra, son of Ranga Krishna Muttuvīrappa Nāyaka, the lord of Madura.
66	Trivandrum Murajapam Special Officer.	...	...	Jupiter in Mētam Makaram 20.	Tamil in Vaṭṭeḻuttu.	States that Kunrummel Sri Vira kerala Mārttāṇḍavarmar made a gift of land to the Bhaṭārakar of Mitrānandapuram for Puja and Amutupaṭi.
67	Do.	...	...	Jupiter in Vṛścikam Mēṭam 10.	Do.	Mentions that Sankaranārāyaṇa and Dēvanārāyaṇa of Sankaramangalam granted some lands for the pujas of Mitrānandapuram Bhaṭārakar.

68	Trivandrum Murajapam Special Officer.	...	...	Jupiter in Mēṭam Kanni, 7 Sunday Utrāṭam Pañcami.	Tamil in Vaṭṭeḷuttu.	Records that the members of the Eṭṭarai yōgam assembled and granted some lands to the Bhaṭāraka of Mitrānandapuram.
69	Trivandrum Museum plate of Tiruvelunnaṇṇūr temple.	Ilayaṭa svarūpam	Virakōṭai varman.	Ko. 711. Mēṭam 4.	Malayalam.	Records gift of lands by the agents of the King for the morning service of God Endalayappan at Tiruvelunnaṇṇūr.
70	Trivandrum plate of Tiruvelunnaṇṇūr temple.	...	Do.	Ko. 715. Mithunam 4.	Do.	Records gift of lands in Karakulam by the king's agents for the maintenance of a torana of lamps in the same temple.
71	Trivandrum Museum plate of Tiruvelunnaṇṇūr temple.	...	Virakerala Ramavarman of Kilappērūr.	Ko. 663 Kumbham 8.	Do.	The year 663 of Tiruvelunnannur Bhaṭāra is mentioned. It records gift of land to the temple for the maintenance of a torana of lamps.

No.	Place of inscription.	Dynasty.	King.	Date.	Language and Alphabet.	Remarks.
72	Trivandrum, Museum plate of Tiruvelunnaṇṇūr temple.	...	Vīrakerala Ramavarman of Kilappērūr.	Kollam 793, Kumbham 8.	Malayalam.	Records gift of lands to the temple for the conduct of the early morning service.
73	Do.	...	...	Kollam 878, Iṭavam 7. Rōhiṇi, Thursday, Su. 3.	Do.	States that Sankaran Kandan of Idamana paid 288 panam as prāyascitta for assaulting certain temple servants.
74	Do.	...	...	Kollam 878. Iṭavam 16 Saturday, Hasta, Su. 11.	Do.	Relates to certain sākṣikkāṇam of the same Idamaṇai pōṟṟi.
75	Do.	..	...	Kollam 839, Kanni 26.	Do.	States that the property of Mukkuvan was confiscated to the temple by a Muhammadan pārvatyakāran for entering the temple premises.
76	Do.	...	...	Kollam 240 Mithunam 12, Wednesday Makayiram. Pañcami.	Do.	Records gift of lands by Kandan Kandan and Manlan Kandan for the maintenance of a torana.

77	Trivandrum Museum plates of Vaṭaśēri.	...	...	Sa. 1691 Kollam 945 Puraṭṭāsi 27, Su. 10 Monday Tiruvōnam.	Tamil.	States that the two widows of a certain Ramalinga Bhaṭṭa of Vaṭaśēri confirmed the gift of certain lands made by their deceased husband some years previously for the conduct of worship and feeding of Brahmins in the temple of Rūpanārāyāna Viṇṇakar Emperumān at Vaṭaśēri alias Ādityavarma caturvēdimangalam.

Cadjan Records.

1	Akapparampu Jacobite Church.	...	...	Ko. 923 Mithunam.	Malayalam in Vaṭṭeluthu.	Records a വിലയാധാരം of Kumaran Sirukanda Tirumulpadu of Maññadu to Akapparampu Church.
2	Akapparampu Jacobite Church.	...	...	Ko. 926 Dhanu 8.	Malayalam.	Records the settlement between പുത്തൻകൂറ്റുകാർ & പഴയകൂറ്റുകാർ.
2 a.	Do.	...	...	Ko. 926 Dhanu.	Malayalam.	This is a continuation of previous record.
3	Alakiyapandyapuram Periyavīṭṭu Mudaliyar.	Travancore	...	Ko. 810 Māsi 22.	Tamil.	Records the royal order of relinquishment on taxes on account of the invasion of Tirumalai Nayakkar.

No.	Place of inscription.	Dynasty.	King.	Date.	Language & Alphabet.	Remarks.
4	Alakiyapandyapuram Periyavīṭṭu Mudaliyar.	Travancore.	...	Ko. 878 Alpasi 1.	Tamil.	Records the resolution of the Nāṭṭārkūṭṭam at Vaṭaśēri.
5	Do.	...	...	Ko. 889 Mārkaḻi 14.	Do.	Records the resolutions of the Nāṭṭārkūṭṭam at Āśrāmam.
6	Do.	...	...	Ko. 894 Vaikāsi 15.	Do.	Records the resolutions of the Nāṭṭārkūṭṭam at Īśāntimangalam.
7	Do.	...	...	Ko. 896 Māśi 26.	Malayalam.	Records the royal order to the people of Nānjināṭu.
8	Do.	...	...	Ko. 898 Āni 25.	Tamil.	Records the royal order to the people of Nānjināṭu.
9	Do.	...	—	Ko. 898 Kārtikai 16.	Do.	Records the resolutions of the Nāṭṭārkūṭṭam at Kadukkara.

10	Do.	...	...	Ko. 899 Āni 20	Tamil.	Records the royal order for the tax exemption to the people of Nānjināṭu.
11	Do.	...	...		Do.	Incomplete. Records the Royal order for the tax exemption to the people of Nānjināṭu.
12	Alakiyapandyapuram Periyavīṭṭu Mudaliyar records received from Mr. S. Desikavinayakam Pillai, Putheri.	...	...	Ko. 732 Kārtikai 5.	Do.	This records that the Sri Paṇḍārakāriyam of Sriparānkusanallūr maṭham received a loan of 10 kōṭṭas of paddy from Udaiya Nayinan Udaiya Nayinan of Atiyanūr alias Alakiyapandyapuram for conducting pūja.
13	Alakiyapandyapuram. Do.	...	...	Ko. 915 Cittirai.	Do.	This is a royal Nīṭṭu sent under command to the people of Southern portion of Northern sub division of Nānjināṭu reducing certain taxes on account of the invasion of Mukilan's army.

No.	Place of inscription.	Dynasty.	King.	Date.	Language & Alphabet.	Remarks.
14	Do.	...	....	Ko. 957 Iṭavam 30 Sunday.	Do.	This is a royal Nīṭṭu sent under command to the Nāṭṭār of Tenmītināṭu informing that the illness of Queen Mother is getting serious.
15	Do.	...	...	...	Do.	Records that the temples of Śiva in Quilon having been demolished through constant war and pūjas have been neglected in the ruined temple near the Putukuḷam Palace, it may be reconstructed and the Goddess Ānandavalli be consecrated of whose idol was made at Trivandrum, and Putukuḷam be renamed Ānandavallīśvaram.

16	Alakiyapandyapuram PerIyavIṭṭu Mudaliyar records received from Mr. S. Desikavinayakam Pillai. Putheri.	...	...	Ko. 970 Āṭi 30.	Tamil.	States that owing to the invasion of Tippu Sultan, money having been received on loan from merchants in advance and new taxes having been introduced, the lands and fields in Nāñjināṭu have also been included for additional taxation.
17	SucIndram Vaṭṭappaḷḷi Paṭṭar.	Travancore.	VIra Kerala varmar.	Ko. 305 Mēṭam 6 Śu 14 attam, sun.	Malayalam.	The record is a copy of the original and to recopy has been made on Ko. 865 Chittirai 9. It states that the then Vaṭṭappaḷḷi Paṭṭar died without heirs and as there was none in the family to hold the title of Vaṭṭappaḷḷi, Nārāyaṇa Suvaran of Padiññāre Iṭam of Vaikkam, his wife and son were installed as Vaṭṭappaḷḷi and they were ordered to perform the duties of Vaṭṭappaḷḷi and to enjoy the privileges thereon.

No.	Place.	Dynasty.	King.	Date.	Language and Alphabet.	Remarks.
18	Tṛppūṇittura, Mr. Rama Pisharoti B. A. L. T.	Onaṭu.	Ravi varma Ravi varma	Ko. 507 Tulām.	Malayalam.	It is a copy of the temple records and states that the 'janam' of nine houses, the ūrāṇma of Kūṭalmāṇikkam Temple received the Māṇikkaratnam from Ravi varmar ravi varmar, Onaṭu and in return the 'janam' gave him Kārāyma Melayma etc. of the said temple and the privilege to install a Taccuṭaiya Kaimal.
19	Trivandrum Central Records Office.	Travancore.	Mārttāṇḍa varma.	Ko. 925 Makaram 5.	Do. in Tamil.	Records the historical episode known as Tiruppaṭi dānam.
20	Do.	...	...	...	Malayalam.	Describes Sarkētam, Samudāyam, Adālam, Akakōinma and Purakōinma elaborately.

21	Do.	...	...	Ko. 951 Kumbham 20.	Tamil.	Is a variyōla referring to the agreement between Paliyattu Menon etc., and some of the Travancore officials at Ernaculam in settlement of the Perumpaṭappu Svarūpam dispute.
22	Trivandrum Records in bulk.	...	...	Ko. 1046.	Malayalam and Tamil.	These record the answers given by private individuals of various taluks to about 25 questions regarding some of the social customs, Government, law etc., during the time of King Rāmavarman (933-973).
23	Trivandrum Central Records Office.	...	...	Ko. 985.	Tamil.	Refers to the expenditure of Rs. 25000 in connection with the capture of Dalavay Velu Tampy.

No.	Place of inscription.	Dynasty.	King.	Date.	Language and Alphabet.	Remarks.
24	Trivandrum Central Records Office.	...	...	...	Malayalam.	This is a ninavu written by Kanakku Subramanyan Cokkanāthan, and refers to the proper arrangement of business at Kampam in Pūnjār.
2	Do.	...	...	...	Tamil.	Records a dettu (adoption) by Ramavarma Koyiladhikari of Palladu.
26	Do.	Mysore Sultan.	Hyder Ali.	Dhatu year Avaṇi 20.	Do.	This is a Sādhanapaṭṭayam of the transaction between Hyder Ali Sayibu of Mahisura Pandārakāryam and the King of Kūṭalūr, the former giving Kampam to the latter in return for 7 elephants and 75000 pon.
27	Do.	...	...	Ko. 922 Dhanu 15.	Malayalam.	Records the collection of cardamom in the hills of Madappalli Kaimal and of the Pūnjār chief.

28	Trivandrum Central Records Office.		...	Ko. 947 Tai 9.	Tamil.	Is an atimai muri executed by Kulaśēkhara Paṇḍaram Kolarien of Manjamalai giving his son Ayyappan as atimai to the Paṇḍāratti cinni of Viradenda Paṇḍāram.
29	Do.	...	...	...	Do.	Conferring the title of Vīradenda Paṇḍāram on Ramanathan (Kanden) Ayyappan and pattu and valai as a token thereof.
30	Do.	...	...	Ko. 9 (64) Kumbham.	Malayalam.	This is a ninavu written by command by Valiamēluttu Sankarakumaru on the seige of Kampam.
31	Do.	...	...	Ko. 990 Mīnam 10.	Do	Is a sadhanam referring to privileges of Cānnār and Elava converts.

No.	Place.	Dynasty.	King.	Date.	Language and Alphabet.	Remarks.
32	Do.	...	...	Ko. 985 Kanni 12.	Do.	This sādhanam sent by Dewan Mārttāṇḍan Iravi to the Sarvādhikāryakkār of Muḷakumaṭissīla, records that Kūli labour should be exacted from the prisoners and they should each be provided with 3 nāḷi rice, a kalam and a caṭṭi per day.
33	Do.	...	...	Ko. 974 Mēṭam 19	Do.	Is a copy of a nīṭṭu given to Jayantan Sankaran Nampuri by command that he was appointed Valiya Sarvādhi and he should see that Isvarasēva, Tingal ūttu, Paṭṭāḷam. Kuñju kūṭṭam puḷḷī, Kōṭṭappaṭi Veṭippura etc. were administered properly.

	Do.	Travan-core.	Padmanābha Sēvini Vañci Dharmavardhini Rāṇi Pārvati Bāi.	Ko. 994 Karkatakam 1.	Do.	Is a royal proclamation cancelling the old trakkasu and issuing cempu kāśu of four kinds 16, 8, 4 and 2 per cukram struck with nāmam, panantēr malai and cintalanāgam
	Trivandrum Central Records Office.	...	...	Ko. 974 Kanni 3.	Tamil.	This is a sādhanam sent to Sarvādhikāryakkār of Mulakumatissīla by Raja Kēśavadas that he should see that expenditure on account of toppu should be incurred as first.
36	Do.	....	...	..	Do.	Records the insignificant defeat at Cenkōṭṭa and a lak of chukrams to be sent to Nāyars of two taluks who are to be sent to the front.
37	Do.	...	...	Ko. 952 Kanni 10.	Do.	Records that 4000 Kaliyan should be sent to build Kṛṣṇan Kōṭṭai and Melurkōṭṭai.

No.	Place.	Dynasty.	King.	Date.	Language and Alphabet.	Remarks.
38	Do.	...	...	Ko. 937.	Tamil.	Is a ninavu sent to Mārttāṇḍan Mārttāṇḍan of Muḷakumaṭissīla at Māvēlikkara that the amount required to put up the forts at Varāppuḻa and Ālappuḻa be sent to Mārttāṇḍa Pillai and Suppayyan.
39	Do.	...		Ko, 945 Āvaṇī 29.	Do.	This is a ninavu sent to Mārttāṇḍan and Vīrēśvaran Raman that from the amount of 1000 panams received on loan from Sankara Sastriyal and others for incurring expenditure in building a long line in Vaṭṭakōṭṭa, 2400 panams be repaid by the amount that may be got from Udayan Aḻaki Cokkanāthan for honouring him with tirumukham.

40	Do.	...	...	Ko. 959 Makaram 12.	Do.	This sādhanam sent to Kaṇakku Cempakarāman Ayyappan, the Vicārippu of Cirayinkīl Paṇḍakaṣāla, states that the amount of 500 paṇam be spent in the construction of a Kalippura in the parade of Añcuteṅgil Kōṭṭa.
41	Trivandrum Central Records Office.	...	...	Ko. 962 Kanni 3.	Tamil	Registers the purchase of Kaṇṭam, parampu and salt pans of Lantakkummañi (the Dutch) for Rs.1001331 and the balance of 54161 should be paid off by Narasimhan(Kōṭṭu) Anantan who owes the same on account of the duty on dry ginger camphor, kopra etc.
42	Do.	...	...	Ko. 975 Tulām 12.	Do.	Mentions that 64331 varāhans due to Major Bannerman of Pāḷayamkōṭṭa were paid.

No	Place of inscription.	Dynasty.	King.	Date.	Language and Alphabet.	Remarks.
43	Trivandrum Central Records Office.	...	...	Ko. 951 Vṛścikam 12.	Tamil.	This is a ninavu sent to Mārttāṇḍan Śankaran that as information has been received that Tippu Sultan and his army have reached Kōḻikkōṭṭu Mukham soldiers be mobilized in forts and a lak of panams should be sent for their meals.
44	Do.	...	...	Ko. 950 Tulam 16.	Do.	Is a ninavu sent to Parappan Kumāran of Muḷakumaṭiśŗla ordering 461000 panam for digging a trench around the Vaṭakkēkōṭṭa at Pārūrkōṭu.
45	Do.	...	...	Ko. 985 Āṭi.	Do.	Records that 10000 Kaliyan be paid for providing the Kunjukūṭṭakkār with rice.

46	Trivandrum Central Records Office.	...	...	Ko. 931 Ciṅgam 29.	Tamil.	This is a ninavu sent to Mārttāṇḍan that a lak of panams be paid as travelling expense to Nāyars who encamped at Māprāṇam.
47	Do.	...	...	Ko. 925 Mārkaḷi.	Do.	In a copy of the original agreement written to Parantrīse Kalpittān under command and refers to the treaty between the Dutch and the Māhārājā.
48	Do.	Travancore.	Parvathi Rani.	...	Malayalam.	Is a translation of Pārsi-Kaṭudās addressed to the Governor of Bengal that captain McLeod may be retained in Travancore.
49	Trivandrum Central Records Office.	Travancore.	Vancipāla Mārttaṇḍa Rāmavarman.	Kollam 964 Karkaṭakam 19.	Tamil.	Refers to the sale deed in favour of Dewan Kēśava Pillai by the Honourable Dutch East India Company, of the forts at Munambam and Koṭungallūr and to the conditions thereof.

No.	Place of inscription.	Dynasty.	King.	Date.	Language and Alphabet.	Remarks.
50	Do.	Do.	...	Kollam 1027 Karkaṭakam 15.	Malayalam.	Refers to the committee constituted to settle who should be the Metropolitan of Malankara viz., Mar Kurilose supported by 28 churches including Valiapaḷḷi, or Mar Athanasius supported by 26 churches including the Quilon Church and to the royal proclamation confirming Mar Athanasius as Metropolitan of Malankara for the reformed Syrians.
51	Do.	Do.	Bālamārttāṇḍa Varman	Kollam 925 Makaram.	Tamil	Is a copy of a letter from Yiraṇyanallūr addressed to Captain Mayya of France and refers to concessions allowed to the French for trade.

52	Do.	Do.	...	...	Do.	Refers to the defeat Kāśavuṇikkunnu sustained by the soldiers went to the Iṭavaka of Gñavakkāṭu Kaimal.
53	Do.	...	...	Kollam 991 Makaram,	Tamil in Vaṭṭeḻuttu.	Is a paṇaya-ōla executed by Dēvan of Tāmarassēri on account of the money received by him on loan from Rāman Śaṅkaran of Kiḻakkē house in Ceruturuttu at Kuṇṭūr dēśam.
54	Do.	...	...	Kollam 890 Ciṅgam 1.	Do.	Is a tīṭṭu (writ) ordering Dāmōdaran of Kaḷḷiyam and his nephews to write out accounts of vastu and ulpatti of Purattūr dēśam of Perumana devaswom.

No	Place of inscription.	Dynasty.	King.	Date.	Language and Alphabet.	Remarks.
55	Trivandrum Central Records Office.	...	...	Ko. 993 Dhanu.	Tamil in Vaṭṭeḻuttu.	Is a paṇaya-ōla relating to a loan received by Devan Devan of the Samudāyam of Tāmarassēri from Rāman Śaṅkaran of Kiḻakkē house in Ceruturutti at Koṇḍūr dēśam.
56	Do.	...	...	Ko. 920 Makaram.	Malayalam.	Is a copy of the original record in regard to the paṇḍāram of Maṅṅāṭṭu Accan.
57	Do.	Parur Svarūpam.	...	Ko. 895 Kanni.	Do.	Is a tīṭṭu referring to the Samudāyam of Peruvāram.
58	Do.	...	...	Ko. 504 Mēṭam 4.	Do.	States that Iṭṭivāsu of Perumpiḷḷi was installed as the priest of Tṛkkāriyūr temple and refers to the interesting incident that a cobra was found round the tiruvaḻutinaṅga offered to the deity.

59	Do.	...	...	Kali......	Do.	Is a Vaypōlakāryam executed by Ponnambi Sankaran of Navakkara in Karattedam and Kumaran Iravi Kaimal of Vallārakkōṭṭu, the former to enjoy the titles, rights, shares, thousand Nayars, tiṭṭu, Kai, karaṇḍakam, vastu, adiyār and koda kartṛttuam of the senior member of Kurumalasvarūpam and the latter the titles, villu, vela etc. belonging to the Junior member of the said svarūpam.
60	Do	...	...	Ko. 508 Tulām 29.	Do.	Records that Īśvaran of Cerukarataravāṭu was installed as priest.
61	Do.	...	...	Ko. 881 Mēṭam 18.	Do	Refers to the decision by the yōgam of Tṛkkāriyūr and by the assembly of Tṛkkaṇṇapuram and by Paḻur Namburi re: the capture of elephant.

No.	Place of inscription.	Dynasty.	King.	Date.	Language and Alphabet.	Remarks.
62	Trivandrum Central Records Office.	Neṭi-yirippu Svarūpam.	Kunnalak-kōnar tampurān.	Ko. 724 Dhanu.	Malayalam	Refers to the Brahma-kūrcam ceremony performed by Karuttedattu Namburi by the command of Kunnala-kōnar Tampurān.
63	Do.	...	...		Do.	Damaged. Seems to refer the region of Taliyātirimār and of Cēramān Perumāḷ.
64	Trivandrum Palace Library Āyakeṭṭu Kaṇakku.	Travan-core.	Sri Padma-nābha dāsa Venrumaṉ Koṇḍa Bhūtala Vīra Rāma-varman.	Ko. 695 Mēṭam 25.	Do.	Refers to a pāṭṭayōla exe-cuted by king Sri Padma-nābhadāsa in favour of Vātuppāṭi Kaṇḍan Kaṇḍan for conducting Venruman Koṇḍa Bhūtala Vīra Rāma varman pūja in Sri Padma-nābha Perumāḷ temple.

65	Do.	Do.	Sri Padmanābhadāsa.	Ko. 722 Alpasi 14.	Do.	States that Sri Padmanābhadāsa of Venrumaṇ koṇḍa bhūtalavar Rama varman tirumaṭam borrowed on behalf of Sri Padmanābha Perumāḷ 6200 marakkāls of paddy from Vātuppāṭi Kaṇḍan Kaṇḍan.
66	Do.	Do.	Do.	Ko. 696.	Do.	Refers to the pāṭṭayōla executed by Sri Padmanābha dāsa on behalf of Sri Padmanābha Perumāḷ.